The Veronal Mystery

Supressed Evidence, Missing Witnesses - Was it Murder?

Norena Shopland

WORDCATCHERpublishing

The Veronal Mystery
Supressed Evidence, Missing Witnesses – Was it Murder?
WORDCATCHER HISTORY

British Library Cataloguing in Publication Data.
A catalogue record for this book is available from the British Library.

Published in the United Kingdom by Wordcatcher Publishing Group Ltd
www.wordcatcher.com
Tel: 02921 888321
Facebook.com/WordcatcherPublishing

First Edition: 2020

Print edition ISBN: 9781789422894
Ebook edition ISBN: 9781789423358

Category: History / True Crime

Picture Credits

Front cover images, as per list below.

The following images have been taken from the Cambria Daily Leader *Brighton Inquest: Some pictures* (4 Feb. 1913) a public domain newspaper on Welsh Newspapers Online:

Roe family shop, p.14
Albert Roe, p.19
The Coroner Mr Benson p.40
Eric Trevanion, p.43
Miss Geneste, p.63
James Lumb, p.73
Joiner (the Butler), p.109
Mr Trevanion's flat, p.110
Mrs Trevanion, p.127
Albert Roe, p.152

Images from Wikimedia Commons are public domain and include:

Veronal bottle, cover
Orotava ship, cover
Postcard of Brighton, p.29
Hove Town Hall, p.37
Dr Bernard Henry Spilsbury, p. 43

Other images:
Eric Trevanion, Cambria Daily Leader *Hove Mystery Inquiry* (28 Jan. 1913) Public
    domain p.16
Albert Roe, Cambria Daily Leader *The Will Case* (17 Jan. 1913) Public domain.
    p.38
Henry Cyril Paget, James Gardiner Collection: photograph album labelled
    'Drag', 5th Marquis of Anglesey, seated in drag by a tree (1905), Wellcome
    Library. Public domain. p.25
Table of fatal cases Willcox, Sir William H, Pickworth, F A; Young, Helen M
    A *The clinical and pathological effects of hypnotic drugs of the barbituric
    acid and sulphonal groups,* Proceedings of the Royal Society of
    MedicineVol. 20 (9) (July 1927), Public domain. p.49
Inspector Ward in Swansea, Cambrian Daily Leader (7 Feb. 1913) Public domain.
    p.209

CONTENTS

FOREWORD..1

ACKNOWLEDGEMENTS...2

INTRODUCTION 3

1: A WARRING FAMILY: THE TREVANIONS 7

    ERIC 12

    ALBERT ROE...14

    THE MEN'S TRAVELS..15

    ALBERT'S ILLNESS 23

2: DEATH AND EXHUMATION.....................................29

    LIFE IN BRIGHTON AND HOVE 29

    THE FATEFUL DAY 33

3: DAY 1 – FRIDAY 24 JANUARY 1913: THE NEW INQUIRY 37

    THE UNDERTAKER 41

    THE EXHUMATION..41

    THE PATHOLOGIST...43

    THE VERONAL EXPERT 45

4: CONTRADICTORY EVIDENCE COMES TO LIGHT 48

    DR BAINES 50

    THE CHEMISTS...55

    GIBSON..55

    MARSHALL...56

    DOUTHWAITE 57

    ANALYSIS..58

5: SHARING BEDS AND DISAPPEARING MONEY 62

    THE GOVERNESS 63

    ERIC'S RAPIDLY DISAPPEARING MONEY..................70

6: DAY 2 – MONDAY 27 JANUARY: CONTROVERSIAL WILLS AND A SHOCKING NOTE..73

    THE CURIOUS WILL...73

    THE CONTENTIOUS EVIDENCE OF NURSE RICE 83

    THE OTHER NURSES 91

    WAS VERONAL SOLELY TO BLAME?.........................92

7: DAY 3 – TUESDAY 28 JANUARY: 'VERY WEAK MINDED'.......... 104

    THE HAIRDRESSER.. 105
    THE PICTURE FRAME MAKER 107
    THE BUTLER.. 109
    ERIC'S APPEARANCE.. 123
    THE HOUSEKEEPER 125
    ERIC'S MOTHER SPEAKS.. 127
    THE VERONAL EXPERT RECALLED 136

8: DAY 4 – THURSDAY 30 JANUARY.. 139

    MR BRIDGES – THE SOLICITOR'S CLERK............................ 139
    CONRAD WILLMORE - THE CHAUFFEUR............................ 143
    WHY ALBERT?... 151
    ALBERT EDWARD ROE – 'THE BOSS' 152

9: DAY 5 – TUESDAY 4 FEBRUARY... 159

    ALBERT AGAIN 159
    NURSE HAWKINS 184
    CHARLES CECIL TREVANION.. 184

10: DAY 6 – FRIDAY 7 FEBRUARY 186

    NURSE RICE AGAIN 189
    DR BAINES RECALLED 194
    MARY JOINER RECALLED 198
    THE BUTLER AGAIN 202

11: DAY 7 – FRIDAY 14 FEBRUARY: THE MISSING WITNESSES...... 203

    A ROPE AROUND HIS NECK.. 205
    JACK, DON'T YOU SIGN ANYTHING 207

12: SUMMING UP 211

    THE CORONER'S BIAS 220
    THE VERDICT 220
    WHO GETS THE MONEY?... 222

13: THE AFTERMATH.. 223

    WHAT HAPPENED TO...?... 225
    THE DAMNING LETTERS... 225
    NURSE RICE'S MISSING NOTE 229
    A SIMILAR TRIAL 231

14: CONCLUSION... 235

INDEX.. 238
REFERENCES... 241

FOREWORD

I first covered the true-life story of *The Veronal Mystery* in my book *Forbidden Lives: LGBT stories from Wales*. I gave a short round-up of the facts behind a case concerning the relationship between two men, Eric Trevanion and Albert Roe, and raised the question of whether Albert could be held accountable for Eric's death in 1912. However, I felt there was a lot more to this story and so set about researching and analysing it in greater detail. There was, as I suspected, a far richer story... and the results were shocking.

The main facts in this book have been compiled using two sources: contemporary newspapers; and the *Records of Coronerships in Eastern Sussex (1882-2002)* held at The Keep, East Sussex Records Office (ESRO) in Brighton.[1] Other records, such as those taken in interviews by the police could not be found and appear to have been lost over time.

Due to the sensitive nature of the case and suggestions of 'unnatural vice', it is interesting to see how the press of 1912 reported the details. While the newspapers present a more dramatic account, the official records and letters from the Coroner's reports offer a more neutral view, but do flesh out facts that journalists omitted. In addition, letters held at ESRO shed new light on how the Office of Public Prosecutions tried to deliberately suppress certain aspects of the inquest.

The outcome of the case is very much open to personal interpretation: was it accidental, a suicide or did Albert kill Eric? Even without a conclusive reason for Eric's death, the story is certainly an interesting look at the attitudes towards homosexuality in the early twentieth century.

ACKNOWLEDGEMENTS

To my wonderful wife, Julie Carpenter, who helped so much by reading through my manuscript and clarifying several points; Pam and Bob Shopland for their never-ending support; the Wellcome Library; Royal Pharmaceutical Society Museum; and the extremely helpful staff at The Keep, East Sussex Records Office.

INTRODUCTION

The first inquest into the death of Eric Trevanion was held inside his own Brighton flat on Thursday 12 September 1912. Eric had died the day before, apparently of a drug overdose. Nobody who knew him seemed surprised so for most people it was seen as very much an open and shut case.

Not everyone was so convinced.

At the inquest, Eric's mother, Mrs Florence Trevanion, harboured suspicions and said so in her evidence, claiming it to be 'a case of murder' but she was persuaded to drop her objections by her son, Claude. However, she could not rest and took her suspicions to the police. While there is no record of what she told them, it was certainly enough to convince officers to reopen the case.

For two weeks, the police carried out extensive interviews and what they learnt deeply concerned them, so much so, that they ordered Eric's body to be exhumed for further tests -with startling results.

As a result of the exhumation and four months after Eric had died, a request was sent to the London Divisional Court of the King's Bench from a man regarded as the greatest prosecutor of the time, Richard David Muir. He had taken part in a number of sensational trials and just two years previously had a prominent role in the Crippen case, one of the most sensational murders in British criminal history. After receiving the results of Eric's new autopsy, Muir was sufficiently concerned to enter an affidavit on behalf of the Director of Public Prosecutions,[2] for a ruling under Section 6 of the Coroner's Act 1887. In it he asked the Lewes District Coroner to quash the results of Eric's inquest and order a new one be held.

Muir's affidavit detailed why he thought the original verdict should be overthrown. He explained that the twenty-seven-year-old unmarried Eric had, for about six weeks before his death, rented a flat at Hove with his good friend, Albert. A manservant called Joiner, with his wife and baby daughter, moved in with the two men.

3

Since the age of twenty-one, Eric had been in the habit of taking the drug Veronal for his insomnia, warning those around him that he may still be in a deep sleep the following morning. On the night of his death, Eric told no one he was intending to use the drug, and nobody saw him take it. It was not until after they had eaten dinner that Eric, according to Albert, stated that he had taken an overdose. He then lapsed into unconsciousness, leaving Albert to call in Dr Baines, the local GP. Eric never recovered and on the 11 September he died.

There had been no indication of suicide. Eric's mind was quite normal; fairly cheerful on the day; and he was perfectly sober. Dr Baines was in no doubt that death was caused by accidental Veronal poisoning and in this he was supported by the two other doctors he consulted.

The first inquest was held in Eric's flat the day after his death. This was nothing unusual, during this period, inquests had to be carried out within forty-eight hours of a suspicious death and could be held at a local pub, workhouse, town hall, or in the building in which the death occurred. Only a small number of deaths were considered suspicious so most did not require an inquest, compared to the one third of deaths that are examined today.[3] Until 1927, juries were also present at inquests and consisted of between twelve and twenty-four men who were required to examine the body and hear the witnesses. Jurors were supposed to be householders taken from an area outside that in which the death occurred, but given that male householders only made up about around 23%[4] of the male population in England and Wales, it was not always easy. Considering Eric's inquest took place the day after he died, obviously the jury was one the Coroner could call in quickly.

As the black-coated jurymen stood around the dining room, with the Coroner sitting in Eric's black oak, throne-like chair, Mrs Trevanion was asked if she was satisfied that Eric had died from accidental Veronal poisoning. Sitting close to her son's body, she replied no, she thought it 'a case of murder'[5] adding she was also very disturbed by the number of other 'poisons' on Eric's bedside table, including bromide, aspirin and morphia. At the mention of poisons, Albert, who had been sitting quietly listening to the

4

evidence, suddenly leapt to his feet shouting, 'Does Mrs Trevanion accuse me of murdering her son?'

Ignoring Albert's outburst, Mrs Trevanion explained that on previous occasions when she had seen her son under the influence of Veronal or morphia he had 'lain as if dead'[6] but before he died, his breathing had been violent and he appeared to writhe in agony.

When Dr Baines was asked about this, he argued that Eric would not have been in pain and that the seemingly violent breathing was due to the fact that the drug acted quickly as he had taken it on an empty stomach, having eaten nothing at dinner.

The Coroner, turning back to Mrs Trevanion, asked if she was suggesting improper administration and she, suddenly less certain, drew back from the murder charge saying, 'Not by anyone else, but I believe that he took something else'.

Was it not possible, she asked, for a post mortem to be carried out?

Despite the fact that inquests were called to investigate suspicious deaths, the Coroner's Act 1887 stated that a post mortem was not always necessary. However, it could be requested if interested parties wanted one. The Coroner told the jury that Mrs Trevanion, or indeed themselves, were entitled to ask for one and that he would adjourn the process if they, or the family, wished it. Claude Trevanion, Eric's brother, then intervened persuading his mother it was not necessary and under his influence she withdrew her request. After some discussion between themselves the jury also decided they did not want an autopsy[7] and a verdict of death by misadventure was returned.

However, Florence Trevanion could not come to terms with the verdict and shortly afterwards instructed her solicitor to write to the public prosecutor, asking how a jury could have come to a verdict of overdose when they did not know the quantity of drugs in Eric's system. Charles Mathews, the Public Prosecutor, agreed and ordered the exhumation of the body and the post mortem.

Eric was exhumed on 8 October and a chemical analysis of samples taken from the body showed that at least 150 grains of Veronal must have been taken within an hour of him becoming unconscious, thirty to fifty grains were a fatal dose.[8] Dr Willcox, who attended the exhumation and who had taken the samples, expressed the view that the quantity could not have been accidental and his report concluded:

> I am of opinion that the large dose of Veronal taken by the deceased shortly before the onset of coma must have been either:
>
> 1. Wilfully taken by the deceased, and since he had knowledge of the effects of Veronal the large dose taken by himself must have been taken with suicidal intent, or
>
> 2. The large dose taken must have been wilfully administered by some other person and if this other person had full knowledge of the poisonous effects of a large dose of Veronal the intent must have been homicidal.[9]

It was primarily this report that was used by Charles Mathews to ask for a new inquiry. In addition, in a series of letters to Coroner Benson, Mathews (careful not to criticise Benson for his handling of the first inquest) admits that the original jury had no option in their verdict, but adds, 'there is fresh evidence, apart from D. Willcox's report, directly implicating the friend.'

Was it, as Mrs Trevanion said, a case of murder?

1

A WARRING FAMILY:
THE TREVANIONS

The new inquest into Eric's death generated enormous press interest. Eric was very wealthy and his relationship with Albert was curious, to say the least.

However, this was not the first time that Eric's family had created a media sensation - his parents had created their own storm not just once, but twice.

Florence Eva Cooper was born in 1856 in Sydney, Australia, the fourth daughter of Sir Daniel Cooper. Her father had been born in Bolton, Lancashire in 1821 but had moved to Australia aged fourteen when his father, Thomas, relocated there. They may have moved to join an uncle, also called Daniel Cooper, who had been transported in 1815 for stealing, but pardoned six years later. While he was in Australia, Uncle Cooper had met another convict, Hannah Dodd, and the two married. He then established a number of highly successful businesses, became extremely wealthy and a substantial land holder.[10] It was the atypical success story so beloved by nineteenth century novelists, the ex-convict becoming rich and powerful. Uncle Cooper and Hannah, having no children of their own, made his nephew, Cooper junior, their heir.

Cooper junior built on his uncle's successes and gained his own riches and influence. He owned a great part of Sydney; became an elected Council member in the first New South Wales Legislative Assembly; and its first Speaker in 1856. As a result, he gained a baronetcy in 1863. He and his wife Elizabeth (nee Hill) had seven children and with his son, yet another Daniel Cooper, became prominent in the world of horse racing. Sir Daniel was also a founder and first president of the Philatelic Society of London and amassed a vast number of Australian stamps which he sold in 1878 for £3,000 - the first four figure sum for a collection of stamps. He died in 1902 and the Royal Philatelic

Society still hosts the Sir Daniel Cooper lectures in his memory.

When Florence was twelve, she had moved to 100 King's Road, Brighton with her mother and several siblings. As with many wealthy families who had contacts both in Australia and the UK, her family often travelled back and forth between the two countries but Florence never returned to Australia.

As a young woman, she met and was courted by the dashing Hugh Arundell Trevanion and while details of how and when they met are not known, they quickly became involved - too quickly some said.

Hugh had been born in 1859 in Cornwall and was a nephew of the 12th and 13th Earls of Strathmore. He was the only son of Hugh Charles and Lady Frances Trevanion of Lowndes Square in London. Frances was part of the Bowes-Lyon family whose most famous member was Queen Elizabeth, the current queen's late mother.

It is not known why Hugh's family objected to their son having a relationship with Florence. Perhaps it was because he came from the aristocracy whilst her family were nouveau rich and had inherited their fortune from an ex-convict; or possibly because the relationship was just moving far too fast. Whatever the reason, Hugh 'got impatient at the obstacles put in the way of his marriage with Miss Cooper ... so took the law in his own hands and had the ceremony quietly performed without anyone's knowledge.'[11] They married on 10 June 1882, she was twenty-six and he was twenty-two, and the families were not told until an hour after the ceremony.

A year later their first child, Florence Nellie, was born in London but died before she was a year old. Seven months later, Eric was born, but Hugh was beginning to show his true colours and just a week after their son's birth, he had pulled Florence out of bed, seized her by the throat and cut her left eye open. That same year, he came home intoxicated and assaulted her again and when they visited Ireland to stay with Florence's sister, he gave her a black eye. In April 1886, their second son, Charles Cecil was born in London. However, in October that year Hugh beat Florence so badly, she determined to leave him.

Shortly afterwards, Florence discovered a letter implying that not only was Hugh having an affair with a woman called Alice

Evelyn Savage but that she had borne his child. Florence wrote to Miss Savage demanding an explanation and the reply confirmed the child was Hugh's. Florence, always with one eye on social appearances, later paid Savage £200 to get her letter back.

Despite his affair and illegitimate child, Florence decided to forgive Hugh and they reconciled on the promise that he would treat her better. She was keenly aware of what a separation, or worse a divorce, would do to the family's social standing, particularly if a woman left a man, so Florence was keen to keep her private life out of the papers and societal gossip. She was equally determined not to let her tangled marriage affect her sons' social positions.

Having reconciled, the family moved to Teignmouth in Devon, possibly thinking that by getting away things would change. Their final child, Arundell Claude, was born in Newton Abbot in 1887, but things did not change and Hugh's violence began to escalate. He would come home late and when Florence asked where he had been, he would beat her. Finally, after another violent kicking, she left him and fled to her father's house with the three children, where she was confined to bed for ten days.

Hugh was charged with assault.

In the subsequent court case, Florence's doctor produced an affidavit confirming her injuries. She was, the doctor wrote, bruised all over her body, the marks appearing to have been made by pinching and kicking. Florence's sister also gave evidence of Hugh's violence towards his wife during their stay with her in Ireland. On another occasion, after a dinner party when the guests had left, Hugh rushed at Florence and swore he would kill her. 'On that occasion,' Florence told the court, 'I sat up in the dining room all night', presumably too afraid to go to bed with Hugh.

To heighten Florence's shame, Evelyn Savage was brought into court to testify about their affair and confirmed that she had given birth to Hugh's daughter.

Florence's bitterness boiled over and she flung in new charges against her husband: that he had squandered her fortune; that he had been disowned by his own father;[12] and that he was 'very much given to drink.' The squandering of a fortune may have some truth, as in May 1886 Hugh filed for bankruptcy, just a month after Charles Cecil had been born.[13]

In court, Hugh threw in his own counter claims saying that he had found Florence in a guest bedroom but then backed down, admitting he did not feel any indiscretion had taken place. He tried to accuse her of assaulting him but that too was dismissed and Hugh was seen for what he was, a violent bully of a man, at least towards Florence.

Hugh was found guilty on two offences of assault and sentenced to three weeks' hard labour for each, spending a total of six weeks in prison.

Florence sued for divorce.

At this time divorce was extremely rare and confined largely to the wealthy, who could afford the great cost. Nonetheless it was a scandal, even more so when it was the woman who brought the suit. Florence would have been keenly aware that what she was doing was not only going to adversely affect her social standing, but negatively impact on her three boys. Perhaps Hugh had this in mind when, despite not contesting the divorce, he insisted that the three children were brought up by Florence's parents, Sir Daniel and Elizabeth Cooper and they were not to be removed without giving him notice. Perhaps it was simply revenge, or spite. Florence could have sued for full custody of the children as the early twentieth century courts did favour the mother and Hugh would have been an unlikely choice following his conviction for violence, but Florence chose not to. Leaving the children with the Coopers seems to be an arrangement which suited them both. While it is unknown how the three boys felt about this, Eric himself was very close to his grandmother.

The divorce was granted, resulting in Florence's worst fears being realised as their 'runaway marriage'; subsequent divorce; and Hugh's trial for cruelty were sensationally covered in the international papers.

As to Hugh's sentence, the *Pall Mall Gazette* thought it derisory: 'Is Mr Trevanion, who is a barrister, to be allowed to remain a member of his clubs and to be received into society?' they asked with some astonishment, 'If he is, what combination of cruelty and vice justifies the social boycott?'[14]

Despite the prison sentence, there was no boycott so within just a few years of his release, Hugh was once again a practicing barrister and had regained his former life.

Florence moved into her parents' house with the three boys but life was still not always smooth. In September 1896, she sued her cook, Rose Norris, for assaulting nine-year-old Claude by injuring his ankle with a toasting fork. Apparently, twenty-seven-year-old Rose had only been working there a week but the 'situation did not suit her' and she handed in her notice. Since her resignation, the children had been persistently teasing her and had on one occasion refused to leave the kitchen, so she lost her temper and threw the toasting fork. It had entered Claude's ankle which subsequently became swollen. Claude was brought into court to give evidence, admitting that the cook had told him to leave the kitchen and that if he did not, she would throw the fork at him.

Rose countered that she had not thrown it *at* Claude but onto the floor when it bounced. However, Florence pointed out that Rose had also thrown a knife at Eric. He too was called into court to give evidence, a stressful time for anyone but particularly for the two children, aged just twelve and nine.

Eric said he had taken the governess' dress, which was wet, into the kitchen to have it dried, but Rose threw a carving knife at him. Annoyed by this, Rose shouted out that there were no carving knives in the kitchen, so Eric changed the description to a large knife, which he said hit him on the boot. Rose denied the charge and besides, as she pointed out, she was not on trial for that. However, the judge still found her guilty of throwing the fork at Claude, saying it was an 'unwarrantable act' and fined her 20s or seven days' imprisonment.[15]

Meanwhile, the tangled affairs of Eric's parents continued. Hugh had re-married in 1888 to Charlotte Amy Key, a woman he had already had an affair with and who had borne him a daughter in 1881, also called Charlotte Amy, a year before he married Florence. However, tragedy was to strike when Hugh's new wife died in April 1900, followed closely by his daughter, Charlotte, just two months later.

It is not known if Florence knew about the affair or the daughter, when she married Hugh. She did not cite them in the divorce proceedings. It is also not known whether she was aware that he had another daughter, May Lloyd, born to Caroline Margaret (surname unknown) in 1890, whilst he was still married to Charlotte. It seems that Hugh simply could not be faithful to any woman. Considering how angry Florence was over Hugh's infidelity, it seems probable, had she known about Charlotte and Caroline, that she would have mentioned them in the divorce.

Nevertheless, once free again and a mere three months after Charlotte's demise, Hugh married for the third time, not to Caroline, the mother of his last child, but to Florence.

Some reports state Florence was concerned that her sons would be denied a proper place in society[16] and that made her suggest they re-marry; while others claimed it was Hugh. 'When his second wife died,' wrote the *Brisbane Telegraph*, 'he approached his former wife, and suggested that they should be remarried. After a great deal of consideration, Mrs Trevanion came to the conclusion that as her sons had grown up it might be right to take this step and she married him.'[17]

It may be that Hugh was so traumatised by losing his wife and daughter in the space of three months, he needed to be with someone he knew. Whatever the reason, the press was certainly fascinated. Divorce was rare enough but the novelty of a couple re-marrying, particularly given his cruelty, was an irresistible story and they salaciously rehashed the old trial, asking why would a woman want to go back to such a man?

Despite their hopes, this marriage was no better than the first and Hugh went back to Caroline Margaret, living with her 'as his wife' for all to see.[18]

Regardless of his womanising, there is no record of Hugh ever being violent towards Evelyn, Charlotte, or Caroline, or to any of his children. He may have been abusive but nobody other than Florence went on record claiming violence. Florence does seem to have been a little, as we might say today, 'high maintenance'; and Eric was often estranged from her later in his life, although it is not known how his two brothers got on with their mother.

Despite Hugh agreeing not to molest Florence, he was still behaving badly and they divorced for the second time.

ERIC

It was into this tumultuous relationship that Hugh Eric was born on 4 December 1884 in fashionable Stamford Road, Kensington. Queen Victoria had been on the throne for forty-seven years and

William Gladstone was Prime Minister; and in May of that year Oscar Wilde had married Constance. In the January, Dr William Price had been arrested for attempting to cremate his dead baby son at Llantrisant but was acquitted as no law had been enacted to prevent cremation. When Price carried out the ceremony, it was the first in modern times.

Just a week after the birth of his first son, Hugh apparently dragged Florence from her bed and cut her eye open. Two months later, Eric was baptised on 23 February 1885 at St Peter's in South Kensington, an imposing Anglican church with a soaring steeple.[1] He was only four when his parents divorced, so possibly knew little about it but the subsequent family's scandals continued until the second divorce in 1900 when Eric was six. Whether from the psychological impact of this dysfunctional family, or inherent medical conditions, Eric grew up a sickly child.

Eric never really fitted into his wealthy and prominent family. He had suffered an accident when he was three years old which brought on convulsions[19] and had an appendicitis operation at fourteen. His mother later testified that 'he became very delicate. His palate had something wrong with it. He had an impediment in his speech. His heart was weak.'[20]

He did not attend school but was taught by private tutors and usually wintered abroad, often in Egypt and for the most part lived away from his family. Due to ill health, he was constantly tortured by insomnia and convinced it was incurable, Eric decided to spend his life travelling the world, a feat made much easier by his family's enormous wealth. Sir Daniel had died in 1902 leaving an estate valued at £558,690 (over £58 million today) out of which Florence inherited £10,000 (about one million today) and, on her mother's death, she was to inherit a further £30,000. Her three boys inherited even more and when Eric came of age, he had between £80,000 and £100,000 (about £9 million in today's money).

It was on his travels that Eric first met Albert.

---

[1]Now the St Yeghiche Armenian Church

ALBERT ROE

Albert Edward Roe was the opposite of Eric in many respects. Born in October 1878 and brought up in Swansea, South Wales, he was the third child of six, and a member of a well-known local family. His mother was Sarah (nee Rogers) and they lived at 18 and 19 Greenhill Street, which was being operated as a shaving salon.

For several years, his father, also called Albert Edward Roe, was the landlord of the *Upper Lamb Inn* and also owned the *Ale and Porter Store*. Both were in Greenhill Street and Albert helped out there.

Albert senior was prosecuted in 1884 for selling spirits in unlicensed premises and selling beer on a Sunday. A PC. Ferguson had dressed up as a sailor on a Sunday and loitered around the Porter Stores until he met a man and asked where he could get a drink. They went to a house opposite Roe's and the constable gave a boy (not Albert junior, who would have been too young) a florin to get some whisky. The boy ran across to Roe's house and soon returned with Roe's daughter who said they had no whisky but would rum do? The constable said yes, he would have a shilling's worth of rum. PC. Ferguson then went to another house for half a gallon of beer and a woman there went across to the *Ale and Porter Store* to get it. This provided enough evidence for the police to arrive at Roe's house with a warrant to search for alcohol. They found several jugs of beer in the kitchen and in the cupboard and several bottles of spirit which Roe said were for his own use.

At the hearing, Roe claimed that the second amount had been supplied by his daughter without his knowledge but the magistrate ruled that Albert senior, as landlord, had to be held fully responsible saying: 'this great evil must really be stopped at once.' Albert was fined £25 for the sale of spirits on unlicensed premises but the second charge was dropped.[21]

When Albert senior died in 1896 aged only fifty-six,[22] the pub continued to be run by his widow and family until the licence was removed because local justices believed there were too many public houses in the area. Then the family took to managing lodging houses. However, this did not end their brush with the law and in 1904 Sarah, who had recovered the *Upper Lamb Inn* and was now the landlady, was fined 40s and costs for selling liquor on a Sunday.

Albert junior had grown into a strong, muscular man with a desire to travel and, at his father's request, was given an apprenticeship on board a ship, where by hard work he climbed steadily up the ranks. In Britain, four levels of achievement were available to merchant sailors: Second Mate, First Mate, Master and Extra Master, the last being the highest professional qualification any mariner could achieve. In 1900, aged twenty-two, Albert achieved his 'second officer of a foreign going ship certificate'; in 1903 he became a first mate; and in 1905 received his Extra Master's certificate, which meant he could captain a foreign-going ship. In 1906, he was on board the *Orotava* which had been launched in 1889 but sold in 1906 to the Royal Mail Steam Packet Company to carry mail to Australia. After a refurbishment, she set sail to take mail to Ceylon, Australia, New Zealand, via Naples - a round trip taking between eight to ten weeks.

THE MEN'S TRAVELS

Every night, as part of his duties, Albert was required to patrol the sleeping quarters of the *Orotava* to ensure that everything was in order. About a week out at sea a noise caught his attention - a low sobbing coming from one of the cabins. He knocked and after being told to enter, Albert opened the cabin door to find Eric sitting alone on the floor weeping bitterly, his head resting on the bunk. Somewhat alarmed, Albert asked what was wrong and, between tears, Eric told him of how depressed and lonely he felt. He had recently received news of the death of his grandmother, Lady Elizabeth Cooper, who had brought him up after his parents' divorce. His grandmother was, said Eric, his only friend.

Eric went on to tell Albert that he was being completely

neglected by his travelling companions: his younger brother, Charles Cecil, and his brother's friend, Herbert Montgomery.[23] These two had agreed to accompany Eric on one of his trips to Ceylon but during the voyage they had paid him little attention and shunned his company.

Having helped Eric off the floor and onto the bed, Albert solicitously enquired if there was anything else he could do for him. Eric said he wanted more pillows as he slept in an almost upright position. Albert rang for the stewardess to arrange this and  instructed her to keep an eye on the young man in the future. He reported the matter to the chief officer on the bridge and thought that was the end of it.

Eric was very touched and grateful for the kindness Albert had shown him. Every night, as a high-ranking officer, it was Albert's duty to sit at the head of one the smaller tables at dinner. Eric, Charles and Herbert usually sat at his table, taking places in the middle. However, after his meeting with Albert, Eric had his seat moved next to his.

Over the following days their friendship grew and Eric tried to be with Albert as much as possible. When Albert and other offices sat on deck, Eric would join them. To them he appeared lonely and somewhat pathetic. At the investigation into Eric's death, Albert said, 'Generally he was cheerful but at times he was very despondent.'[24]

To Albert the young man poured out his problems: his difficult childhood; his parents' tempestuous marriage; and all the details of his illnesses. He described how he and his family did not get on; and how estranged he was from his mother whom he found cold and controlling. He did not mention his father and he called himself Eric, not his first name, Hugh; Claude was also known by his second name, and not Arundell. Whether this was tradition, to avoid confusion, or because the two boys were rejecting Hugh is not known.

It is also not known if Eric or his brothers knew of their two half-sisters. Eric never spoke about them but then he rarely spoke of his brothers or of his grandfather Sir Daniel who had died just four years earlier. The only person, according to Albert, whom he did speak of regularly was his grandmother and the close relationship he had with her.

At the inquest into Eric's death, Albert claimed that during the voyage he had continued to show the sickly young man kindness and attention, so much so that when Eric disembarked at Ceylon to return to England for his grandmother's funeral, he was anxious to keep in touch. Could he write to him? Albert agreed and, as the *Orotava* continued on to Australia, at every port there would be letters from Eric.

This record of a kindly older professional man taking time out of his busy life to care for a depressed ailing young man is touching but much is questionable.

The first voyage the *Orotava* made to Australia in 1906 departed on 23 February, taking seventy-five days. The date of this voyage matches Albert's testimony that Eric was crying over the death of his grandmother who had died on 1 April. It is also supported by the testimony of Eric's old governess, Mary Geneste, who said that she had received a letter from Cecil telling her that Eric was on the way back from Ceylon after being notified of his grandmother's death. However, while the outgoing passenger list of the *Orotava* shows a passenger called Trevanion, the initial given is 'C', not 'E' and there is no mention of an H (or C) Montgomery. C. Trevanion is also listed as forty-nine years old but in 1906 Cecil would have been twenty and Claude nineteen. Had a mistake had been made, this meant Cecil and Herbert were not with Eric on the voyage. In addition, why would Cecil who, Albert said, had accompanied Eric, send a letter stating that 'Eric' was returning and not say 'they' were returning? This could just have been an error on the part of Mary Geneste, speaking at the inquest seven years later. It would seem illogical for Albert to lie about this and Cecil certainly does not counter it, either in the press or at the inquest but then the brothers rarely spoke in public and Mrs Trevanion only occasionally. There is also no known reason why Mary Geneste would lie about receiving the letter.

There may well have been a voyage in which the events

described by Albert took place, but no voyage, either in 1906 or earlier, identifies Eric and either of his brothers on any ship's passenger list so far published.

Albert stated that as soon as the *Orotava* returned to the UK and prepared to turn around back to Australia, Eric booked a berth - this time alone. Eric is indeed listed alone on the passenger list although his age is shown as thirty-nine when he would only have been twenty-two. Having left on 15 June, the ship arrived in Australia on 3 August. This can be borne out by the arrival notices in the Australian newspapers and raises the question; did they really meet on the second voyage of 1906?

At the second inquest into Eric's death, Mary Geneste testified to a conversation she had with Eric in which he said he did not mind going on the voyage alone as he knew so many of the officers, implying that he had indeed been on a ship with Albert before. There is a record in the Australian newspapers of Eric arriving in February 1907 on board the *Orotava*, and he does appear on the passenger lists for this voyage but again his age is wrong; it is given as thirty instead of twenty-three.

It would seem more likely that the first voyage they met on was in June 1906 but rather than immediately jump on the next ship back, Eric did not sail again on the *Orotava* until February 1907. In which case why would Albert lie about Eric crying over the death of his grandmother and being accompanied by his brother? Perhaps he was simply mis-remembering; after all it was six years later when he was recounting the story of how they met.

Albert said Eric was particularly ill on this journey, especially so when they reached Australia. Already addicted to Veronal and alcohol, Eric was a highly-strung individual of a nervous temperament. He was frequently seen by the ship's surgeon who told Albert that Eric was taking drugs to help with insomnia. He was concerned, Albert said later, that Eric was overdosing but neither the surgeon nor Albert took any measures at this time to help Eric in controlling his intake; that is, if we can believe Albert's story about the surgeon's involvement as there is no corroborating evidence.

Arriving at Sydney, Eric was very ill for about two days; he was weak, unable to exert much effort; and remained in bed. He had relations in Australia, according to Albert, called

Montgomery although some newspaper reports cite the name McNamara, who may be relatives of Claude's friend. Eric went to stay with them to recuperate. Albert's account reinforced the notions of gratitude and friendship when, on Eric's suggestion, the Montgomery's/McNamara's invited Albert to the house for dinner. Albert reciprocated by inviting them on board the ship for lunch.

On the trip home, Eric was ill the whole time they were at sea. Albert tried to make him as comfortable as possible and even encouraged him to take part in sports on the ship but to little effect. Once they had docked in the UK, Eric was determined to show his gratitude and offered a lift to London in his chauffeur-driven car to Albert and another officer who had been kind to him. They went as far as London Bridge and had tea before parting.

At the inquest, Albert went on to explain that after this he departed for Australia and eight months later returned to find Eric and his friend, Charles Montgomery, waiting at the dock. Eric took Albert on a visit to his flat and the two men went on to spend much time together over several weeks before Albert shipped again.

They were an incongruous pair. Eric was 'shy, delicate, averse from sports, and fond of indoor life, rather a dandy, tall, slim and pale with almost girlishly small hands and feet' whilst Albert was 'robust, a well-built man, with a clean-shaven face and thick black hair, keenly interested in many forms of sport and a devoted motorist.'[25] Despite their differences, Eric had become so attached to his friend that it seemed Albert was the only person who could influence him, so much so that Eric's family began to reach out to him. Albert received a telegram from Eric's aunt, Ellen Sophia Cooper, asking him to visit her. When he showed it to Eric, the younger man replied sardonically, 'I expect it is something about me. You had better go and see her.' When Albert called, Miss Cooper told him that Eric had spoken highly of Albert to the family and his obvious affection and high regard for him had persuaded them to see if Albert could stop Eric taking drugs. He promised he would try.

At this early point in the narrative, Albert was keen to show how favourably the family regarded his friendship with Eric. Considering how toxic this relationship became after Eric's death, none of the family contested this version of Miss Cooper's intervention. However, Claude had not contested Albert's false claim that he was on board the *Orotava* in 1906 and, on a number of other issues, family members made no comments, making it difficult to verify many of Albert's accounts. In addition, why was it an aunt who spoke to Albert and not Cecil whom, according to Albert, he had known on the first voyage?

Albert told Miss Cooper he did not really know what he could do as the two men were often travelling in different directions, nevertheless he promised he would try and curb Eric's drug intake. Albert was then busy with his own family and affairs and consequently the two men did not meet for several weeks. He had also been promoted to 3rd officer on the *Orotava* and she had been sent to Belfast to undergo alterations. Eric, who Albert said was related to one of the Royal Mail Steam Packet Company directors, also got a passage to Belfast. The young man was now becoming well known to other ship officers and at Belfast Albert had a fortnight's leave and so he, Eric, and other offices spent ten days travelling via Dublin and back to London.[26]

Most of the information available about how the two men spent time spent together comes from Albert. Eric left nothing in writing, and no other testimony of this early relationship has been given by anyone else. One of the interesting aspects of these early versions is that Albert always puts himself in company with Eric alongside other people. Describing the first journey, Albert pointedly told the court that Eric was accompanied by his brother and his brother's friend but that was not true. He went on to say that when he and other officers sat on deck Eric would join them and it was to *them* that he appeared 'lonely and somewhat pathetic'. In Australia they supposedly spent time with Eric's relatives, the Montgomery's, and after they returned from the second journey to Australia, Eric offered to drive Albert, and 'another officer who had been kind to him' to London. At Belfast they were with other officers. Only once does Albert admit to being alone with Eric when, at the end of a journey, he was greeted at the quay by Eric and the two men subsequently spent time together. Despite these claims none of the other officers ever wrote their versions in the newspapers, but after the inquest one man claiming to be a fellow officer did write to the Coroner, painting a not very flattering portrait of Albert. Nor did any of the officers ever appear at the inquest to provide corroborating evidence as to Eric's weak state of mind.

Albert's stories always have him as the kind, caring older man, even though there was only a six-year difference describing how he looked after the sickly, weak younger man whom he often called a 'boy'. With no other alternatives available to us, it is his stories which are left to outline Eric's life. Whilst they may well have been true, it is also worth bearing in mind that as Albert narrated these stories at the inquest, he was protecting himself, the money he had acquired, and the need to promote the idea that this sickly young man was, according to him, suicidal.

Albert's questionable veracity can be seen in other evidence he gave to the inquest.

Albert stated that, during the time the *Orotava* was being refurbished in Belfast, he was transferred to another ship, the *La Plata*, that was also part of the Royal Mail Steam Packet Company. However, this cannot be true. There were four different ships named *La Plata* in the Royal Mail Steam Packet Company but none corresponds to the dates of Albert's travels. His claimed reassignment to the *La Plata* must have been around 1907/8, but the last ship of that name was sold by the company in 1901, so it had been disposed of before Albert supposedly met Eric on the 1906 *Orotava* voyage. Once again, we are left questioning Albert's versions of the truth. Why did he find it necessary to pretend he was elsewhere? Was it to avoid the question of where he really was?

Albert also slips up in other accounts. Having carefully built up an image of always being in the company of others alongside Eric, he revealed that every time the ship docked in Southampton, Eric was there to meet it, and he would stay with Albert often for two or three days at a time.

Albert testified that in December 1907 he was transferred to a third ship, the newly built *Asturias*,[2] returning to Belfast. Her maiden voyage was from Tilbury in Essex to Australia and, when the ship returned, Eric and Claude booked passages to Egypt on the second voyage in early 1908. When he arrived, however, Eric was so sick that he had to be carried on-board on a portable couch. His mother, who had accompanied him to Tilbury, asked Albert to give him as much attention as possible and Albert managed to get him upgraded to a better cabin.

For the first three days of the voyage, Eric was very ill but by the time they reached Port Said he was much recovered when he left the ship with Claude.

This account is again loaded with errors. The *Asturias* was indeed built in Belfast, but her maiden voyage was from London, not Tilbury which lies further down the Thames in Essex. The second voyage which Eric was supposed to be on did not return to Australia until 7 April 1909, not 1908 as claimed by Albert. For a professional seaman, Albert seems to have a dreadful memory of his voyages.

As usual, neither Florence nor Claude countered these earlier accounts that were steeped in errors. The passenger lists show that Claude did make a trip to Egypt in January 1908 but abroad the *Asterias* not the *Asturias*, a ship owned by the Orient Line, not the Royal Mail Steam Packet Company for whom Albert worked.[27] What is interesting is that Eric is not shown as a passenger on that journey either. He does appear on the manifest of the *Cap Blanco*, of the Hamburg South American Line, travelling back from New York to Southampton over a year later in March 1909. Claude is not listed as a passenger but his friend, Charles Montgomery, is with Eric and this voyage ties in with an extract from the *Cambrian Daily Leader*:

> Whatever the steamer, on which Mr Roe was
> engaged went, there Mr Trevanion insisted on going
> also. At a later period Mr Trevanion's friend was
> transferred to a boat in the Canadian trade, but Mr

---

[2] She was requisitioned in 1914 as a hospital ship in World War 1 and was torpedoed in 1917 by a German U-boat. She went on to work as a cruise liner until retired and scrapped in 1933.

Trevanion found the climate too severe for his constitution, and the Canadian voyages were accordingly discontinued, although the two friends remained in constant communication.[28]

Ships travelling to Canada would often stop off in New York and Eric may have made his way back via the *Cap Blanco*. This account again raises a number of questions. There is no other evidence that Albert was transferred to a Canadian ship. He may well have done so while the *Orotava* was being refurbished in Belfast, but why would Albert, an experienced sailor, get the ship name wrong? It is possible that journalists may have written the names incorrectly, particularly with the case of the *Asterias* and *Asturias* which sound alike, and a number did call the *Orotava* the *Oratara*, but journalistic mistakes cannot account for all of Albert's errors.

It was on the supposed return trip from Australia on board the *Asturias* that Albert was taken ill.

ALBERT'S ILLNESS

In 1908, Albert had been playing cricket on board ship when he was struck in the foot with the ball and sustained what he thought at the time was a trifling injury. During his correspondence with Eric, he mentioned his illness. At first, he said Eric was with him on this voyage but later said he wrote letters, implying Eric was not there and when he returned, Eric invited him to his apartment at St Stephen's Crescent in Bayswater, London. Concerned about his health, he asked his physician, Dr Sandifer if he would examine Albert and the doctor duly advised an operation. Albert went to Southampton and stayed in a nursing home for a short period.

Having recovered, Albert went back to sea and travelled to the West Indies but the ship suffered an unknown mishap, so the officers were returned to the UK in October 1909. On the way back, Albert had a relapse and doctors on board diagnosed his condition as blood poisoning caused by the dye from his coloured socks. He returned to Swansea where he recuperated for nearly a year, at times quite ill and on one occasion hovering 'between life and death.'[29]

According to Albert, Eric corresponded with him and went to see him on just one occasion, although other evidence supports a different story.

The coverage in *The Cambrian Daily Leader* suggests that Eric was frantic about Albert; wrote to him almost daily; and sent parcels of papers, magazines, fruit and other delicacies. He arrived in Swansea with an 'intense craving' to be with Albert as he felt 'morose and depressed when they were separated.'

Eric stayed one night at Albert's family house which, since the loss of their pub licence, had been turned into a grocer's; but on other occasions he stayed at the *Singleton* or at the *Cameron Hotel,* belying Albert's version of Eric's sole visit.[30]

'On the first occasion,' an unnamed hotel staff member told the *Cambrian Daily Leader*:

> ...he arrived on a Saturday and remained over the weekend. I am not sure about the second occasion, but I believe he stayed here once later for a single night. I remember him well. The name is not a very common one, and as soon as I read the story in the 'Leader,' I recollected at once who was referred to. Mr Trevanion was very affectionate in his ways; in fact, in this respect he was more like a lady. During his stay here he occupied room No 219. I went up to him on one occasion, and was surprised to see the quantity of powders, puffs and cosmetics he had lying about. It was just like a small chemist's shop. Mr Trevanion appeared to be of a generous disposition, and was seemingly not a man who drank much; in fact, I should say quite the contrary. He wore a watch fastened round his wrist, and several rings; indeed his fingers were almost covered in them.[31]

Eric's appearance generated comments from almost everyone: Albert's neighbours described him as 'over six feet in height, of slender physique, a perfect gentleman in his manners, and somewhat fastidious in his method of dress. He also used to 'wave' his hair.'[32]

The description of Eric as 'more like a lady' conforms to a number of descriptions of effete men of the late nineteenth and early twentieth century, who may or may not have been homosexual. Perhaps the most well-known is the fifth Marquis of Anglesey, Henry Paget, who ten years before Eric's death had almost his entire jewellery collection stolen in a highly publicised robbery.

Henry Cyril Paget, 5th Marquis of Anglesey, seated in drag by a tree. 1905.

While much of the press was sympathetic, notes of ridicule crept in to some articles, such as when the *North Wales Express* commented:

> ...people are laughing at the idea of a man carrying so many jewels with him in order to adorn his person. With a woman, of course, it would have been altogether different; but a bejewelled man, be he prince or peasant, is looked upon as being troubled with effeminacy.[33]

Paget had appeared in the press on many occasions due to his flamboyance: 'In appearance,' wrote the *Yorkshire Post* 'there was ... an almost total absence of the masculine quality in his character, and he went with easy facility from one extravagance to others greater still.'

The colonial press, less restricted than the staid British newspapers, was more open and critical of Paget. 'He is a thoroughly effeminate-looking young fellow,' wrote the *West Australian Sunday Times* 'and he may be seen when in Paris walking around with a toy terrier under his arm, the pet being heavily scented and bedizened with bandages and bows. The fingers of the Marquis fairly blaze with rings. His favourite dogs had jewelled collars and their hair curled and perfumed.'

One writer, 'T. P.', in the New Zealand paper *Otago Witness*, tried to understand him and others like him:

> I am driven to the conclusion from much that I have
> seen that there are men who ought to have been
> born women, and women who ought to have been
> born men ... Bearing the form of a man, he yet had all
> the tastes, something even of the appearance, of not
> only a woman, but, if the phrase be permissible, a
> very effeminate woman.

The German physician, Magnus Hirschfeld, ran an annual journal, *Jahrbuch für sexuelle Zwischenstufen,*[34] where he also discussed Paget in 1904. Hirschfeld was an important theorist of sexuality and a prominent advocate of the rights of homosexual people, believing homosexuality was natural. He thought that a scientific understanding of sexuality would promote societal acceptance, something which was slow to happen. His comments about Paget were later used by Iwan Block in his 1964 book *The Sexual Extremities of the World:*

> ...the Marquis of Anglesey... also seems to have had
> homosexual tendencies, or at least to have been
> effeminate to a high degree ... resembled a
> pampered eccentric woman with all the whims and
> weaknesses of the latter. He really had the
> appearance of a pretty women attired in male
> clothing. Silky locks surrounded a pink face,
> distinguished by the softness and gentleness of its
> features. In order to appear even paler and more
> interesting he didn't hesitate to use the powder box
> or blanching toilet waters. He was always strongly
> perfumed and his dainty long fingers were enmeshed
> in rings.[35]

Henry's excessive spending on jewels and costumes finally bankrupted him and he fled to France, dying there in 1905.

Another man, Charles Frances Seymour, brought a libel action against the *Daily Telegraph* for defamation. In court the defence stated: 'We will show you that this man ... disgraced his family name, painted his face, roughed his neck, painted his arms and breast, wore petticoats, and assumed the dress of a female ballet dancer.'

One of the main planks of the *Telegraph's* defence was *to* argue that Seymour's associates alone proved his guilt - that in the UK he had been friends with Lord Alfred Douglas, the lover of Oscar Wilde, and the Marquis of Anglesey.

It is possible that Eric was familiar with the press stories about Henry Paget. He was twenty-one when Paget died, and the media coverage had been extensive. There were many similarities in the ways the two men dressed and acted and at the inquiry into Eric's death, more details would emerge. However, during his lifetime the sensational reporting around Henry Paget and others does not seem to have impacted on Eric either in the way he dressed or behaved in public. It can be argued that both Henry and Eric were extremely wealthy and could afford to go their own ways, opportunities not so easily available for others with diverse sexual orientations and gender identities. Newspapers across the world are littered with examples of working-class people who cross-dressed and cross-lived - and who had been arrested, simply for wearing clothes of the opposite sex.

Meanwhile in Swansea, as Albert recovered from his severe blood poisoning, Eric tried to convince him to stay with him at the hotel, with no success. Eric went to the family, insisting on taking his friend back to London and they and Albert finally agreed. However, in later testimony, Albert changes this story and said he went to Aberystwyth to recuperate.

Once again, the narrative is driven by Albert who is cast as a neutral observer, whilst Eric is described as 'frantic', sending 'daily parcels', and having an 'intense craving' to see his friend, all reinforcing the idea of a neurotic character. Yet the description from the hotel staff member does not conform to this image, there is nothing frantic in his behaviour, only observations as to how eccentric and how 'like a lady' he was.

In March 1911, Albert was well enough to resume work but when his doctor advised that he not return to sea, his brother-in-law found him a job as a colliery clerk. However, just nine months later he was employed by Eric and had gained control of both Eric and his fortune.

It was generally considered, by various witnesses for both sides at the inquest, that Eric had been living something of a chaotic life and that Albert's training as an officer was helping Eric regain control. Apparently so successful was he that when the pair returned from their world trip, Eric's lawyers were said to have expressed their appreciation of his excellent work and as a consequence Albert received a pay rise from Eric.

In this new calmer version of Eric's life, a decision was needed as to where they were going to live. The pair had frequently visited Brighton and Hove so Eric decided he wanted to move there.

2

DEATH AND EXHUMATION

LIFE IN BRIGHTON AND HOVE

Postcard, dated 3.9.1913 "Brighton – Aquarium and Marine Parade"

In the early 1910s, Brighton and Hove[3] were popular places, easily accessible from London by rail and with a rapidly growing population. Many of the imposing buildings had been constructed during Victorian times and, in 1883, the majestic Grand Avenue Mansions were the first purpose-built apartment blocks in Britain. Running from King's Gardens on the sea-front to the main street in Hove, the Avenue was one of the most fashionable and exclusive in the area.

Eric knew the area well: his mother had lived in King's Road when she was twelve and Eric, like many wealthy people, often visited the area. He and Albert would motor down and with Eric's 'eccentric' appearance they were often recognised in hotels across the south coast. The two men travelled a great deal, either with

---

[3] The area was merged with Brighton in 1997

Albert driving or later with a chauffeur and would often stay at the imposing and exclusive Grand Hotel in Brighton, still one of the most expensive hotels in the town.[4]

Later investigations by the police revealed that the first occasion the two men stayed at the Grand Hotel was 1 to 10 December 1910, when they occupied a suite of rooms consisting of three bedrooms, a sitting room, a bathroom and a W.C. They returned on 30 September 1911, staying until 16 October and again on 15 to 22 May 1912, each time occupying the same type of suite. The last time they stayed was 31 July to 17 August 1912 when they occupied one bedroom containing two beds and it was from here that they moved to take up residence in the flat.[36]

Eric had been impressed with the Grand Avenue Mansions so the two men moved into No 10 on the fourth floor,[37] in a flat previously occupied by a Baron von Bissing.[38] Another neighbour was General Sir Thomas Kelly-Kenny, a famous Boer War soldier. The rent was £275 a year (about £22,000 today) on a seven-year lease and Eric keen to move in his antique collection and furniture, set about:

> making his home a miniature palace. His ambition was achieved. His flat was an amazing storehouse of treasure and works of art collected in his travels. Imagination showed in every nook and corner, reflecting the sybaritic temperament of this wealthy young man. To make his flat perfect in every detail was his hobby. He spent his time thinking out combinations of wonderful colour schemes. He was a commander-in-chief of a small army of workmen, who carried out his ideas. Perhaps he reached the height of his craving for artistic effect in a scarlet sitting room which was called "The Den." Here a deep rich red is made the predominant colour. The walls, the carpet, the curtains, and the lamp shades are of red. In striking contrast is the sombre but imposing dining room, of black oak, whose walls are hung with oil

---

[4] It came to fame in 1984 during the Conservative Party Conference when the IRA attempted to assassinate Margaret Thatcher.

paintings, some by Romney, of the Trevanion's ancestors.[39]

There were three reception rooms and three bedrooms in the flat. The main bedroom was large, furnished with costly art objects from all over the world. The wallpaper was a dark grey with a cream-flowered border and the floor was laid with a thick Turkish carpet as Eric was particularly fond of expensive fabrics. One of the most striking pieces of furniture was a tall-backed chair of a dark highly polished wood which a neighbour thought was a present from the Pope. The walls were hung with great pictures, including a portrait of Boadicea reputedly worth some thousands of pounds,[40] and a painting of the Madonna by Leonardo de Vinci.[41]

An unnamed person, who was obviously very knowledgeable about antiques, was in the flat a few days after Eric's death and told the *Daily Express*:

> I do not believe that I have ever visited a flat which combined such costliness and taste. The walls of Mr Trevanion's bedroom for instance, were covered with portraits in oil. These pictures were illuminated by a clever arrangement of electric lights so contrived as to show each to the best advantage. The effect against the background of the torpedo-grey walls was a striking one. This bedroom must have contained thousands of pounds worth of articles. It was a treasure house of art objects gathered from all lands. Shelves, cabinets, and tables ranged about the room supported a high of valuable articles, each of which seemed to be a gem. I noticed particularly some fine bronzes of the Italian school, half a dozen or more exquisite little ivory statues, and specimens of Meissen ware, as well as examples of rare porcelain from several countries, a set of Crown Derby ware, and some old silver. The cornices of the walls seemed to be of silver or a substance like silver and the thick Turkey-red carpet with a blue pattern, added richness to the room.[42]

The neighbours were certainly aware of the unusual couple. After Eric's death, a number came forward to describe them:

> Three things must have impressed the most casual observer who saw Mr Trevanion for the first time, even for a few moments,' one said to the Daily Express, 'The first was his peculiar walk, which I can only describe as a sort of stagger, the second, his habit of wearing a gold bracelet sometimes on the right wrist, sometimes on the left; and the third his extraordinary high-heeled boots. These boots were all the more striking because his feet were as small as a girl's and he stood nearly six feet in height.[43]

According to a variety of descriptions, Eric was slender to the point of fragility, his hair fair with a reddish tinge and his face pale with sunken eyes, perhaps a result of his chronic insomnia. He was regarded as somewhat eccentric as he wore his hair artificially waved and was usually adorned with jewels of great value. One item was a cross set with diamonds, valued at several thousand pounds that he wore on his breast. He was known by everyone to be very wealthy and very generous to his friends,[44] the majority of whom were of his own sex. Albert later said of Eric that he would never pass a beggar in the street without giving him money.[45]

Neighbours thought he suffered from heart weakness: 'The least exertion fatigued him,' said one, 'and he had to be assisted into the lift when he descended to the motor-car in which he and Mr Roe took almost daily drives.'[46]

Eric owned two British made cars, a Rolls Royce and a Siddeley-Deasy. The latter rumoured to have been used by the King George V at the 1911 Delhi Durbar, a celebration to mark his succession as Emperor of India. Whether true or not, the upholstery and fittings were of the most elaborate style. On the seats were four cushions that had cost four guineas each (about £1,000 today) as well as numerous expensive electrical devices, including a button that released bunches of artificial flowers and another that opened a container of cigars and a cigarette lighter.

An unnamed friend said of Eric's car: 'It was the most sumptuously furnished vehicle of the kind I have ever seen.' Eric's lavish spending was evident; he even paid his chauffeur £4 10s a week, when the average wage was around £3.

'The two men were scarcely ever apart,' said another neighbour of Eric and Albert, 'Mr Trevanion seemed to think a tremendous lot of his friend, and always wanted to be with him. In his company he would seem, so far as his ill-health would permit to enjoy life, but in Mr Roe's absence he would become almost spiritless.'[47]

Eric initially referred to Albert as 'Rex' (Latin for 'king'), possibly to reflect the control Albert had over his friend but later Eric changed it to 'Bear'; for whilst Eric was tall, frail and delicate with a slight stoop, Albert was robust and muscular and, said Eric, often 'gruff on times.'

Eric showered gifts on Albert as he had, according to Albert's later testimony, saved his life on the ship. Among the many presents were a beautiful sable coat and a gold cigarette case set with diamonds, inscribed with the word, 'Rex'.

THE FATEFUL DAY

Eric loved beautiful things and once moved in to their new flat, he threw himself into decorating. On 9 September, he was fitting blinds and gilding chairs with every indication that he was making plans for the future, yet two days later he was dead.

Albert arrived back in Brighton at 7.40[48] on the 9th and they dined together, but Eric ate very little. After the meal they had coffee and Eric went to the bedroom where his man-servant, Joiner, opened a bottle of sparkling hock (white wine) for him. Later Albert went to look for him and, according to his testimony, they were talking together about ordinary things when suddenly Eric said, 'Bear, I've taken an overdose. Ring Dr Baines'[49] and those were the last words he spoke.

When Albert phoned the doctor, he repeated what Eric had said and Dr Baines quickly arrived, immediately attempting to administer an emetic. Baines was the same doctor who had treated Eric just a few weeks earlier when he had become unconscious due to an overdose.[50]

There was nothing the doctor could do and Eric lingered until 11 September when he died.

At the first inquest, Dr Baines had declared that death had

been caused by an accidental overdose and with no suspicions aroused, the body was taken back to London and buried in the family vaults at West Norwood Cemetery.[5] However, nearly a month later, due to Eric's mother's concerns, the body was exhumed on 8 October 1912.[51]

The exhumation took place at night to avoid public scrutiny, and only those deemed absolutely necessary were allowed to attend:

> Screened from all observation and working solely by the flickering light of lamps in the dark and silent cemetery at West Norwood, the stonework of the vault was removed, the coffin was raised and opened, and a doctor removed the contents of the stomach and placed them in vessels for expert analysis. Then the coffin was closed again, reverently lowered into the vault, and the head-stones placed in position once more.[52]

As a result of the expert analysis, a new inquest was ordered by Charles Mathews, the Public Prosecutor because it was deemed that the jury had been denied information on how much of the drug Eric had actually taken.

The press was avid for details and attempted to interview any of those involved. Albert, still stinging from Florence's reference to 'a case of murder', refused to be drawn out, telling the *Cambrian Daily Leader:* 'I have nothing to hide, and when the proper time comes for me to speak I shall do so. Until then I have nothing to say on the matter. My solicitors are acting on my behalf, and until they instruct me to speak my lips are sealed.'[53]

An unnamed friend did, however, speak for him, saying that while Albert knew Eric's will was being contested, he had not been informed of the Trevanion family's decision to apply for a second inquest. He had only heard about it through the newspapers the night before he left for London. 'I can assure you,' continued the friend:

> That Mr Roe, whilst still feeling the loss of his friend, is not in the least perturbed by recent events. The

---

[5] It was one of the first private landscaped cemeteries and is one of the 'Magnificent Seven' cemeteries of London

circumstances concerning his relationship with Mr Trevanion, and the extent to which he benefits under the will, were, as the "Leader" has already explained, well known to many people. Mr Roe has concealed nothing, because he has nothing to conceal, and when his story is told, as it will be at the inquest next week, it will be found that what Mr Trevanion did was by way of making his appreciation of the honourable manner in which Mr Roe had acted in connection with his affairs throughout. It is quite true that overtures were made with a view to a compromise over the will, and that these were declined on the advice of Mr Roe's representatives, who had been fully acquainted with Mr Trevanion's intentions.[54]

The press was not so easily put off and avidly followed Albert's movements.

He was supposed to have driven back and forth from London to Swansea in a car but this was denied by friends. Other reports said he had not been seeing his mother which was untrue as he visited regularly.[55] On Saturday 18 January 1913, a relaxed Albert returned to Swansea having been to Cardiff to watch the Wales and England rugby match.[6] He arrived at High Street Station at 8pm, spent the night with his family and left again for London the following day by the 3.10 train.[56] One of the *Leader's* journalists who saw him reported him as looking:

…particularly cheerful. He is apparently little concerned with what is going on, and chatted and joked with the friends who saw him off. Mr Roe was accompanied by an intimate personal friend in the person of Mr Andrew Paton, the well-known local golf and billiard player, who will remain with him until the completion of the coroner's investigation.[57]

Albert was intending to meet his lawyers in London before heading to Brighton for the inquiry which was predicted to last three days.

As the press sensationally covered Eric leaving the whole of

---

[6] Wales lost 0-12

his fortune to a 'close' friend, Albert's family had, supposedly, been taken completely by surprise. They knew, they told the local press, that Albert was friendly with a wealthy young man who had shown an interest in him but were stunned to hear that Eric's estate had been left to Albert. The *Cambrian Daily Leader* was not convinced of the so-called 'shock', pointing out that most of Albert's friends knew of his situation, so it is unlikely the family would not. What was the point of lying? Albert had been receiving large gifts of money from Eric for several years, and was in receipt of a large salary. Yet there does not seem to have been any money passed to the family. They continued to live in Greenhill Street, Swansea moving up and down the row of terrace houses, living first at 18 and 19, then at 32 and finally at number 30. Wherever they lived in this poor neighbourhood, the family took in lodgers. In the 1911 census, Sarah, Albert's mother, had three boarders living at her address, making a total of nine people crammed into the house. Albert registers this as his address in 1911 with his profession listed as a 'colliery clerk'.

The press, having gained little information from Albert's side, turned to Eric's family but they too were tight lipped; Mrs Trevanion telling a *Daily Express* reporter on 15 January:

> At present it is not my intention to say anything concerning my son's death. I can only await the result of the second inquest. One statement, however, I should like to correct. Mr Roe was not, as I have been quoted, a lifelong friend of my son Eric. My son met Mr Roe on board ship, while on a voyage home, not so very long before his death.

Perhaps Florence was genuinely mistaken about the length of contact between the two men. Certainly, both Albert and Eric are on record as being aboard one of the *Orotava's* journeys six years previously, but the amount of contact between Eric and his mother is debatable. Most of it is dependent on Albert's version, and he claimed that Eric was estranged from Florence for some time. If that was true, she may have genuinely believed that it was not until the world tour in 1911 when they met.

3

DAY 1 – FRIDAY 24 JANUARY 1913: THE NEW INQUIRY

Hove Town Hall in 1907

The second inquiry was set to take place in the banqueting hall at Hove Town Hall. The police court, which would normally be used, was not going to be large enough to cater for the expected crowds caused by the enormous interest the case had generated. As it was, Hove Corporation had to make alterations to the Town Hall to cater for thirty official pressmen and as many of the public who could squeeze in. All witnesses who had attended the first inquest were subpoenaed and fresh witnesses were going to be called.

The inquest opened on Friday 24 January 1913 at 12.30 by the East Sussex Coroner, Dr G. Vere Benson, the same coroner who had carried out the initial inquiry. Highly experienced, Benson was well thought of and had been Deputy-Coroner for West Middlesex 1894-99 and Coroner for East Sussex in 1899. From 1908 to 1910, he was vice-president of the Coroners' Society of England and Wales and had contributed to the *Encyclopaedia of the Laws of England*, the *Dictionary of National Biography* and other publications.[58] Benson and Charles Mathews, the Public Prosecutor, thought it would be a very speedy inquiry lasting no more than a day or so. It was to last for seven sittings carried out over three weeks.

As the doors of the banqueting hall opened, there was a rush for places and great crowds gathered in the vicinity of the Town Hall hoping to get in. The stained-glass windows and high pew-like wooden seats of the banqueting hall made it look like a chapel and a number of fashionable dressed women had places in the public gallery. Once they had secured their seats, many of them did not leave the court during the interval, preferring to go without lunch than risk losing such coveted places.

ALBERT EDWARD ROE,
(from a photograph taken some years ago).

About fifty journalists managed to squeeze in, sitting in a long row of seats under the public gallery. The case was covered extensively in international newspapers: 'No case for many days has aroused such a great amount of public interest, especially in London,' wrote the *New York Times*, 'where Trevanion's eccentricity in dress had been the subject of much comment in the hotels where he stayed.'[59]

The *Cambrian Daily Leader*, determined to cover 'local boy' Albert, boasted that they were 'the only journal which has given a verbatim account of the proceedings, a special staff of reporters having been engaged on the case.'[60]

R. D. Muir, who had requested the second inquest, would represent the Attorney General; Frederick Palmer represented Albert; and Eric's family were represented by renowned barrister, Oswald Hanson.

Florence, accompanied by one of her sons, was swathed all in black, with a heavy fur boa and a large picture hat.[61] However, it was Albert the press wanted to see and they watched him carefully, noting his manner and appearance. He was described as dark, curly-haired, a clean-shaven man 'with a face suggestive of a seafaring life'. On his wrist he wore a watch bracelet, had gold rings on his fingers, and a diamond pin glistened in his tie. He wore 'a dark lounge suit which set off his broad shoulders and compact figure'[62] and sat with his arms folded listening to the evidence, at times smiling at one of the two male friends who had accompanied him.

Coroner Benson, in his introduction, told the fifteen-strong jury that the first case had been heard by him on 12 September,

The Coroner Mr Vere Benson

death having occurred on the morning of the 11 September 1912. The evidence that death had occurred by misadventure with an overdose of Veronal was 'so clear' that there did not appear any reason to order a post mortem.[63] However, evidence supplied after the inquest led to the body being exhumed on 8 October and a chemical analysis was performed by two of the most distinguished experts in Britain. They found that Eric's body contained in the region of 150 grains of Veronal, taken in the hour before he became unconscious. Benson said that was an astonishing result and certainly one not expected by himself or anyone on the jury. The question had to be asked, how was it that such an enormous dose came to be taken?

The usual recommended dose for general insomnia was from five to ten grains, but Eric would take doses of between seven, or seven and a half grains in cachets. Cachets were made of gelatinised starch paste, or rice paper, and looked a little like ravioli. The packets had the white crystalline powder sealed inside, odourless but with a bitter taste. Several cachets would be contained in a long glass phial with a cork stopper and a number of phials placed in a box, one box containing a dozen cachets. The cachets themselves would usually be circular, stuck down around the edges and would dissolve in liquids, although they could also be pulled apart to free the powder. The most common way to take them was to hold the cachet by the fingertips and dip them in a liquid to create a soft, slippery surface and then swallow them whole like eating an oyster.

On nights when Eric could not sleep, he would often take two cachets. Could he really, asked Benson, have taken twenty-one by misadventure? They had all been taken at the same time about thirty-six hours before death and he would have been unconscious within the hour. In addition, the coroner pointed out that as Eric knew Veronal so well he knew he would not have to take 150 grains to kill himself, as fifty would have done the job.[64] If suicide was to be put aside, he told the jury, they would have to suspect foul play and consider whether there were any suspicious circumstances. Was there any opportunity? Was there a motive? Was there anything to suggest that anybody else had any hand in it? These had to be considered by the jury and Coroner Benson advised them to spread their inquiries as widely as possible so they might miss nothing.[7]

There were three questions to consider, said Benson: was it suicide; was the poison given to Eric deliberately with homicidal intent; or was it misadventure. He admitted it was all a bit of a mystery:

> I am bound to say that there are difficulties in regard to accepting any one of the theories, the possibilities, which I have mentioned to you … and it will be very necessary for you to give your best attention, and to spread your inquiries as widely as possible, so as to miss nothing that might throw any light upon what I think may fairly be ascribed as somewhat of a mystery. I mean to say by that the thing is not explained satisfactorily by anything that has been as yet made public; and I do not know that even with the further knowledge that I have of the facts I should like to anticipate what your verdict would be.[65]

Benson admitted in his introduction to details not made public and it was those details which were to prove so troubling.

---

[7] Inquest juries were allowed to ask questions

THE UNDERTAKER

After the Coroner had spoken for forty minutes, George Baker, a Brighton undertaker, was called. He had conducted the funeral and was present at the exhumation to identify the body alongside Eric's mother.

The first question put to Baker was why a cremation order had so rapidly been given when there was a family vault for the Coopers. It certainly was an interesting point for had the cremation gone ahead, the enormous overdose would never have come to light.

Baker testified that it was Dr Baines who told him that Eric was to be cremated and so he had taken the forms to be filled out; one by the coroner and another by a family member. On 12 September, Coroner Benson refused to fill out the papers, presumably because it was the day of the inquest and Benson was waiting for the verdict before proceeding. In the meantime, Baker went home but later received a telephone call from Cecil Trevanion, Eric's brother, asking him to return to the flat. He did so and they met at the door but instead of inviting him in, they remained outside on the landing. Cecil told Baker that he was to take no instructions from anyone except himself. The cremation forms were never completed and Eric was subsequently buried in the family vault on 14 September, three days after he had died.

This raises a number of questions. From whom did Dr Baines receive instructions that Eric was to be cremated? Certainly, he had not consulted the Trevanions as they wanted him buried in the family vault. Conversely, he didn't seem to be hiding anything as he told the undertaker that a member of the family needed to sign the form. A doctor would not have taken it upon himself to decide on burial or cremation so Albert most likely told him.

THE EXHUMATION

After the undertaker had given evidence, Dr Willcox and pathologist, Dr Spilsbury, who did the analysis of Eric's remains, were called to present their reports which contained detailed descriptions of the body, the post mortem, and the test results.

Before they began, Muir asked the Coroner if he could hand

the reports of the two men to the jury to read as, 'It is undesirable they should be read out in public,'[66] but this was overruled.

The first part of the reports contained no difficulties as they related the removal of the coffin from vault No. 3561 at Norwood Cemetery, a vault originally built for Eric's grandfather, and inscribed 'In memory of Daniel Cooper, Esq. 1853'. Other inscriptions showed three additional family members had been interred there.

Eric's coffin, which bore the inscription 'Hugh Eric Trevanion, Born 4th December 1884, Died 11th September 1912', was taken into the cloisters to make it easier for the pathologists to carry out their work. It also meant strong lights could be provided as the work was carried out at night to discourage press intrusion. The coffin itself consisted of an outer shell of oak; a lead shell soldered shut; and a second oak coffin within. The body was covered with cotton wool and flowers. In Eric's right hand were three handkerchiefs, 'the size of a lady's', each with a 'W' embroidered in the corner; the reason for the 'W' is not known. Next to Eric's head was a towel with the monogram H. E. T. 1, and the date 1897. The initials were for Hugh Eric Trevanion, but the significance of the 1 and the  date is also not known. Eric did not meet Albert until 1906 so the event being commemorated predated that relationship.

Eric was dressed in a silk night-gown also inscribed 'H. E. Trevanion'; on the ring finger of the left hand was a plain gold ring; on the right wrist a gold bangle and a brown metal bangle. Attached to the front of the nightgown was a 'curious umbrella brooch of gun metal' (a grey corrosion-resistant form of bronze).

The reports of Spilsbury and Willcox described the remains as that of a well-nourished man about 5ft 11½in in height (about 1.8 metres). There was a small gaping wound on the radial artery of the right wrist but no other marks of violence; some blood staining from the mouth and ears; and some green staining due to putrefaction round the back, neck, thighs and chest; the hair came off readily; the eyes were glazed and the colour could not be recognised; but altogether the body was in a good state of preservation with the features well preserved; which must have made it easier for his mother to view.

THE PATHOLOGIST

Sir Bernard Spilsbury

Dr Bernard Henry Spilsbury, later Sir, was a pathologist who worked for the Home Office and at St Mary's Hospital. He was a boyish-looking, clean-shaven man who, like Muir, had worked on several sensational cases including the Crippen case, the 'Brides in the Bath', 'Brighton trunk' and 'Blazing Czar' murders, among many others. Despite his dominance in many cases of the first half of the twentieth century, Spilsbury's reputation has since been reassessed and his methodologies questioned. Among many concerns he would often refuse to work with others; keep abreast of developments in research; or to share his work However in this case, there are no reasons to doubt his results.

Spilsbury was asked to read out his report 'slowly and clearly' for everyone to understand. He proceeded to describe the body and organs, which were well preserved with no disease to account for death, their appearance consistent with Veronal poisoning.[67] Eric had a little pneumonia which was frequently found after periods of unconsciousness.[68] This was consistent in other research carried out by Spilsbury on fatal cases of Veronal poisoning at St Mary's Hospital, where he had found bronco-pneumonia present in a large percentage of those cases.

Spilsbury then read out that part of the report Muir had considered 'undesirable they should be read out in public'. It was just one line, but it was to have a significant impact on the case.

The press did not include it in their reporting, and the details remained sequestered away in the files at the ESRO and on four index cards, Spilsbury's autopsy notes, in the Wellcome Library.

On top of the first autopsy card are the underlined words 'Sexual Pervert', and on the second 'the anus was very patulous and skin was loose around it' – patulous from the Latin patēre meaning 'wide open.'[69] The line also appears in his report submitted to the court with an additional comment: 'the genital organs were normal'. Dr Willcox's account, held in the ESRO, also contains the same line about the 'patulous' anus. In an earlier document to the police, also held at ESRO, Spilsbury's account ends with the line, 'the condition of the anus and surrounding skin was not due to post mortem changes but was present during life. I think it is very suggestive of some unnatural vice.' Willcox in his police report concurred, 'In my opinion the condition of the anus is significant. I did not consider it was a natural change occurring from post mortem; I think the condition must have been present during life, and I agree with the witness Dr Spilsbury as to the probable cause of it.'

The press handled this detail in various ways. Some, like the local Welsh newspaper the Cambrian Daily Leader, did not include the uncomfortable testimony at all; while others, including the national Daily Sketch, hinted that the evidence was indicative of a 'habit far worse than that of drug-taking.'[70]

The theory of identifying homosexual men by the nature of the anus had existed since 1857 when Auguste Ambroise Tardieu, a French forensic doctor, published his book 'Etude médico-légale sur les attentats aux moeurs (Forensic Study of Assaults Against Decency). Tardieu, who wrote extensively on various kinds of sexual abuse, outlined six basic criteria which he claimed could be used to identify homosexual men: excessive development of the buttocks; funnel-shaped deformation of the anus; relaxation of the sphincter; the effacement of the folds, the crests, and the wattles at the circumference of the anus; extreme dilation of the anal orifice; and ulcerations, haemorrhoids and fistulas.[71]

As Tardieu's book ran into numerous editions, his method of examination was adopted in many countries, including Britain. Other doctors built on his work with examples of their own. Men arrested on suspicion of homosexuality were often examined by the police doctor and cases will often cite a doctor's name as a court witness.

Perhaps the most well documented case is that of Thomas Ernest Boulton and Frederick William Park or 'Fanny and Stella' as they were popularly known. The Boulton and Park case was a sensation in 1871 when the men, who often cross-dressed, appeared in court on a charge of 'conspiring and inciting persons to commit an unnatural offence', namely homosexuality. Boulton and Park were submitted to extensive and intimate examinations to ascertain if they had anal sex but in the end the prosecution could not convince the jury and they were released.

By the late nineteenth century, the theory of Tardieu and others was completely discredited: there is simply no consistent evidence that can prove anal sex has taken place and 'open' anuses can have a variety of causes. However, the legacy of this flawed examination is a long one and Tardieu's theories are still being used in a variety of countries today to 'prove' homosexuality, despite the UN Committee Against Torture saying that such examinations 'have no medical justification' and campaigners insisting that they violate international law.[72]

THE VERONAL EXPERT

Dr William H. Willcox, the Senior Scientific Analyst to the Home Office, was the best possible person to speak about the effects of Veronal, having studied and written about the drug and other barbiturates. Whilst he was a great believer in the drug's usefulness for a number of conditions, he was also acutely aware of its dangers.

He was a slow-speaking man with ruffled dark hair and moustache. A box of powders peeped out of the breast pocket of his morning coat and he held a glass phial containing 150 grains of Veronal.[73]

As Willcox gave his evidence, there was a brief discussion about the reason for the gaping wound on Eric's wrist. Willcox explained that many people were afraid of being buried alive so it was a common practice to have such an incision made, in order to be quite certain that the person was dead.

They then started to discuss Veronal. Replying to a question from Palmer, Albert's lawyer, about the amount needed to become immune to the drug, Willcox explained that a person who had been taking Veronal for years would be able to take a larger dose. However, although long-term users could take two or three times the proper dose, constant use did not have the same effect as morphia, in that the more you took the more resistant you were to it. The average recommended dose was up to ten grains and a long-term user could take thirty grains, something that would cause an overdose in most people. Anything over that, no matter how long someone had been taking Veronal, would still kill them.

Palmer asked Willcox what was the largest dose he knew about where the person survived. 'I saw a patient about three months ago,' Willcox said, 'who had taken 45 grains and recovered, but with regard to that patient I may say that he would have died if he had not been medically treated.'

Palmer asked, 'Was that person accustomed to taking Veronal?'

'He had taken it several times before, but not regularly over a long period.'

'If it is proved that this young man had been taking it for years,' continued Palmer, 'could he take a stronger dose than 45 grains?'

'If a man has taken it regularly, 50 grains would be in the danger zone, and serious symptoms would be likely to follow such a dose.'[74]

Coroner Benson then asked Willcox if he knew of cases where people had recovered from doses of the size in question. 'Would it surprise you,' he said, 'to hear that the deceased, who was used to taking Veronal, should take 150 grains with the intention of committing suicide?'

'No,' said Willcox, 'It would not.'

The Coroner was not convinced, '150 grains is an enormous dose. It would not strike you as unreasonable that a man wanting to be sure to make away with himself would take three times the fatal dose?'

Willcox replied, 'Not at all.' He then handed the Coroner a small phial he had been holding containing 150 grains which was described as being about the same bulk as a pile of twelve old pennies (just under an inch). Such a quantity he said would require two and a quarter pints (just over a litre) of cold water or a teacup of boiling water to dissolve it. When taken in coffee the taste would be very bitter and would be easily detectable but it would be less noticeable if taken in wine or spirits.

In order to show how the amount of Veronal present in the body had been calculated, Willcox explained that Veronal was a poison which when absorbed into the system circulated in the blood and so spread evenly throughout the body. In Eric's liver there were 2 grains, in the kidneys 0.56 grains, the intestines 2.87 grains, the brain 1.28 grains, the blood 0.87 grains, the stomach 0.28 grains and the stomach wall 0.8 grains. The total was 8.66 grains. There were no traces of other poisons.

Willcox explained that the quantity found would then have to be multiplied to account for the whole body and gave the figure of 75.8 grains. When taken orally, Veronal was quickly absorbed and excreted by the kidneys but it did not cause death rapidly, a large dose did not kill within twenty-four hours, but much later. The face would become flushed and the breathing rapid and frequently the temperature rose with signs of pneumonia, just as Spilsbury had found. The person then usually went into a coma for three or four days and no amount of effort could wake them. By the time Eric had died, a large amount of the Veronal would have been excreted by the kidneys and at least half the amount would have disappeared from the body. Therefore, by doubling the dose, Willcox arrived at his estimate of 150 grains taken in one dose within thirty-six hours of death.[75]

The Coroner asked if all the Veronal would be dissolved in a tumbler full of hock and whilst Willcox did not think all of it would dissolve, most of it would.

At the end of his testimony, Dr Willcox took the opportunity to strongly urge that Veronal be placed under restricted sale due to the frequency of deaths which had taken place over the last few years. Even the 1911 edition of the *Encyclopaedia Britannica* had drawn attention to the fact that people were calling for it to be restricted by the Pharmacy Acts. It was not on the poisons schedule and it could be sold by, and to, anybody. The jury and the Coroner agreed with the doctor and thanked him for his observation.[76]

4

CONTRADICTORY EVIDENCE
COMES TO LIGHT

Dr Willcox had been right that Veronal had caused a number of deaths; since its first use the number of fatal overdoses had been steadily rising.

The drug had been developed in 1902 by two Berlin physicians, Professor Emil Fischer and Joseph von Mering. One explanation for the name is that von Mering was in Verona at the time and named it after the city; others believe it is derived from the Latin *verus* meaning true. Fischer and Mering published their discovery in 1903 just nine years before Eric's death.

It was a drug that was quickly adopted and extensively advertised as a cure for insomnia, as well as other conditions including heart and lung diseases; mental disturbances; acute alcoholism; morphinomaniac (addiction to morphine); and kidney disease. It was fast acting. Within an hour of taking the recommended dose, the individual would be asleep and stay asleep for six hours or more. A Dr Lillenfield, who had treated sixty patients of all ages suffering from insomnia, said that each morning following the taking of the drug 'the patient was fresh, and felt as if the sleep had been wholly natural.'[77]

However, by 1908 it was becoming clear there was a problem. From July that year, reports were creeping into the media about comas and deaths resulting from Veronal use. William Ewart Maw in London was one of the first to die, thinking it was a relatively safe drug so he could take any dose he liked. At the same time, an unnamed man took 150 grains and slept for a week;[78] the media may have been mistaken here, as that dose would certainly have been fatal.

The following month, Henry Arthur Wolverton, also of London, was driven to despair because of his inability to sleep and used Veronal to commit suicide. Shortly after this, author Gilbert Charles Hutton Wintle accidentally took an overdose, followed a year later by another author, Ernest Wilhelm Sutton Pickhardt. Artist Ernest Morris Jessop drowned in his bath after taking about sixty grains of Veronal.[79]

It was in 1909 when a doctor from Brighton became the first person to publicly speak out against Veronal. Dr Wyborn had told his wife, Adriana, not to buy it, offering to prescribe something else, but she bought the drug against his advice and accidently overdosed in the August of that year. He said it was 'a wicked thing that such tablets could be purchased.'[80]

By October 1909, at an inquest into yet another death, that of Beatrice Mary Short, the jury expressed the opinion that the drug should be scheduled as a poison, the coroner noting that he had two or three similar cases in the last two months alone. Coroners across the country were commenting that these cases were becoming increasingly familiar and by the start of the 1910s, people were using Veronal to commit suicide as a result of the publicity.

Willcox believed that the statistics of death by Veronal were low as many doctors not familiar with the symptoms were attributing these deaths to pneumonia.

VERONAL AND BARBITURIC ACID GROUP. FATAL POISONING. ENGLAND AND WALES.

Year	Male	Female	Total
1905	0	0	0
1906	0	1	1
1907	1	0	1
1908	4	0	4
1909	6	7	13
1910	9	6	15
1911	8	11	19
1912	12	4	16
1913	14	12	26
1914	12	18	30
1915	14	10	24
1916	5	5	10
1917	8	8	16
1918	6	6	12
1919	3	3	6
1920	3	6	9
1921	4	4	8
1922	3	3	6
1923	7	1	8
1924	4	4	8
1925	10	15	25
Total ...			257

Table of fatal cases[81]

Despite this, at the time of Eric's death, Veronal was still freely available in chemist shops.

DR BAINES

The next witness at the inquest was Dr Harold Athelstan Baines of Brighton, the local general practitioner who had previously attended Eric. Baines said he had only known Eric since the beginning of August, some five or six weeks earlier, when Eric consulted him about muscular rheumatism. Baines said did not know he was taking Veronal, Eric had complained about great pains to his side when he breathed so Baines simply strapped his chest.

Later that month on the 24th, Baines again attended Eric when he was called by the butler, William Thomas Joiner, (Albert was away). The doctor found Eric insensible and sent for a colleague as he felt the condition was serious and required a second opinion. Eric remained unconscious for about three or four hours. When he finally woke up, he was warned by Dr Baines about his dangerous behaviour and Eric promised he would not do it again. According to Baines, Eric had said he had taken 105 grains of Veronal and had taken even bigger doses in the past. When asked what bigger dose, Baines replied, 'He said he had taken 190 grains, which, of course, I did not believe.'[82] Baines added that, firstly, he did not generally believe anyone who took drugs and, secondly, it was patently absurd as both doses would have killed him. After the overdose, Baines engaged a nurse to look after Eric for two or three days, perhaps a week.

Eric boasted to the doctor that he understood all about Veronal, having taken it for years, so when Albert called Baines about the overdose on 9 September the doctor was not surprised, telling the court he knew it would happen sooner or later.

Baines had received a telephone call about 11pm from Albert asking him to go to the flat at once as Eric had taken an overdose of Veronal. The doctor instructed Albert to give Eric an emetic but when he arrived Eric was unconscious and the emetic could not be administered. They kept him warm by putting hot bottles on his feet and body and he was injected with strychnine and digitalis to stimulate his heart which was beginning to show signs of failure.[83] Albert suggested calling other doctors, so Baines called Dr Hobhouse and Dr Sandifer to assist him. They too agreed it was Veronal poisoning. Albert also suggested that other doctors from London who had previously treated Eric should be called and as far as Baines knew, Albert then called those doctors, as well as Eric's solicitors, so they could inform the Trevanions.

Baines said that as he could not delivery an emetic, he tried putting a feather down his throat.[84] 'But why', asked Muir, on behalf of the prosecution, 'had he not pumped Eric's stomach?' Baines was evasive and there followed a heated discussion on whether Eric's stomach should have been pumped both that night and on the previous time Eric fell unconscious.

Muir, starting with the earlier event asked, 'Did you use a stomach pump on August 24th?'

The doctor replied with an odd statement: 'No; I should have killed him the second time if I had,' before going on to say that if he had put a pipe down Eric's throat while he was unconscious, it could have asphyxiated him. He did, however, agree that in the case of Veronal poisoning it was best to empty the stomach as quickly as possible.

Muir asked Baines what he meant by the 'second time' and Baines replied that the chauffeur had told him of another occasion at Tunbridge Wells when Eric had taken an overdose and had returned in a state of collapse; which did not really explain what he meant by 'I should have killed him the second time.'

Muir was unhappy with the doctor's decision not to pump the stomach. 'Do you,' he said 'suggest that it is dangerous in the case of an unconscious person to use a stomach-pump?'

'Yes, I do in his case.'

Muir was not convinced, 'Can you indicate in any book in which I shall find such a statement?'

'No.'

'Why in his case?'

'Because he was so far gone.'

'But he lived for 32 hours after,' said an incredulous Muir, 'Do you say that to a man in that condition it would be dangerous to use a stomach-pump?'

'Yes, I do.'

'Less dangerous than to leave the Veronal in the stomach?'

'The two other medical men agreed with me.'

'I want to know your opinion. Is it that it would have been

dangerous to use a stomach-pump on that unconscious man?'

'Undoubtedly.'

'Have you any authority for that proposition?'

'No.'

Muir, still unhappy with Baines' testimony, decided to recall Willcox to ask the pathologist's opinion. Willcox confirmed that, in his opinion, it was very important that the stomach be pumped as soon as possible. Personally, he would have inserted a tube and washed the contents out as, if it was done with great care, there would be no danger of killing the patient. 'I do not see any reason why the stomach pump should not have been used,' said Dr Willcox. He added that in a case where the patient was unconscious for thirty-two hours, he would also have administered nourishment. Overdoses of Veronal rarely caused death in less than twenty-four hours and long comas were characteristic. However, help arrived very quickly for Eric before there had been time for the drug to be absorbed. Had they washed out the stomach out as quickly as possible they could have saved him, as records of recovery exist even after a dose of 120 grains. Overdoses higher than this almost always resulted in death.

Muir asked Willcox about Baines' refusal to give food to an unconscious patient as the doctor claimed it could not be done through the mouth. Dr Willcox stated that food being passed through the nose, or elsewhere, could be done and the patient could receive nourishment even though unconscious.[85]

Muir recalled Baines and asked if there was anything else he could tell them about Eric. 'Yes' was the reply, but he didn't elaborate. Muir asked Baines if he had seen him later in the evening on the 24 August, after he had revived him, but Baines could not remember. This is curious as Veronal overdoses, although becoming more well-known, were still not that common and it seems odd that the doctor did not recall such an unusual event that had happened just a month earlier.

Muir, unwilling to accept that Baines simply could not remember, pushed him for an answer. Journalists noted his irritation with the doctor and the tension beginning to grow between them. Baines seemed inattentive and nervous and several times questions had to be repeated. Turning to the Coroner, Muir complained in an oddly disjointed sentence, 'This gentleman is not treating properly and I don't know why.'

Baines snapped back, 'You seem to be doubting my evidence that is why.'

But the Coroner disagreed and admonished him, 'I do not think you have any justification for saying that,' and Muir echoed Benson's comments, 'There is not the smallest justification for such a statement, I ask you simple questions to elucidate facts.'

Baines prevaricated, saying, 'I cannot hear what you say, for one thing.'[86]

The Coroner admonished him once again making it very clear that he supported Muir, 'If you do not hear what is said, you can say so, and Mr Muir will repeat the question in such a way as you can hear. These questions Mr Muir is (sic) asking with my authority.'[87]

People were noticing Baines' strained behaviour and almost all the press included Baines' quarrel with Muir in their stories. Why was he so nervous? He was simply a doctor giving evidence at an inquiry, something he must have done many times during his career. Perhaps he was nervous because of the press coverage, or did Baines have something to hide? It seems he did, but the truth was not going to come out until a couple of days later.

Muir continued to push the doctor for information. He demanded to know what time Baines had arrived at the flat on the day Eric had died. Once again, the doctor replied that he could not remember and instead complained to the judge about Muir 'Bullying me in this manner.'[88]

Muir switched back to the subject of the emetic that he had told Albert to administer. Baines said both Albert and the butler had been trying to do this when he arrived.

'Didn't Roe tell you whether they had succeeded?'

'No; I could see they had not.'

Muir continued to worry at the question of the stomach pump and Baines continued to insist that it would have been have been dangerous in view of Eric's unconscious condition. 'As I have previously explained, how could I use it? If he had died when I was using it they would have blamed me for it.' Baines seemed more concerned about his own reputation than Eric's life.

'Will you,' demanded a frustrated Muir, 'state quite calmly why you did not use it – without any heat at all.'

Baines replied, 'I thought if I put the tube down his throat I should have asphyxiated him.'

Muir took one last attempt to drive the point home, 'It is very important, is it not, in Veronal poisoning to try and get rid of the poison that may remain in the stomach as soon as possible...'

Baines interrupted saying it depended on the patient's condition.

As it was clear he was going to get no further with the subject of the stomach pump, Muir turned to the question of the cremation forms, 'Did you say anything to the undertaker with regard to the funeral?'

Baines initially denied it, then said 'probably'.

'Are you sure?' Muir prompted and Baines changed his mind again, saying yes, but then paused and added, 'I may have told him that they wanted the body cremated. Possibly I did.'

'Was that said of your own motion or someone else's?'

'I cannot have made it on my own motion.'[89]

Muir was starting to boil over again, 'I wish you would answer the questions, Dr Baines,' he complained, 'they are simple questions, and smiling does not make it a bit plainer.'

Baines replied that he 'understood' there was a document in which Eric had stated he wanted to be cremated but he did not know what it was or what happened to it.

When Muir finished his questioning, the Coroner asked Baines what sources he was using which advised not to use a stomach pump. All Baines would say was that it was his own personal experience and when the Coroner pushed him for a reference in a book or journal, Baines knew of none. Muir interceded expressing his amazement that Eric had been left for thirty-two hours with the Veronal still in his system.

As the lawyers ended their questioning, Benson turned to the jury, inquiring if there was anything they would like to know. When the foreman asked what the doctor's qualifications were, Baines replied that he was a Licentiate of the Royal College of Surgeons, Edinburgh, and a Licentiate of the College of Apothecaries, London and had been practicing for thirty-three years. The foreman of the jury also seemed unhappy with Dr Baines' responses and added, 'My colleagues and I wish to state that we think the evidence of the doctor most unsatisfactory.'

Throughout his testimony Baines seemed evasive and had an unfortunate habit of constantly smiling, which seemed to irritate almost everyone. He continued to smile as Benson tried to defend the doctor by stating, 'I cannot but think that Dr Baines is willing to give you any information he is asked for.'

Baines was released from the stand, but there lingered an uneasy feeling about his testimony.

THE CHEMISTS

The next series of witnesses were an attempt to work out exactly how much Veronal Eric was buying and how much he had in his possession at the time of his death - not an easy task.

There were two chemists that Eric would regularly visit, one in London and one in Brighton.

GIBSON

William Humphrey Gibson was a registered chemist on King's Road, Brighton and testified that he had supplied Eric with two prescriptions of Veronal. The Coroner quickly interrupted, 'Are you correct in saying two, because I think at the inquest you said four?' Gibson denied that, saying he had only ever said two. This was a problem that was to surface several times during the second inquest. The record of testimonies from the first inquest are brief, amounting to around one page per person and so there were differences in what people could, or could not, remember saying.

The prescription presented to Gibson for a dozen cachets was written in French but why Eric had a foreign prescription was not explored. It was also the reason why Eric's doses were measured out at 7½ grains and not 7, the usual British recommended dose, according to Gibson.[90] It is possible that Eric had two prescriptions, as he would collect doses of both a dozen or two dozen and, while Veronal was available to buy over the counter, both chemists say they only supplied Eric on prescription.

Gibson supplied Eric on two occasions, 15 August and 2

September, to the same French prescription. His assistants, said Gibson, had frequently pointed out the danger of Veronal, but Eric had told them he knew as much about the drug as they did as he had been taking it for years.

Palmer, representing Albert, asked the chemist about Eric supposedly visiting the shop on five other occasions; could he have bought the drug over the counter on those occasions? Gibson said no, as all sales of Veronal were logged in the ledger regardless of whether the sales were prescription or not. Palmer continued to push for the possibility of Eric paying cash but Gibson insisted he always paid everything on account.

'Did he boast how many grains he could take?'

'I think not. He used to buy large quantities. But there is nothing in that,' said Gibson. The chemist appeared anxious to distance himself from accusations that they had made up incorrect amounts. 'It was put up in cachet form,' he said, 'which makes it easy to determine the correct dose.'[91] He was certain, he told them, that there had been no mistakes in making up the doses as he and his staff personally weighed the medicine and put it in the cachets.

He was wrong.

MARSHALL

Next in the witness box was John David Marshall, a registered pharmacist.[92] He had been called simply to confirm his findings and so his testimony was brief.

Marshall stated that Eric's brother, Claude, had brought him nine cachets to examine. Seven were in a box with Gibson's logo and the contents of each ranged from 5.8 to 6.3 grains of Veronal, none was exactly the same. One, which had been delivered in an envelope marked 'in the bottom of the box' had the remains of 0.1 grains; and another, a different kind of cachet as it appeared to be made of rice paper, was labelled 'A.C.T.' and contained 8.2 grains. He affirmed that there was nothing else mixed with the Veronal.

Arundell Claude Trevanion, who lived near Regent's Park and was described as being 'of no occupation', was Eric's youngest brother. He was put in the witness box to confirm Marshall's testimony as he had stated at the first inquest that after Eric's death their mother had found a box of cachets in the bedroom cupboard. When it became apparent there was little interest in them, Claude approached Inspector Ward asking if the police intended to keep them. The Inspector replied, 'No, I think not', and this had troubled Claude. He asked if he could keep them, and the Inspector handed the box to him which he later took to Marshall to be analysed. The odd cachet had been found by his mother on Eric's dressing table and Claude had put it in the envelope.

DOUTHWAITE

The second chemist to take the stand was Henry Londesborough Douthwaite, from Bayswater who stated that Eric had been introduced to him by Mary Geneste, Eric's old governess and friend of the Trevanion family. He added that he had probably sold drugs to Eric before the introduction and confirmed a cash sale in May 1911.

Eric opened an account on 15 June and from that time, Douthwaite regularly supplied prescriptions of 7½ grains of Veronal, presumably on the same French prescription Eric used at Gibson's. Douthwaite could not be certain of the dates as he did not begin a new, more accurate, recording system until January 1912. From that new system he could attest that he had supplied Eric with:

13 May 1912 - one dozen cachets (equalling ninety grains)
11 June 1912 - one dozen cachets
24 June - two dozen cachets
9 July - two dozen cachets

On 4 September, he supplied 'one dozen and one'; Eric took the single dose with him and asked that the rest be sent to Brighton with other goods he had ordered.[93] They were despatched on 6 September.[94] Muir asked if it were true that Eric's chauffeur had arrived the morning of the 5 September to pick up a package, but Douthwaite had no memory of the visit and said he would not have been supplied with Veronal because it would have been entered in the book even if it had been a cash sale.

When asked about the cachets found in the cupboard by Mrs Trevanion, Douthwaite confirmed the one marked 'A.C.T.' may well have been his, as it looked very similar but it had not been marked at his shop.

ANALYSIS

Both chemists stated that they had never supplied Eric with as much as 150 grains at one time and were certain that on no occasion had there been a mistake in either the quantity of the cachets, or the quantity within each cachet. However, this was not borne out by the testimony of Marshall.

Cachets of drugs were usually made up by the chemists themselves or their staff. At the inquest, Gibson described the process:

> We make our own cachets; the medicine is weighed and put into cachets. We sell cachets to hold 5, 7, or 10 grains. The cachets I sold to the deceased would hold 10 grains. The utmost they could hold is, I believe 12 grains. We could not make a mistake in the making up of the cachets. Each powder is carefully weighed separately, and put into a small funnel into the cachet, one at a time, on a paper containing 12 holes. The edges are moistened, the lid is brought over, and the cachet is closed at once. Each one is weighed and put in separately. We weigh each powder separately. I am absolutely positive that I could not make any appreciable mistake.[95]

The regular British prescription for Veronal was seven grains and so cachets were made to that size, but to fill out the French order for seven and a half grains a larger 10 grain cachet had to be used. It was this that concerned Muir and he tried to determine if more than seven and a half grains could be accidentally added but both chemists assured him that was not possible.

Of the nine that were analysed the cachet containing 0.1 was evidently just the remnants of one that had been used. The 'A.C.T.' example came from an unknown source but it must have been, according to Gibson, been marked by Eric himself. However, he gives no reason for his suspicions and it is not known what the initials stand for. As the dose in this cachet was higher than the others, Eric may have acquired it in another country.

The chemist went on to explain that marking cachets 'is

sometimes done abroad, but in England there is a prejudice against marking the capsules'. However, Douthwaite admitted that it did look very similar to his but insisted he had not marked it.

Questions arise from this: why would Eric want to label a single cachet, unless he knew it contained a high dose; and why was it in the box which Gibson supplied? When clearing the bedroom, Mary Joiner had supposedly been told by Albert to throw away any drugs so perhaps she, her husband or Eric had put it in the box.

In addition, according to Marshall, cachet No 1 was a different shape from cachet No 2 but he made no comment about why that might be, or if all the others were similar. It is therefore possible that cachet No 1 also came from another source.

The six remaining cachets were probably the last ones supplied by Gibson and they were found in a box bearing his name. It would have been impossible to date a generic box of this kind which could have been used as a store for drugs from any source; but the probability is that they were Gibson's and from the analysis of the contents it was clear he was underselling.

Both chemists had said they had supplied cachets of $7\frac{1}{2}$ grains but pharmacists could act independently. If they believed a client was becoming addicted, they could make an arbitrary decision to secretly lower the dose. If the drugs were all from Gibson then he was either cheating Eric or acting in his best interests.

In the five months prior to Eric's death, from 13 May (Douthwaite's first record) to the day Eric lapsed into unconsciousness on 9 September, there are one 109 cachets recorded. There is no evidence to suggest that Eric bought the drug elsewhere as he never went out on his own and would only travel with either the chauffeur or Albert, neither of whom gave evidence that they bought Veronal elsewhere, or on Eric's behalf.

There is also no evidence that Eric kept a store in the flat, certainly none was found. With a chauffeur readily at hand, and Veronal being available to anyone over the counter, Eric did not need to stock pile, he could just send the chauffeur out. In his testimony, Gibson admitted that it was possible that Eric could have bought drugs for cash but they would still have been entered against his name and Gibson had not checked the cash records, only the accounts.[96] Of course this does not mean Eric did not keep a store, only that one was not found. Eric does not seem to have been hiding drugs in the flat as he had done with the morphine because none was found after his death. Besides, Albert and the Joiners knew he was taking them. Mary Joiner testified that she had found a little bottle of cachets at the flat but she did not know what type of drug it was, so she threw it into the bin. She states 'I thought it better to throw it away, for the deceased's sake. I cannot remember that Mr Roe told me what I should do with any drugs which I found lying about.' Yet elsewhere she specifically says Albert told her to throw them away which if she had not been instructed to do so, shows a surprising familiarity that a servant should throw away an employer's possession.

Eric's buying pattern, from both Douthwaite and Gibson, varied in frequency: the lowest number of days in-between doses is fourteen, with the largest gap being thirty-seven. Using the testimony given at the inquest and dividing the number of cachets bought by the number of days between purchases, it would seem that on average Eric was taking less than one a day. Only during the sixteen-day period between 24 June, when he bought twenty-four cachets, to 9 July would Eric be able to take one and a half a day. At all other times during the five months (assuming there was no store), there would not have been enough for Eric to take one cachet a night. This supports testimonies that Eric only took the drug when he had a bad night, not every day but without his purchasing record for earlier years, we cannot be certain how often and how much Eric bought.

There is also the overdose in August to account for and, while the exact dose is unknown, it must have been a minimum of three cachets as Eric often took two without any effect. To be able to do this, he must have had a store at that time.

In September, Eric bought just over two dozen doses in a period of two days (twelve from Gibson on 2 September, and thirteen from Douthwaite on 4 September), amounting to 180 grains. As Gibson was underselling to an average of an 18.4%, this would reduce the amount of grains available to 160, enough for the overdose.

The analysis of Eric's purchases does not support the impression he was addicted to Veronal alone unless he had a store which is unaccounted for. It is possible that he continued to take morphine, as Mrs Trevanion found some on Eric's bedside table but if he was alternating it with the Veronal it would be more in keeping with his supposed addiction to drugs in general.

5

SHARING BEDS AND
DISAPPEARING MONEY

The Town Hall, although quite spacious, was not really suitable
for an inquest that hundreds wanted to attend. Early that Monday
morning, a large crowd was fighting for seats. Scores of journalists,
photographers and artists had arrived, many of whom had to write
standing up or rely on reports written by those who had more
favourable positions. Indeed, so great was the number of press
articles being generated that the Brighton Postal Authorities had
to put on twenty additional staff to cope with the amount of copy
being dispatched.[97]

The broad-shouldered Chief Inspector Ward of Scotland
Yard, who was in charge of inquiries, could be seen at intervals
flitting around the court doing general administration and
arranging for witnesses to be brought in. Clerks were directing a
crowd that included some of the most fashionable people of
Brighton and Hove, notably 'the presence of many well-dressed
ladies.'[98] Mrs Trevanion was not among them, as she had been
taken ill. Eric's brother, Cecil, was also absent. He had to appear
at Bow Street Police station on a charge of insulting behaviour and
causing a disturbance outside a West-End hotel about midnight.
He was fined 5s but it is not known what the altercation had been
about.[99]

On day two, the crowd had grown for one reason; Albert's
was going to give his version of the story. As he sat behind his
counsel, immediately beneath the dock, he seemed relaxed and
unconcerned but he must have been a worried man. If he was
connected in any way to the supposed evidence of Eric's
homosexuality, he could be arrested.

Before proceedings began, the foreman of the jury stood and
addressed the Coroner regarding the disagreement over Dr
Baines' testimony. He wanted to set the record straight: 'the jury
wish me to say, in justice to Dr Baines,' he said, 'and also in

reference to the remark I made at the close of his evidence that they were dissatisfied with his evidence, that this remark referred only to the manner in which he gave his evidence. I think it is fair to Dr Baines that we express that.'

The Coroner agreed, 'I am glad you have made that clear,' he said, 'I took that to be your meaning but I saw it was open to the other interpretation.'

THE GOVERNESS

The first witness of the day was Mary Geneste, a London spinster whose age, according to the 1911 census, would have been forty-five. She lived with her mother, her two middle-aged sisters, and a thirty-five-year-old niece, all spinsters of 'private means'. Despite being single, Geneste is often referred to as Mrs throughout the inquest and by people who knew her. She was a daily governess who had known the Trevanion family for about fifteen years and Eric since he was twelve. That Eric left her money in his will indicates they shared a close relationship. When he had his appendicitis operation at age fourteen, she had assisted the nurse in his recovery at home and believed that since the operation Eric had been in delicate health.

Geneste continued to see Eric even after she had stopped being a governess for the family. He would write to her often and in one of his letters, shortly after he came of age, he told her that he had been in dispute with his family and so was going to live with his grandmother. He later went abroad and Geneste mentions that his brother and Charles Montgomery accompanied him. It was this voyage, on the *Orotava*, that Albert supposedly found him sobbing in his cabin. Lady Elizabeth Cooper had died on 1 April 1906 and on 8 April, Geneste received a letter from Cecil Trevanion telling her that Eric had left Colombo in Ceylon and was heading home for the funeral. On returning to the UK, Eric went to live, not with his family, but with Genestes as a paying guest at St. Stephen's Crescent.

Coroner Benson asked, 'on his return did he mention the names of any of the officers whose acquaintance he had made?'

'He mentioned Mr Roe as having been very kind to him on the voyage, and also the name of the chief officers. In fact, I think he had made great friends with all the officers.'

'Was that the first time he had made any mention of Mr Roe?' Benson continued.

'Yes,' she said. This contradicts Mrs Trevanion's statement to the press that the two men had only known each other just a short time. Geneste added that Eric went abroad again in the autumn of 1906 to Australia.

'Did he say anything about not requiring a travelling companion?'

'Yes; he was going on the *Orotava*, on which he had travelled before, and knew all the officers and was very happy with them.'

Benson asked, 'Did he mention any names?'

Geneste admitted that Eric had mentioned a few, but she was not asked about them. Her main recollection was Eric talking about his friend, Mr Roe, and that he 'wished to introduce him to us.' Perhaps she did not remember them, but throughout the trial no other names were ever made public and none of the officers voluntarily came forward. Although two men who claimed they knew Albert wrote damning letters to the Coroner, they were not included in the inquest and there is no evidence that the police or solicitors sought them out. Only now, with the writing of this book, can the letters be made public and they appear later in the story.

Back at the inquest, Muir was still questioning Geneste, 'Was Mr Roe on that voyage, do you know?' he asked.

'Yes.'

'You went to see Mr Trevanion off?'

'Yes.'

'He returned the following August, did he not?'

'Yes. I could not quite ascertain the date.'

'He came to live with you then?'

'He came to live with us in 1907.'

Before doing so however, Eric went on a short motoring tour with a friend, Dr Rees, and it was not until October that Eric went to live with her, remaining for five years.

'At first,' Muir asked her 'did he occupy one room only in your house?'

'Yes, that was so.'

'During that period from October 1907 until the autumn of 1911, did Mr Roe visit him at all?'

'Yes, occasionally.'

'Did he stay with him at all?'

'Yes, occasionally; four weekends.'

'Where did Mr Roe sleep?'

'In Mr Trevanion's room.'

'Did Dr Rees visit Mr Trevanion?'

'Yes.'

'Where did Dr Rees sleep?'

'I think he also slept in Mr Trevanion's room. I think he stayed the night.'

'Are you sure that Dr Rees slept there at all?'

'Well, that I cannot be certain of.'

She went on to say, 'He had frequent visits from friends in that way' but did not name the friends. 'I think Dr Reece (*sic*) came up several times, but I am not quite certain as to whether he actually slept with the deceased.'[100]

In the autumn of 1911, Eric took two additional rooms in her house, adding furniture and pictures that he had inherited from his grandfather. He continued to occupy the three rooms until July 1912.

'During that period did Mr Roe come to your house at all?'

'Mr Roe was very seriously ill for about a year in 1907 I think.'

'Did Mr Roe visit him between the autumn of 1911 and July 1912?'

'Oh yes.'

'Did he stay the night at all during that period?'

'I think he stayed one or two weekends.'

'What room did he occupy?'

'The same room.'

'Mr Trevanion's room?'

'Yes.'

'With Mr Trevanion?'

'Yes.'

The testimony of Geneste is interesting for a number of reasons. Albert elsewhere claimed that he and Eric always asked for separate rooms whenever possible but there is no evidence that he asked Geneste for another room. The fact that Eric took two additional rooms means there was space available but Albert continued to sleep in the same room as Eric. There was no discussion about the beds at the inquest so it is not known if there were two beds or just one in Eric's room. Elsewhere it was stated that Eric hated to sleep alone and that occasionally his butler and his chauffeur were required to sleep in the same bed as him in order to calm his nerves. Geneste also said she had to sleep in Eric's room to take care of him. Of course, it would have been socially unacceptable for a woman to share a bed with a man she was not married to, so the likelihood is that there was somewhere for her to sleep.

If the situation had involved a man and a woman, it is almost certain questions would have been asked about whether the couple shared a bed but throughout the inquest, despite questions around 'unnatural vice', there was little effort to pursue the matter in detail.

This was in keeping with how homosexuality was portrayed at the time. Although sodomy had been illegal since medieval times, the actual nature of the crime was rarely discussed. It was feared that by openly discussing it in court and the media, it would encourage the public to think this was a common part of human nature, but the authorities wished to present it as rare. In addition, by making the facts known, the authorities worried that it opened the possibility of people trying it for themselves so it was buried in deliberately vague terminology. In 1795, Judge William Blackstone in his book, *Commentaries on the Laws of England*, described it 'as a crime not to be named'[101] and Oscar Wilde at his 1895 trial quoted a line from a poem by his lover, Lord Alfred Douglas, of 'the love that dare not speak its name'.

Instead the crime was couched in terms such as *gross indecency, unnatural crime*, and many other euphemisms which could and did mean anything from paedophilia, pederasty, bestiality or even a heterosexual couple having sex in a public place. By providing such wide-ranging terms meant that the media did not have to specify what the nature of the crime was and even if it went to court there was a concerted effort to keep any details secret. In this context, skittering past details surrounding Eric and Albert in bed would not have been unusual.

Geneste's testimony continued with the trip Eric and Albert made in the winter of 1911-12, visiting Egypt; Sicily; Italy; and then Paris. The governess said she received frequent letters from both men and on their return, Eric told her they were moving out because he 'had arranged for Mr Roe to come and live with him permanently.'

Muir turned his questioning to the taking of Veronal. 'Did Mr Trevanion tell you at any time that he had taken Veronal?' he asked.

'Yes once,' said Mary.

'Or more than once?'

'Oh, he took it frequently if he had bad nights. He did not tell us until after he had taken it because he knew we objected.'

Geneste said Eric had taken Veronal for years as he always had a good night's rest as a result. He would boast that he had taken enough Veronal to kill two people, although he rarely stated what that dose was. It was common knowledge, she said, that he sometimes took two cachets. As that would have been around fourteen grains, it was not enough to kill someone. Three doses would have been twenty-one grains, still not enough to kill but sufficient to induce a coma-like sleep so a killer dose would have been at least four cachets.

Geneste spoke of how Eric's friends and family warned him about his extensive use of Veronal. According to her, Eric would smile and tell them that he had become so resistant to the drug that he could take alarmingly large doses without it having the slightest effect.

Palmer, acting for Albert, pushed Geneste on Eric's belief that 'he had extraordinary ideas as to the amount of Veronal he could take?' and she agreed that was true. She added that she had often seen empty packets of Veronal about the room as Eric had no secrets from the household, everything was left lying about. This lends support to the hypothesis that there would have been no secret store of cachets given the amount Eric had bought in the five months prior to his death.

In August, when Eric had taken his penultimate overdose and had subsequently been treated by Dr Baines, Geneste had been staying at the flat in Brighton.

'Did Mr Trevanion tell you he had taken Veronal then?' Muir asked.

'Yes, he said he had taken a sleeping draught, and he thought he would be better now.'

She went on to relate that the door had been locked and had to be burst open with an axe, but she did not say why the door had been locked. Later, when Eric had recovered, he claimed he had fainted. 'He said he felt ill, and we sent for the doctor', Geneste added.

'Did a nurse come also?'

'Yes.'

'The doctor was Dr Baines?'

'Yes. He sent for a nurse.'

'Was Mr Roe at the flat at that time?'

'No, he was away.'

'He was always very nervous about sleeping alone?'

'Yes, he did not like to be alone.'

'I don't say it offensively, but you have had to sleep with him?'

'Yes, I had to sleep in the room when he was ill. I had nursed him since he was a boy.' Once again, the question of how many beds was not considered. Geneste specifically says 'in the room' implying that she slept either in a chair or another bed. Considering how long Eric had lived with her, it would seem that most nights Eric did sleep on his own. During her testimony she said that 'whenever he was ill he would not be left alone at night. We used to make him beef tea at all hours of the night, and would wait until he fell asleep, and then would withdraw quietly.'[102] If, as Albert claimed, he slept with Eric due to his nerves, why did he not adopt the same methods as Mary Geneste?

Muir then turned his attention to Eric's money. 'Did Mr Trevanion ever tell you anything about his having given money to Mr Roe?'

'Yes.'

'What was that?'

Geneste explained that Eric had said something about Mr Roe being 'a nice fellow,' and that he wanted to give him money. 'I said why did he want to make over £10,000 to Mr Roe, and I think it was explained that he wanted Mr Roe to have £400 a year.'[103] According to her understanding, he was to pay his share of the flat and all the expenses out of the money. It was agreed that £8,000 was to be returned to Eric's estate in the event of Albert's death, while £2,000 was to be left to Albert to will to his mother or anybody else. This is about £200,000 today, so still a sizable inheritance.

Muir asked if Geneste knew Albert had been made the main heir of Eric's estate and she confirmed that yes, she had known. She explained that Mrs Trevanion had told her, but didn't say when. Eric had died on the Wednesday and on the Thursday Albert had gone to see her. During their conversation she mentioned Mrs Trevanion's comments about everything in the will being left to him. He confirmed it and later sent her a copy of the will. It is not known why he did this but it may have been to let her know that Eric had left her some money.

When Muir asked if Albert had made any comments about Eric's family, Geneste replied that Albert rarely had anything to do with them, adding, 'I think he realised a little of why Mr Trevanion had found it difficult to live with them. He said that they were rather inclined to quarrel amongst themselves.'[104]

When asked what had been discussed about the will, she said, 'I don't think I can say exactly. I think he said he had spoken to the boys and told them he did not want all the money or the family pictures, and that if they would deal fairly by him, he would like to come to some arrangement with them.'

Muir then briefly covered the previous overdose asking, 'Do you remember an occasion when Dr Sandifer was called in?'

'Yes,' said Geneste.

'Was that when he had taken an overdose of morphine?'

'Yes.'

'By himself?'

'By injection.'

'Who had injected it?'

'He had.'

Geneste confirmed that this was the day Eric left hospital after treatment for a hammered toe (a toe which bends downwards instead of forwards now called hammer toe) and that he was intending to go on a motoring tour to Cornwall the following day.

Turning to the night of the death, Muir asked Geneste what her understanding was of the events. She replied that she had been staying at the flat when Albert had knocked on her door, saying that Eric seemed ill but he wasn't sure if it was an overdose. 'He said he (Eric) complained of feeling ill, and that he was sick and dizzy. He sent for the doctor. He said he thought he would pull through. He said that his pulse was very strong for a good part of the time, but afterwards he said he was like wax.'

After Muir had finished his questioning, Palmer was anxious to push home the fact that there had been no secret that Eric had given Albert the £10,000 and Geneste agreed.

'He gave it to Mr Roe to make him independent?' Palmer asked.

'Yes', she said.

Palmer then brought up a subject not covered before: the cutting of a phone line at the time of the overdose. The reason he did so was to distance Albert from the act and, in answer to his questions, Geneste confirmed that one had been cut but there was a second wire in the room. She had no idea who had cut the wire.

Geneste continued: 'Dr Sandifer was called in and he stayed with deceased until 7 o'clock next morning. I and Mr Roe and Dr Sandifer and my sister took turns in giving artificial respiration, and we also gave him strong coffee. The doctor said that Mr Trevanion nearly died that night. Mr Roe rushed off to the chemists to get some oxygen.'

An interesting aspect of Geneste's testimony regarding the previous overdose is that even though Eric was unconscious 'we also gave him strong coffee', which means they were feeding him through a tube, something Dr Baines had refused to do on the night of Eric's overdose.

ERIC'S RAPIDLY DISAPPEARING MONEY

On 22 May 1906 Eric sold a sum of 'Consols', not through the bank but through brokers. A Consol was issued by the Bank of England as British government bonds, a form of annuity or income paid at regular intervals either for a fixed period or for life. The sale of Eric's Consols realised £3,103 but he did not sell or transfer any monies, Consols or stocks again until 1911.

Eric inherited and had access to his fortune sometime in 1910 and began to withdraw significant amounts. Taking into account other overdrafts and debits in the twelve months before his death, Eric had withdrawn approximately £7,100 (nearly £800,000 today) and Gale confirmed he had no other income other than the sales of the Consols and other minor assets. In other words, Eric was rapidly eating into his inheritance.

Gale confirmed that Albert's account had been opened on 1 February 1912 and he had described himself as a colliery agent, a false statement as he was a colliery clerk. It is possible Gale got the job title wrong but Albert could have been trying to appear more important than he actually was.

The two men had known each other for six years and maintained a reasonably close relationship, Albert spending many weekends with Eric although he was away at sea a great deal. It was not until after Albert's illness in 1910/11 that they began to spend more time together and Eric's money started decreasing rapidly. Eric often showered Albert with expensive gifts yet it is not until the last four months of Eric's life that he started to transfer large amounts of money into Albert's name. Eric could have been passing cash to Albert ever since they had known each other but Albert, a proud and domineering man, may have found it demeaning to be given handouts and wanted freedom to control the money himself. In the end, almost all of Eric's disposable fortune was transferred or 'caused to be transferred'[105] as the *Cambrian Daily Leader* put it, into Albert's account.

The opening balance of Albert's London account was £50 (about £5,000 today) which came from Eric. He had written a letter instructing Gale to transfer the money and to also credit Albert's account with £50 on the 1st of January, April, July and October, his pay for being a companion. A further letter dated 13 May 1912 increased the amount to £75 a quarter.

Later that month £4,000 in Japanese bonds was transferred to Albert by Eric; and another month later, £3,800 of Brazilian bonds were also transferred, bringing the balance moved to Albert's account to £7,800.

On 11 July, Albert deposited more Swansea Harbour Trust shares to the value of £2,200 and on 30 July, a further sum of £1,600 in the same stock. These amounts were later explained by Albert in his testimony.

Muir asked Gale if he had examined Albert's bank account and Gale confirmed he had. He was also asked if Albert had other sources of income besides Eric and Gale replied that apart from £219 from the Swansea Harbour Trust shares, and 14s 3d from Swansea, there was no other income. Obviously, there was because Albert had a job. No transfers were made to any other account held by Albert and probably why they were never mentioned. Nevertheless, in the year that Albert was Eric's 'companion', around £800,000 in today's money was withdrawn from Eric's account but no checks were made to see if any of it ended up in Albert's Swansea account.

6

DAY 2 – MONDAY 27 JANUARY: CONTROVERSIAL WILLS AND A SHOCKING NOTE

THE CURIOUS WILL

As day two progressed, Eric's lawyer, James Dillon Lumb ,managing clerk to solicitors Messrs Mackrell, Maton, Godlee and Quincy,[106] was called to give evidence. Lumb had worked for the company for nearly thirty years and had known Eric well for about six.

Eric constantly changed his will and so was often in his solicitor's office. He had originally been dealt with by one of the partners, Maton who, when taken ill in 1912, handed over to Lumb. Maton had not only been responsible for all the transfers of money to Albert but had also overseen the changes in Eric's wills.

The first time Albert is mentioned in a will is the version dated 16 November 1906, just a few months after he returned from the voyage to Australia. In it, Eric left him £250. A new will in January 1908 did not mention Albert at all but by December the same year the £250 had been reinstated. In July 1910, that amount was increased to £2,500 and this was repeated in other wills on 10 August, 3 November, and in October 1911. By 7 December 1911, a codicil was added leaving him £300 a year for life but six days later on 13 December, Eric had left his entire estate to Albert.

In the four years before his death, Eric bequeathed large amounts of money to Albert, so it is likely that he was also giving him cash.

In September 1911, a year before he died, Eric asked Lumb to call on him at the St Stephen's flat as he was going travelling again with Albert and wanted to re-write his will before they left. They met on the 11th during which Eric declared his determination not to leave anything to his two brothers, despite the fact that in all his previous wills he had done so. He gave no reason to Lumb for this change of heart. While Eric was often estranged from his mother, his two brothers continued a close relationship with her and perhaps Eric resented this. Eric instructed Lumb to leave the majority of his estate to Albert and the will was finalised on 13 December 1911. This must have come as something of a shock to the solicitor and as his testimony progressed, it was clear he attempted to prevent Eric from taking such a step.

Eric also told Lumb that he would start paying Albert an allowance, as he wanted his friend to have enough money to last until the end of the year. He was to be paid £50 a quarter and Lumb was instructed to set up the regular transfer; this amount was later increased.

On Monday 18 December, Eric called into the office again and went through the draft will, repeating that he would not leave anything to his family. On 19 December, the will was executed and Albert became the main beneficiary to Eric's vast wealth.[107]

Coroner Benson intervened in Lumb's testimony to ask when he next saw Eric and Albert. Lumb said this was on 20 April 1912 when they called into the office together but Albert only stayed a few minutes. While they were alone, Eric told Lumb that he and Albert were taking a flat together and that he wanted £5,000 to be transferred to Albert.[108] The payments were for the flat and removals, both of which were going to be paid in cash by Albert. Lumb was asked if he made any comment to Eric about the £5,000 and he replied that he had told Eric of his concerns. If Albert died, the £5,000 might get into other hands, consequently he tried to block the proposal. This infuriated Eric and he began to express his annoyance that Lumb was not carrying out his instructions promptly enough. Muir, pressing Benson's point home, asked Lumb if he had pointed out to Eric that there might be an intestacy. Lumb confirmed that he had warned Eric of the dangers that, if Albert was to die before Eric, there would be, for all intents and purposes, an intestacy but Eric had done nothing about it.

The following Saturday, Lumb met Albert for the first time and took him to the bank where he introduced him to the manager. However, it was not for another month until Albert opened the account.

Lumb told the court that Eric had a habit of regularly changing his will and during these exchanges, the media were avidly watching Albert for any reaction. The *Daily Express* noted that he listened 'without apparent surprise' that Eric had made thirty-six or thirty-seven different wills.[109]

On 22 June 1912, Eric telephoned the solicitor and revoked one or two of the minor legacies. On 24 June, he telephoned again, revoking yet more legacies and amending others. No details of those changes were mentioned at the inquest.

Sometime after this, Eric told Lumb he wanted the £5,000 that was left to Albert to be increased to £10,000, to give Albert £400 a year which would pay his half of the rent and expenses of the flat. Lumb tried to argue against this but Eric was determined, giving the solicitor no options but to carry out his instructions

When asked about his opinion of Albert, Lumb stated in neutral terms that Eric spoke very highly of the man and when Muir asked if he had any doubts about Eric's intentions to leave everything to Albert, he replied that he no doubts at all.

The Coroner wanted to know if Albert was aware that he had been made the main beneficiary of Eric's will. Lumb said as far as he knew Albert was aware but then added he could not really tell as Albert was never present at his meetings with Eric.

After the court returned from lunch, Lumb was cross-examined by Hanson on behalf of Mrs Trevanion. Hanson wanted the lawyer to confirm that up to 13 December 1911, all the numerous wills that Eric had made were in favour of his two brothers and Lumb duly confirmed that they were. In December 1911, he explained, Eric had spoken of a letter he had received from his brother, Cecil, which annoyed him but as far as he knew there was no animosity between Eric and his other brother, Claude.

Something serious had obviously happened, because Eric

received Cecil's letter on the 11 December and just two days later, he was at the solicitors' changing his will. At various times, the press noted the tempestuous relationships of the Trevanions and that Eric often fell out with his mother but had never split from his brothers before. What could Cecil have said in his letter to upset Eric so much that in two days he cut not just him but Claude out of his will? One possible reason is that there was a growing unease of Albert's influence in Eric's life and they had warned him about his friend. Given Eric's level of devotion, any criticism of Albert would not have been taken lightly.

On 13 December, Eric revisited Lumb with new instructions to leave his entire estate to the National Gallery in the event of Albert's death. Perhaps Lumb's concerns about intestacy had played on Eric's or Albert's mind as, with no valid will, if Albert died, then Eric's fortune would have been returned to his next of kin. Eric was determined not to allow that to happen, as he wanted nothing of his to go to the family, confirming the seriousness of the rift.

Unfortunately, the wording of the will did not reflect Eric's wishes, as was apparent when Hanson read out the altered clause:

> out of the monies to arise out of sale and conversion the funeral and testamentary debts shall be paid, and the whole of the residue shall be held in trust for the trustees of the National Gallery.

Lumb agreed the wording was correct but was then asked by Hanson why Albert's death was not mentioned. Who exactly was supposed to be inheriting what? Lumb's testimony was confusing, said Hanson, he had said that on the 13th that Albert was the beneficiary but by the 18th he had changed that to the National Gallery: just who were the main beneficiaries? Lumb seemed to become confused at this point, agreeing that the wording of the clause was completely different from that he believed he had agreed with Eric. He also could not remember if he settled it on the 16th or 18th December. What he was certain about, he insisted, was that when Eric spoke to him on the 18th, it was not to change his mind about Albert inheriting the estate but to clarify that in the event of Albert's death, everything was to go to the National Gallery.

Lumb agreed it was all a bit confusing: an astonishing admission for a solicitor to make. This was an estate valued at millions of pounds in today's money, yet the clause was so badly worded that it was possible to legally challenge the will which is what the Trevanion family were doing. Had Lumb taken matters into his own hands and left the will open to a challenge?

Hanson continued to press for more details of how the will had come about. Had Eric, Hanson asked, come to the office alone? Lumb replied that he had gone to see Eric at St Stephen's Crescent, not his office. Albert had not been in attendance and Lumb did not meet him for the first time until 16 December, three days after he had been instructed by Eric over the will. He did not see Albert again until about 20 April after they had returned from their trip.

Hanson asked Lumb if he knew that Eric was contemplating making the trip at the time the will was written and Lumb replied, 'Oh, yes.' However, when Hanson referred to Albert as Eric's secretary, Lumb said that he was more like a travelling companion. Clarifying, Lumb said he never understood Albert to be Eric's secretary, adding, 'The idea was that they should be the same.'

This was reflected in the lease for the flat. Lumb said the solicitors for Grand Avenue Mansions had sent him a copy of the draft lease, asking for a reference. He expressed surprise to see Albert's name listed first but thought this was just because he was the elder of the two men.[110]

When he was asked at the inquest why Eric had wanted to leave everything to Albert, Lumb replied that Eric had fallen out with his family. Hanson asked him if he thought this was strange but Lumb didn't think so. However, when asked about leaving money and items outside the family, Lumb admitted that he did find that odd and had asked Eric about it but had received no answer.

One of the more curious points of Eric's will was his apparent defying of inheritance laws by willing away items which had been left to him for lifetime use only. Charlotte Georgina Fitzgerald, a cousin of Eric's father, had left the heirlooms to Hugh but he had sold his interests to family members when he became bankrupt. They were then passed to Florence and she in turn passed them on to her three sons but they were intended for life use only in order to keep them for future generations. On death, they had to be re-willed to another family member's lifetime or they reverted back to the head of the family to re-allocate. According to the conditions of his own inheritance, Eric could not will them outside the family. He would have been very aware of that, as would his solicitors, and it gave the Trevanions another reason to challenge the will. Why then had Lumb not driven home the point to Eric that his will was open to being challenged? Or was he deliberately leaving loopholes, something he hinted at when admitting that he had advised Eric not to tell Albert about being the main beneficiary.

'Why did you tell him not to tell Roe?' Hanson asked.

> I did what I could to smooth matters over, so that he should not be so harsh on his brother, and I thought that at some future time there might be a reconciliation with both the brothers, or one of them, and in that case the testator might wish to make an alteration in their favour, and I thought if he told Roe that he had made him residuary legatee it would rather shut the door to that.

This is quite a revealing statement for Lumb to make. He knew that Eric had frequently changed his will but seemed to think that if Albert was aware he was the beneficiary then it would 'shut the door' to any further alterations. Was he implying that Albert dominated Eric?

Hanson certainly seemed suspicious, 'You know perfectly well that could hardly be the reason,' he said, 'because you knew there were 36 or 37 dispositions before this since 1906 to one brother or another?'

It is uncertain what point Hanson was making here. Lumb had made it clear that the change came about as a direct result of the letter Eric had received from Cecil, even though all previous wills had favoured his brothers. It is possible that Hanson was trying to push Lumb into making revelations about the true nature of the men's relationship.

'It is quite clear,' Hanson said, 'that his brother, Cecil, would not have anything?'

'Yes, and he was equally determined about Claude.' This directly contradicts Lumb's earlier statement that, as far as he knew, there was no animosity between Eric and Claude.

Hanson then asked, 'During this week, from the 13th to 19th December, were you not busily engaged in drafting clauses to put the will in favour of Cecil?' Where Hanson got this information from, he did not say but there is a possibility it was from testimony of the first inquest which has not been kept. Lumb did admit that in all other wills the pictures, jewellery, and other items were left to the brothers in order to keep the heirlooms in the family.

Hanson then wanted to establish just how much Albert knew about Eric's wealth. Lumb told the inquest that while he could not give an exact date, an order in the Chancery Division under his grandfather's will was enacted at some time in 1910. This enabled him to take immediate possession of considerable sums of money and as far as Lumb knew Albert was fully aware of how much money Eric had, at least from 1910 onwards. It seems highly unlikely, given the close relationship between the two men, that Eric would not have told Albert he now had free access to his fortune.

'Did Mr Trevanion ever tell you what it was that Roe had done to deserve the whole of his property?'

'No.'

Hanson returned to the question of the pictures and jewellery, things of considerable value. The pictures, Lumb explained, were family portraits and as such not worth a great deal, although a few were by good artists and might have some value. In a previous draft will, Eric had left all the family pictures to Cecil and this may have been the clause, written between 13 and 19 December, that Hanson had been referring to. If that was true, said Hanson, just how upset could Eric possibly have been towards Cecil if he was leaving him these pictures?

'I supposed he wanted to keep them in the family,' Lumb replied, 'That was the impression he gave me.'

After Hanson had finished his questioning, Palmer, on behalf of Albert, rose in order to push home the discord with all the Trevanions. 'He has been on very bad terms with his family?' said Palmer.

'I would not like to say further,' answered Lumb, 'than that I simply knew he was not at all on good terms with his family.'

'Do you know that he went down to Brighton with a view to reducing expenses?'

'That was what he told me.'[111]

This last statement may sound odd for someone so wealthy, particularly given that when details of the will were published Eric left £58, 971 17s (about 6.5 million in today's money), not allowing for all of Eric's money still in Albert's account. It did not mean, however, that Eric could easily access money as his capital was tied up in his trust and in buildings he owned or given to Albert. Eric was apparently living on £8,000 a year which was not enough to meet his expenditure so while he was drawing some from his capital, he was also selling securities and getting loans from the bank, loans which then turned into overdrafts.

Palmer asked, 'Did you know that Mr Roe was in the employ of Messrs Cammell, Laird and Co.?' Lumb said he had not known that.[112]

On bank forms and elsewhere, Albert described himself as a 'colliery agent' as he worked in the colliery department of Messrs. Cammell, Laird & Co. However, this job title seems highly unlikely. An agent was the senior colliery manager responsible for the appointment and employment of mine managers who were usually qualified men. The agent would check that employees were conforming to company policies and to the legal requirements of the Mines Act, as well as determining the development of colliery and mining methods. This seems a rather improbable occupation for someone who had no links whatsoever with mining.

Cammell, Laird and Co was one of the leading British ship building companies although, by the early twentieth century, they had branched out and were making rolling stock for the London Underground. The company was based in Birkenhead but would have employed agents at all the main seaports particularly those with stock exchanges, which Swansea had. They owned a variety of concerns, including several coal mines such as the Clyne Valley Colliery. The 1911 census gives Albert's occupation as a colliery clerk, which seems logical as he would not have the experience to be an agent. Later he admitted that he only arranged the selling of coal from the Clyne Valley mine.

Albert spent a large amount of time in Swansea and, in the last year of Eric's life, seemingly more time there than in Brighton. He continued to work despite the massive amount of money in his bank account perhaps, as a fit, physical type of man used to being on the move and being in charge of people, he simply enjoyed it. Perhaps he needed a change from the life of luxury that Eric offered, or simply a break from a man he described as emotionally and physically unstable. Perhaps he was having an affair. At the time of Eric's death, he had already announced that he intended to marry a woman in Swansea. Whatever the reasons, there are multiple testimonies describing Eric's misery when Albert was away from him. One event stands out: Eric's will was executed on 19 December 1911 and the very next day Albert handed in his resignation to Cammell, Laird and Co.

Returning to the question of the will, it is interesting to note the legatees. Albert is the main beneficiary but Mary Geneste was to receive £1,000, understandable as Eric had known her a long time. All the other legacies were to people who were paid to take care of him. Lumb was to get £300, Bridges £50, Dr Sandifer £100, and Dr Winnington Ingram, the Bishop of London (who remained single throughout his life) was also to receive £100. No friends or other family members are mentioned. However, in a codicil Eric did leave his aunt, Ellen Sophia Cooper a diamond cross to use during her lifetime. To his solicitor, Morton, Eric left a ruby and diamond pin, again to use for a lifetime. Morton was also one of the will's executors with Eric's friend Dr Rees, who flits in and out of Eric's story. Both were to receive £300 for their services but Rees received no inheritance.

Who wanted Eric cremated?

After the subject of the will had been dealt with, Hanson wanted to clarify why Dr Baines believed Eric should be cremated.

Cremation was a relatively new way of disposing of the dead. Despite a number of campaigns during the nineteenth century, supported by individuals such as authors Anthony Trollope, George de Maurier, and the painter, John Everett Millais, acceptance was slow. As mentioned above, when eccentric Welshman, Dr William Price, attempted to cremate his dead baby at Llantrisant in 1884 he was arrested but during the court case he argued there was no law against him doing so. He won the case and this, along with campaigning by the Cremation Society of Great Britain, finally led to the Cremation Act of 1902.

Eight years later, Eric signed a document stating that he wished to be cremated. In it he drew attention to his fears of being burnt alive and echoed his instructions to have his wrist cut to ensure he was truly dead. He detailed the cost of the funeral, the purchase of the ground, and the erection of a mausoleum:

> To my Executors – It is my request that you shall take such steps as shall be necessary to make sure that life be extinct. After a competent surgeon shall have certified that life is extinct, my body shall be cremated and my ashes placed in an urn in a mausoleum that you shall erect at a cost not exceeding £900.[113]

A year later Eric produced another document, dated 2 July 1911:

> To my Executors – referring to the memorandum addressed to you, and dated May 18, 1910. I do not wish to limit you as regards the amount to be expended on my funeral and for the purchase of ground and the erection of a mausoleum, but I wish that the ashes of my life-long friend, Albert Edward Roe, if his body is cremated, shall be placed in an urn and deposited in the same mausoleum, and that both the urns shall be above the level of the ground, and I prohibit you or your successors in title from allowing any member of my family to be buried or their ashes placed in such mausoleum or in the ground belonging thereto. Eric Trevanion.[114]

The first document had been written in 1910, four years after Eric and Albert met and when Eric, according to the solicitor, Lumb, was still on reasonably good terms with his family. At this point, Eric, despite changing his will often, was still regularly leaving his estate to his two brothers. The second document had been written after he had inherited and his relationship with Albert was much closer.

The family may genuinely not have been aware of either document and, in the confusion around his death, the paper Eric signed did not come to light. In any event, they buried him in the family vault but they did at least keep one of his requests and check for life by having an incision cut into his wrist.

Cecil may have taken the undertaker into the hall to override the cremation instructions because he thought Albert was interfering and wanted to avoid conflict with everyone present. Lumb said he had not spoken to Albert about Eric's wish for their ashes to be joined but Albert must have been aware that Eric was to be cremated, as he was the only one who could have instructed the doctor.

It also seems that Albert himself was ambiguous about cremation. The wording in Eric's document states 'if his body is cremated', reflecting the uncertainty of the general public towards this new form of disposal.

Even back in 1910, Eric may not have been as close to his family as had been supposed or he deliberately did not tell his family about his cremation plans, knowing his mother would disapprove. Contained in the second 1911 document that Eric signed was a clause that prohibited his executors from allowing the ashes of any relative to be placed in the same mausoleum as Albert and himself. This was included long before he received the letter from Cecil which resulted in Eric disinheriting his entire family.

Albert listened intently to the discussion about the cremation details, sitting with folded arms during most of the hearing but sometimes 'rested his strong chin on his hands as if in thought'.[115]

THE CONTENTIOUS EVIDENCE OF NURSE RICE

Throughout the inquest, the opposing legal teams vied with each other, trying to present a view of Eric's state of mind. The prosecution presented Eric as quite normal but driven to despair by Albert's behaviour towards him; despair which turned into extreme actions testing Albert's patience, perhaps pushing him to murder. The defence was trying to show how unstable Eric was and how his addiction to drugs affected his mind so greatly that he took the massive overdose himself.

Annie Rice was the first of four witnesses who had either dealt with Eric during his earlier overdose, or had been with him on the day he took the fatal amount. She attended him at the August overdose and she with Dr Baines remained the night in Eric's flat to monitor the patient. As she sat next to his bedside, Eric told her to turn her back; as she did so he reached towards a medicine cupboard, took out some aspirin tablets and put two in his mouth.

The first pill form of aspirin had appeared just twelve years earlier but was still relatively unknown. The aspirin Eric had taken contained five grains per tablet, said Rice, and they would not have harmed him. However, as Eric often boasted of how much Veronal he took, she may have been trying to stop him overdosing on yet another drug. 'I had to struggle with him for the remainder,' Rice continued, 'I held his wrists and rang a bell. Someone came and I asked them to call Dr Baines, who was lying down. Dr Baines came, and we got the tablets away from him, except the two in his mouth, which he had swallowed.' Eric's determination to take more than the two aspirins may have been related to his addiction to drugs but he may also have been trying to reduce pain. Numerous testimonies show that Eric suffered a great deal of pain throughout his life, exacerbated by his sedentary lifestyle.

Following the overdose, Dr Baines arranged for Nurse Rice to visit Eric intermittently for the next few days. When she was asked in court about Eric's mental health, Rice said that while he appeared depressed, three days later he sent for a hairdresser to dye his hair and to do a manicure. Albert had not been in the flat when he took the overdose but returned that evening around 8-9pm. Eric was lying on a couch in the bedroom and Albert said to him, 'You have been taking drugs again,' to which Rice replied, 'there are no drugs in the bedroom for the patient to take and he has only been having the medicine which the doctor offered him'.

Albert said nothing further to Rice but asked Eric to get up and have dinner.

Earlier that day the nurse had spoken to Eric about his drug taking but her advice had little effect. Later that night he called to her into his bedroom (in her police statement she says it was the following morning); Eric was sitting up in bed and he asked her to fetch him some Vichy water, Albert was asleep beside him.

In the morning, the two men had breakfast delivered to them

which they ate in bed. Rice commented that Eric had not eaten much but Albert replied, 'he has eaten as much as I have.' Now he was back, Rice said, there was no need for her to remain but Albert advised her to wait and see what the doctor said so she did not leave until the evening of the fourth day. On the way out, she noticed Eric asleep in a chair alone in the dining room.

A juror asked if she had noticed anything peculiar about Eric's dress but she had never seen him in his day clothes whilst she was tending him. When she went into his bedroom, he was sitting up wearing a silk nightshirt with a kind of kimono over it, she had never seen him wear pyjamas. He did wear white kid shoes with heels six inches high (fifteen centimetres), she added, which made him bend forward in an awkward manner as he walked and she didn't think that he was quite right in the head. In fact, she ended her police statement with the comment, 'during the time I was nursing Mr Trevanion he was as mad as a hatter.'[116]

He often cried and told her that several things were making him miserable. 'He was unhappy,' she stated, 'you could not get away from that. People do not cry if they are not unhappy, do they? ... when Mr Roe returned the deceased was very much upset.'[117] According to her, after Albert left, Eric continued to cry all that night.

The foreman of the jury asked her what it was that was making him unhappy and the nurse turned to the Coroner, asking 'Am I obliged to answer?' After some discussion, during which Rice became visibly agitated, she eventually wrote something down on a half-sheet of foolscap paper and handed it to Coroner Benson.[118]

The Coroner, having read the note, asked, 'Did he say that this made him unhappy?' and she replied, 'Yes. He swore by the crucifix that was hanging over his bed that it was absolutely true.'

'Did he say anything that led you to believe that that was one of the things that was making him cry?'

'Yes. He was crying when he told me.'

The Coroner said that for the present he had better not hand the witness statement to the jury. It was hearsay and might be used in a way which the law of evidence did not allow in other courts so, for the present, it should not be put into evidence.

What could Nurse Rice have possibly written which could not

be read out in court? Putting aside the Coroner's argument that it was hearsay, he also added that it 'might be used in a way which the law of evidence did not allow'. The most probable explanation is that the note contained details of homosexuality, which at that time was against the law for men. It was also socially unacceptable and would explain Rice's 'agitation' at being asked what Eric had told her and why she did not want to speak openly in court. The note also put the Coroner into something of a quandary: he must have been aware that opening the question of homosexuality in court could mean Albert being arrested.

For much of the first half of the twentieth century, the evidence needed to arrest a man on suspicion of homosexuality was slight. Unlike many other laws, even the attempt or expressed intention to commit an 'unnatural act' was in itself a crime. In 1952, Alan Turing was arrested and charged simply because he admitted he was a homosexual; he had done nothing except tell the interviewing officer that he had sex with men.[8]

Once the police had arrested someone on gross indecency, they would often confiscate address books and pursue everyone listed. In 1958, a Dr Reid, a former headmaster from Wells in Somerset, wrote an open letter to *The Spectator* outlining the tactics:

> The police go round from house to house, bringing
> ruin in their train, always attacking the youngest men
> first, extracting information with lengthy questioning
> and specious promises of light sentences as they
> proceed from clue to clue, i.e. from home to home.[119]

This practice of tracing men in order to uncover 'rings' of homosexuals may explain why no officers', or other names were produced in court. It must also have been rather worrying for the Coroner as if Albert was arrested it could mean the inquest being halted.

The details of what Eric told Nurse Rice must also have been quite explicit and Rice must have queried them because Eric: 'swore by the crucifix that was hanging over his bed that it was absolutely true'.

---

[8] Turing, a computer genius who is credited with helping to shorten WWII and so save around 14 million lives, was convicted of gross indecency and given the choice of imprisonment or hormonal treatment designed to curb libido. Turing chose the treatment but committed suicide two years later.

This evidence of the nurse had created cause for concern even before the inquest began. Three days earlier, the Public Prosecutor, Charles Mathews, had written to Coroner Benson saying he was so troubled by Rice's testimony that he felt compelled to ask the Attorney General if they should let her appear. Mathews was concerned that 'the relevancy of the unnatural relations between the deceased and Roe to the inquiry which you have to conduct.' The Attorney General's view was that, 'as these relations might be explanatory of the cause of death, evidence in regard to them which would enable a Jury to determine between the issues of accident, of suicide, and of murder, <u>was material</u> to the inquiry and ought not to be excluded.' The underlining of the words 'was material' emphasised Mathews' own views that the details should be included but, he went on to write: 'the statement of Nurse Rice, once it is made in Court, ought, however, to leave so little doubt upon this unsavoury point that I should say the calling of the witness would probably stop any further inquiry.' Mathews was clearly stating that Nurse Rice's testimony would see the inquest stopped and Albert arrested.

It was something Mathews knew only too well as he had seen it all before at Oscar Wilde's trial.

Charles 'Willie' Mathews (1850-1920) had appeared alongside Sir Edward Clarke as one of Wilde's prosecution barristers in 1895 when Wilde sued the Marquis of Queensberry for libel over accusations of sodomy. However, the defence brought in damning evidence as to Wilde's intimacies with several men and Clarke lost confidence in the case and withdrew. When Wilde was subsequently arrested and charged with sodomy and gross indecency, Sir Edward and Mathews continued to represent him.

By the time of Eric's inquest, Mathews had been the Director of Public Prosecutions for five years, the third most senior public prosecutor in England and Wales.[9] His caution over how and when evidence could be introduced into the inquest may have complex motives. Had the inquest been stopped and Albert arrested, he may well have been put on trial for sodomy and gross indecency and if found guilty sentenced to prison. The number of

---

[9] After the Attorney General and the Solicitor General

years varied; Oscar Wilde served two years. However, if Eric's death was found to be malicious and Albert put on trial and found guilty, he could face either a significant amount of time in prison, or even death as the death penalty in the UK was not removed until 1965. If Mathews thought Albert was 'implicated' in his friend's death, he may have been cautious, not wanting him to avoid a possible murder charge. However, it has to be asked, did Mathews' over cautiousness tip the case in Albert's favour?

At the inquest, Benson was clearly concerned about Nurse Rice's testimony, and he suggests that Mathews should have a seat near him at the inquest so they could consult, but Mathews did not agree. He wanted to avoid an implication 'by proximity' adding:

> were any person hereafter to be placed upon trial as the outcome of the inquiry, I ought to be free from suspicion that I, who must then become a prosecutor, had in the remotest sense controlled or even been conspicuous at the preliminary inquiry, upon the result of which my prosecution would of necessity be founded.[120]

Mathews clearly thought that Albert was heading for a trial after the inquest.

However, Mathews urged caution in how the testimony was handled, perhaps because he did not want details leaking to the press. As he returned the two statements Rice had made, he added, 'I am strongly of the opinion that they ought to be shown to nobody, and that you should resist any application by any person, whether interested or not, to inspect them, or any others of a similar character.'

The following day Mathews sent another letter to Benson:

> I have seen the Attorney General, who is of the opinion that Nurse Rice ought not to be called as a witness until quite late in the Inquiry, and that any evidence which refers to the unsavoury side of the case should be reserved until the close of it. He is, however, of opinion that the Reports of Dr Willcox and Dr Spilsbury should be read in the course of

Friday next ... The Attorney General is of the opinion that the matter first to be investigated is the cause of death, and that the painfully disagreeable incidents may, and ought to, be kept until towards the end.[121]

Nurse Rice then was allowed to speak but when it came to the 'unsavoury point', she clearly lost her nerve. Having read the note, Benson steered questions away, asking 'Were there any matters not connected with this that would account for his crying?'

Rice replied that Eric told her he 'was much upset because Mr Roe was away from him. This was also known to the Butler and his wife. I know of no other reasons for his being unhappy. He was in a very collapsed state on the Monday night; he had to lie down on the carpet to have his nails manicured.'

She had been so concerned about his mental health, she said, that she decided to keep all medicine in her possession out of reach and even asked the hairdresser not to leave the dye in Eric's room in case he drank it. She described him as 'very absent, and dreamy, and if he took a very small quantity of whisky he would be very quickly affected by it.'

'Was he in a state of nervous breakdown?' the foreman of the jury asked.

'He was in a state of collapse.'

'Do you think this cause of unhappiness led him to think of suicide?'

Nurse Rice was adamant against this idea, 'I don't think he ever took his life. He was too fond of living.'[122]

This was another difficulty in the case. Suicide in 1913 was against the law as it was believed that those who killed themselves showed contempt for the Creator who had given them life, an unforgiveable sin.

Historically, a range of post-death punishments were imposed on the suicided under the *felo de se* (Latin for *felon of himself*) law, including: only being permitted burial on the outskirts of an urban area, without a headstone or marking; no religious person in attendance; only the authorities could be present; the burial could not take place in daylight; nor could it be notified; and property could be confiscated. It had only been ninety years before Eric's death that the law requiring suicides to be buried at cross-roads with a stake in the heart had been abolished. It was in 1882, just two years before Eric's birth, that the law was changed to allow suicides to be buried on consecrated soil.

Families of suicides faced societal disapproval and were considered in some way culpable. Survivors faced criminal proceedings and were often socially ostracised.

Things gradually improved but in the early twentieth century suicide was still illegal. According to the Office of National Statistics, there were just 155-163 registered suicides between the years 1909-1919, although this figure is probably extremely low as many deaths would have been covered up by families.

Until the Suicide Act 1961, anyone trying to take their life could be criminally charged with attempting self-murder and could face a prison sentence. Anyone assisting, or seen to play any part in causing someone to take their life, could be tried as an accessory to murder. Even today, suicide is still a criminal act in some countries and illegal in most to assist someone in an attempt to take their own life.

In 2017, there were 5,821 registered suicides, a rate of 10.1 per 100,000 population, three-quarters of these were men, a figure which had been consistent since the mid-1990s.[123] 2017 also saw the first case of a man being convicted of manslaughter by driving his ex-girlfriend into committing suicide by his controlling behaviour.[124]

Of the three options Coroner Benson had given the jury in deciding Eric's death: suicide, murder or misadventure; the first two had serious implications for Albert. Although he had appeared nonchalant throughout the inquest, he must have been a very worried man. If the verdict came back as suicide, there may have been further examination into his controlling behaviour, particularly given Eric's statement that he had deliberately overdosed with the morphine to scare Albert. If Albert's behaviour was seen in any way to have caused Eric's death, he could have been investigated and the true nature of their relationship discussed in much greater detail. If those details highlighted any homosexual behaviour then it is almost certain Albert would have been arrested.

If it was murder, then Albert was the only one who had opportunity and motive to do so.

Eric's mother, Florence, seems convinced that Albert was in some way responsible for his death. Eric had already been buried and for the most part forgotten about by the public; and whilst it would have been shameful to have a family member die of a drugs overdose, Eric's bad health could have been used to explain it away. There must have been those who advised Florence that re-opening the case could result in a suicide verdict, which would have brought shame on the family. She had already been through societal disapproval over her marriage and its fallout; another scandal would have damaged not only her but her sons, Cecil and Claude. Perhaps she did not fully realise the nature of Eric's relationship with Albert and the even greater shame of 'unnatural vice'. Perhaps she did come to regret her decision to put her son's life on public display.

THE OTHER NURSES

Nurse Price was called to confirm that it was she and not Nurse Rice who was summoned by Dr Baines to attend Eric on the night of 10 September. Another nurse called Hawkins was already there but it was Price who administered injections of strychnine and digitalis, given to her by Baines. These had little effect and Eric died at 5.20am. Price also noted that Albert came two or three times into the bedroom and stared down at Eric.

Nurse Hawkins stated that she had been the first nurse to attend Eric and had arrived at 8.30am on the 10th. She explained that she had little to do other than to keep him dry and comfortable, as instructed by Dr Baines, adding that Baines told her to try and feed Eric through the rectum with egg and milk, which she attempted on two occasions with no success. This is in direct contradiction to Baines' own testimony that he had made no attempts to administer food. He may not have done it personally and was not present when it was done, but it was Baines who had instructed Hawkins over the telephone. In his testimony, he had admitted to the injections being used but did not mention it was Nurse Price who had done so. It seems odd that he did not also admit his instruction to administer food.

Willcox was asked about Baines' refusal to give food to an unconscious patient, as the doctor claimed it could not be done through the mouth. Willcox stated that food being passed through the nose or elsewhere could be done even if the patient was unconscious. Despite Willcox giving this evidence, Baines did not admit that the nurse had attempted to give Eric food.

WAS VERONAL SOLELY TO BLAME?

Dr Henry Stephen Sandifer, a general GP in the partnership of Sandifer, Phillips and Leigh, gave evidence saying he had known Eric since 29 September 1908 and attended him when he was staying with Mary Geneste. He had, he said, seen Eric 114 times in four years, approximately once every two weeks, but for nothing serious. It was mainly 'influenza, etc, and there would be the depressing influence of drugs as a complication'. This confirms other views that Eric suffered from depression. Many people who knew Eric chalked up his unhappiness to the drug taking but it could of course have been complicated by his apparent sexual orientation.

Sandifer said Eric was addicted to sleeping draughts and would drink more alcohol than was good for him, though he had never seen him drunk. According to him, Eric took a great deal of Veronal and a certain amount of morphine. He told the court that he had frequently remonstrated with Eric, asking him to give them up. Sandifer admitted, in fairness to Eric, that there had been several attempts to quit,[125] even occasionally volunteering to give up his stores. At the inquest, Dr Sandifer produced two bottles which Eric had given him. One was labelled 'Burroughs Wellcome & Co. Veronal' consisting of twenty-five 1 gram (15 grains) tablets amounting to 350 grains. 'These,' said Sandifer, 'must have been purchased abroad'.

Burroughs Wellcome & Co. was owned by Henry Solomon Wellcome and Silas Mainville Burroughs, Americans who had moved to the UK in 1880 and built up an influential pharmaceutical company that challenged the quack medicine so prevalent in the late nineteenth century. The company was multinational and presumably Sandifer made his comment about Eric's Veronal coming from abroad because of the dose. Ten grains were the maximum recommended dose in the UK but the tablets in the first bottle were fifteen, indicating a foreign origin.

The second bottle, labelled the same as the first, contained tablets of 0.5 grams, a little over 7½ grains, which would be more consistent with a UK dosage.[126] Sandifer does not say if the bottles were full or had been used.

Sandifer also does not give a date for this surrender of Veronal, saying only it was 'about a year ago'. As the inquest was held in January 1913, the surrender must have been early 1912, just a month after Eric had changed his will and left everything to Albert, perhaps as a fresh start.

Sandifer did not see Eric again for some six months but on 21 June 1912, he was called to Mary Geneste's house as Eric wanted advice about a hammered toe. It was Sandifer who recommended and subsequently carried out an operation. A hammered toe is often caused or aggravated by wearing tight footwear and several people testified to Eric's habit of wearing tight, ladylike, high heeled shoes. It may also account for the fact that he rarely walked anywhere, as it would have been painful, although nobody mentions his feet specifically when discussing his pain.

Sandifer told Eric he was looking a lot better and asked how he had managed it. 'He said that he was indebted to Mr Roe, who had not allowed him to take more than a very small quantity of drink, and also that he had kept him from taking Veronal and other drugs.'[127] Eric told the doctor that he had made a fresh will leaving all his money away from his family and it was all to go to Albert. 'I told him I thought it was a very extraordinary thing to do, but I did not take much interest in it, as I did not think he was going to die. The operation upon his toe was quite a small one, and he got better and went back to Miss Geneste's house. I knew he had made arrangements to go for a motor trip to Cornwall with Mr Roe and his nurse.'

Things were not as they looked to Dr Sandifer however, the positive picture of Eric giving up his drugs and being reformed by Albert was simply not true. About six weeks before he had seen the doctor, Eric had bought a dozen cachets of Veronal from Douthwaite; two weeks later he acquired a further dozen. Six days before his appointment, he was opening an account and two days after telling Sandifer that Albert had 'kept him' from taking drugs, he bought another two dozen.

No date is given for when Eric went into hospital but it must have been on or around the 26 June as he was there for two weeks and on the 10 July, the day he came out, he took an overdose.

Dr Sandifer was called to the Geneste house between 1-1.30am, where he found Eric unconscious, suffering from morphine poisoning. He had been called by a Dr Nolan but how this doctor had become involved was not made clear although he may have been the Geneste's physician. Sandifer found Eric unconscious and 'dying'. After trying artificial respiration, Sandifer jumped on his bike, cycled home and returned with a stomach pump. He washed out the stomach with permanganate potash, repeating the process three or four times at intervals of half or three-quarters of an hour. He sent Albert to get oxygen from a local chemist, banging on the shop doors in the small hours.

Between Sandifer, Albert, Dr Nolan and the two Geneste women, they managed to revive Eric around 6 to 7am. He had been unconscious for three hours and Sandifer had not thought he would recover saying 'he would not have lived if it had not been for the stomach pump, and the artificial respiration'. A telling statement.

It seems a shame that Albert did not call Sandifer earlier as Eric lay dying. He was not called until two days after the start of the fatal coma. When Albert finally telephoned Sandifer, the doctor asked if Eric was receiving medical treatment and Albert told him Dr's Baines and Hobhouse were there but that Eric was not expected to live. Sandifer said in that case there was little point in his going to Brighton but Albert told him Eric would have wished it and to hurry up or he would not be there in time. Sandifer dutifully came, arriving at 4.30pm and Eric died at 5.20am. While it is unlikely Eric would have survived the massive dose, it seems his best chances of survival would have been with Dr Sandifer.

Returning to the morphine dose of July, Albert said Sandifer had done 'every mortal thing' he could do to help. The following day he returned to check on his patient and asked Eric why he had taken the morphine:

> He said he had taken it to give Mr Roe a fright. He
> told me he had a row with Mr Roe, who had doubted
> his word; he said that he had not appreciated the

great strength of the morphine, and that he took more than he intended to take; that he had only intended to take enough to make himself unconscious. He told me that he did not intend to commit suicide. I found the box in which the morphine amphules (sic) had been bought; it bore the name of a Chemist in Lisbon. The dose was shown in decimals of a gram, and the deceased had mis-calculated the dose. The deceased informed me that he could not remember how many he had taken, but that he thought it was 6 or 7. I found 6 recent pricks above the patella on his right thigh.

Sandifer later found the glass ampoules thrown down the lavatory.

Once again, Sandifer testified he had pressed Eric to give up his drugs. Eric gave him a box with four ampoules which he thought came from the bathroom and Sandifer took them with him. He thought Albert later found some more but he could not be sure. However, this contradicts Albert's later testimony when he says both men searched together, found the drugs and Sandifer took them with him.

After the overdose, Sandifer warned Eric of doing the same thing with Veronal, as he was aware that Eric had a peculiar idea that he could take enormous amounts of the drug. He mentioned amounts that he could take which were preposterous, said Dr Sandifer, who instructed Eric to eradicate such thoughts from his mind. The doctor told him that if he was not careful, he would be found dead one morning, but Eric reassured him that he could take forty or fifty grains with ease.

Perhaps Eric was simply boasting about the amounts he took for, at the time of the morphine overdose, he had not yet tried the same with Veronal. Eric refused to give up the drugs, telling Sandifer that he could obtain them easily in the UK or abroad. Sandifer tried to convince him to stick to morphine as it was 'an easier drug to manage than Veronal when an overdose had been taken as there was no acquiring a tolerance for Veronal as there was for morphine.'

After almost dying from the morphine, Eric seems to give the drug up in favour of Veronal. He had on two previous occasions been rendered unconscious by morphine but they seem to have been accidental overdoses and not a deliberate attempt to scare Albert. He perhaps saw Veronal as safer, despite his inflated idea about how much he could safely take. Even after his deliberate attempt to scare Albert in 1911, he did not appear to use morphine extensively again, although his mother testified that she saw morphine on his bedside table. However, none was discovered in his system at the autopsy. It is possible he took drugs other than morphine or Veronal, but apart from one mention of aspirin, no effort was made to determine exactly what Eric was taking, the inquest was so firmly fixed on Veronal.

At that time, drugs now considered far too dangerous to be freely available across the counter, could easily be bought. Cocaine was regularly used to prevent toothache, even for children; heroine for coughs; chloroform for colds; and opium for pain relief. They were all highly addictive, dangerous and often deadly. For those with ongoing health problems, addiction and overdoses were common, although few recorded cases show accidental death or suicide from anything as large as the dose which killed Eric.

Dr Willcox had shown in his writings that continual use of barbiturates was addictive. In 1927, fourteen years after Eric died, he wrote:

> From a study of my own cases and from a review of
> the literature which has been most carefully collated
> by Dr Helen Young, I have no doubt whatever that
> the continued use of drugs of the barbituric acid and
> sulphonal groups leads to the formation of a definite
> addiction to the drug in question. The mental
> changes resulting from the drug addiction lead to
> serious moral changes, and suicide is most
> unfortunately one of the commonest of these.
>
> The danger of the use of the hypnotic drugs has not,
> in my opinion, been sufficiently realized by the
> medical profession and the public.[128]

Eric had been taking Veronal prior to the 1911 morphine

overdose and used it almost exclusively afterwards, amounting to at least six years of abuse. In one of Willcox's papers, whilst discussing addiction to drugs such as Veronal, Willcox quotes Mrs Trevanion as saying of Eric:

> He took it first for pneumonia and never could give it up... He told me he should never be able to give it up ... He seemed to lose all self-control when he wanted it.[129]

Willcox does not give any indication as to how long a person needed to take the drug before 'mental changes' took place, but these included depressions, hallucinations, paranoia and it may be these changes which affected Eric.

From various sources of evidence, it was clear that a year before they moved to Brighton Albert and Eric were experiencing difficulties in their relationship. The reason Eric gave for the morphine overdose was because they had a row in which Albert 'doubted his word',[130] although in his evidence Dr Sandifer did not elaborate on the details. It seems too extreme an action for one argument - it is perhaps more likely that the difficulties were well established. Eric often stated openly in front of witnesses his unhappiness over Albert's behaviour, distressed at the amount of time Albert spent in Swansea and also with Albert's domineering behaviour towards him when they were together.

Dr Sandifer had remained ignorant of Eric's continued drug use and the effects it was having on him. In fact, he did not see Eric again until he lay dying in the Brighton flat.

At the inquest Dr Sandifer was asked his opinion on the stomach pumping debate. When he had arrived at the flat, he had asked Baines if a pump had been used, saying:

> "No," because he thought it would have killed him. I said, "Would it be worthwhile washing it out now?" He said, "You can if you like; I "dare not." I carefully examined the deceased. I found that he was nearly pulse less; he was breathing extremely shallowly; that on touching him, if one depressed the jaw half an inch, he would stop breathing; and that if one turned his head aside for a few degrees he would stop

97

breathing; and that his lungs were oedematous.[10] I
therefore agreed with Dr. Baines.[131]

While he agreed that by the time he arrived it was not feasible
to use the pump, he did feel it could have been done at the start
as, 'the state of his lungs would have been different at the
beginning of the 15 hours. The first thing anybody would want to
do would be to wash the stomach out, if the condition of the
patient allowed of it. It was impossible to do this when I saw him
15 hours later – I think it would have killed him, because when the
slightest movement was made he stopped breathing.'

Sandifer then made a shocking statement: 'I suspected,' he
said, 'that the deceased had taken something besides Veronal. I
looked over his skin, and found two pricks, but as the skin was so
blue it was difficult to say whether they were recent. His pupil was
not dilated as much as I expected to find.'

This extraordinary testimony was never followed up.

There were twenty-seven days between Eric dying and his
remains being exhumed and morphine mostly leaves the body
after about three days. It can be detected in hair follicles for up to
ninety days but the technique for testing hair samples, although
discovered in 1858[11], was not used regularly in forensic science in
1912, so it is unlikely that morphine would have shown up in the
analysis done by Dr Willcox. Only Mrs Trevanion mentions
seeing the morphine on the bedside table and surprisingly little
attention was given to the drug, particularly knowing that Eric had
used it for an overdose three months earlier. Could morphine have
contributed towards his death? It certainly would account for the
evidence of both Mrs Trevanion and Dr Sandifer that the coma
seemed different from other Veronal overdoses. Mrs Trevanion
said that while he lived with her, she had seen him several times in
a coma caused by Veronal and it was not the same. On the surface
it would seem irrelevant as the 150 grains would probably have
killed Eric irrespective of whether he took any other drugs.

However, there are difficulties with Willcox's figures. He
assumes that all 150 grains were accounted for by the overdose but

---

[10] Swollen
[11] A German Felix Hoppe-Seyler had discovered traces of arsenic in hair in 1858 but further
research was not done until the mid-twentieth century.

Mary Joiner states that when she went to wake Eric that morning he was 'very drowsy.' This is consistent with her husband's testimony Eric was often difficult to wake after taking the drug. Mary Joiner added that Eric 'constantly said he was going to take sleeping draughts' and on other mornings she also had difficulty rousing him.

If Eric had taken Veronal the previous night, or even several nights before, some would still have been in his system as it does not disperse from the blood for around seventy-two hours. And if Eric did take some on earlier nights it reduces the amount available for the overdose itself.

Furthermore, evidence from a 1936 trial of Eric Mareo in New Zealand, who was accused of murdering his wife with Veronal, raises a further complication. The pathologist had adopted the same method as Willcox for calculating the killer dose: assuming Veronal was equally distributed throughout the body and so it was only necessary to double the amount left in the corpse. This was rejected by the defence team, who referenced a standard work by the American toxicologist, Rudolph August Witthaus. Witthaus had appeared as an expert in several famous criminal cases and his great work was to edit and co-write the massive two volume *Medical Jurisprudence, Forensic Medicine, and Toxicology*. Volume two had been published in 1906 so was available when Willcox analysed the Veronal left in Eric's corpse, but as Witthaus noted, post mortem scientific analysis was in its infancy and

> ...the distribution of poisons in the system, i.e., the relative proportion existing in different organs and tissues of the body at various stages of absorption and elimination, has as yet been studied with regard only to a few mineral poisons, such as arsenic, antimony, copper and lead.[132]

This clearly shows that the distribution of Veronal in the system had not been studied in depth.

Furthermore, the dispersal of poisons in the body is generally dependent on many factors, including the person's temperature; what other medicines they had taken and how these may have interacted with the poison; how much urine and faeces had been expelled; the actions of the undertaker; and the temperature within the coffin. As a result,

the amount which was taken by the deceased ... can never be determined by analysis of the cadaver. The quantity present in certain organs may be ascertained with more or less accuracy by analyses, but from the results of such determination only one inference can be drawn, *i.e.*, that the quantity taken was greater than the amount found. How much greater it may have been guessed at, but not determined... In attempting to calculate the total quantity in the cadaver, it is never permissible to assume that the amount separated from a certain fractional part of the body bears the same relation to the entire amount present that the weight of the fraction examined bears to that of the body. The distribution of the poison in the different organs and tissues is uneven under all circumstances, and the quantity in one part is no indication of that in any other.[133]

In his summing up of the 1936 Mareo trial, the judge reminded the jury that Willcox's methods were 'not universally accepted'[134] and this clearly indicates that the estimation of 150 grains in Eric's system may be seriously flawed, but by how much it is impossible to say.

Even if this is ignored, and staying with the prosecution's estimation of dose, Eric would have needed twenty cachets (or twenty-one due to the underselling of Gibson) - and this can easily be accounted for in the two-dozen bought on 2 and 4 September. However, nine of these were found which would leave sixteen, not enough for a 150-grain overdose. The earlier purchase before 2 September meant that Eric had less than one cachet a day to use and this is consistent with most of the purchases going back to May.

According to most testimony, Eric was addicted to Veronal but this is not supported by these figures, unless he was buying elsewhere or hoarding the drug, although there is no evidence for either. If he was addicted to using it every night and taking on average two cachets, then in the five days between the purchase and the overdose he would have taken ten, reducing the amount available for the overdose to six, far below what was required. Even had he been hoarding the drug, his supplies would have been used up before the overdose, as apart from the two anomalous cachets, only those made by Gibson remained. All this lends weight to the argument that the overdose was taken over several days, not a single night.

Irrespective of the errors made in Willcox's analysis, had the supply of Veronal available to Eric been examined in more depth it would have compromised the testimony that he was 'addicted' to the drug. Had everyone at the inquest not been so quick to accept the last two dozen as the fatal overdose more questions could have been asked as to why Eric was being portrayed as out of control with regard to his drug habits. Perhaps had more attention been paid to the possibility of other drugs, or a hoard, a more thorough search could have been made. If Sandifer's observation of the prick marks was explored then perhaps evidence could have been revealed that Eric had injected morphine in which case why would he also take the Veronal?

One answer could be that the drugs 'affected character' - making people think Eric had an addiction problem. As Sandifer pointed out, 'It interferes with the patient's sense of honour, in that he would speak untruths concerning his store of drugs, etc.' However, he added; 'I think that the drug taking by the deceased had only slightly affected his character, and his nervous system. It had not in the least made his life burdensome; he was a boy who thoroughly enjoyed life. The night before he took the overdose of morphine, he was full of plans for his motor trip to Cornwall on the following day.' He explained the crying by adding, 'any big dose of veronal the patient would be likely to weep easily – like the bibulous tears of an alcoholic – and would interfere with his self-control.' On the one hand he is comparing Eric to an alcoholic and on the other saying the Veronal would have 'only slightly affected his character.'

Sandifer also spoke of Albert's state of mind, noting how 'very upset' and concerned he was, telling Dr Sandifer, 'if Eric recovers from this as he has recovered from the last two attempts, I cannot stand it any longer. I shall refuse to live with him, and his own people will have to look after him. It is the third time, and I cannot stand the anxiety any longer.'

Palmer then rose to ask the doctor's opinion on whether Albert had always done all he could for Eric. Dr Sandifer replied, 'From my point of view he has done everything a doctor could wish, because he had kept him off his drinks and his drugs as well as he could. I know very little about him personally. I only know his effect on my patient.' He added that Eric was absolutely devoted to Albert who had done nothing but good for him, and described Eric as a 'very amusing, very clever, very quick at repartee and quite a clever boy altogether'.

The foreman of the jury then asked if Eric was effeminate and the doctor said yes in both manners and appearance.

Today the word 'effeminate' tends to conjure up images of a certain type of man and modern dictionaries reinforce this, with synonyms such as womanish, unmanly, effete, foppish, affected, mincing, and posturing. For the most part it is used a derogatory term as it emphasises the 'weakness' of women, a commonly held prejudice so for many in history it was an acceptable term. The word was also used as a synonym for sodomy and gender diversity. *A Classical Dictionary of the Vulgar Tongue* (1785) by Francis Grose[135] lists: 'Molly. A Miss Molly; an effeminate fellow, a sodomite.' And *The New World of Words* (1706) by John Kersey[136] lists: 'Androgynus (*sic*), one that is both Man and Woman, or has the Natural Parts of both Sexes; a Scrat or Will Jill, an effeminate Fellow.'

By the late nineteenth century, 'effeminate', when used in a derogatory way, was associated with homosexuality.

The foreman of the jury asked Dr Sandifer, 'Do you know that Mr Roe did all he could to cure him of his effeminacy?'

'Yes. He told me that he had stopped dying his hair because Roe objected very strongly to it.' Dr Sandifer does not give a date for this statement, but Eric was having his hair dyed and waved in August, just a month before his death so he had either changed his mind or had never really stopped.

One of the jurors asked, 'Did you ever think that he was addicted to any unnatural vice?'

'No. I am quite sure he was not,' replied Sandifer quickly. He may have been telling the truth as he knew it but as his business partner was friends with Eric perhaps he did not want to see Albert arrested. He may also have been protecting his partner from investigation, a real possibility had he said yes.

The foreman changed tack, 'Would the drug habit have the effect of making his life burdensome?'

'Not in the least. He was a boy who thoroughly enjoyed life,
'reinforcing Nurse Rice's statement that he 'too fond of living' to
commit suicide.

7

DAY 3 – TUESDAY 28 JANUARY: 'VERY WEAK MINDED'

On the third day of the inquest, the media was busy summing up the proceedings: a twenty-seven-year-old extremely wealthy young man had died in suspicious circumstances and of his £100,000 estate only half was left - the other half having been transferred to his friend. It was impossible, they told their readers, to predict the outcome of the case.

> All that can be said is that it is of the most searching
> character; every point bearing or likely to bear upon
> the death of Mr Hugh Eric Trevanion is being carefully
> sifted. Nothing, in fact, escapes the famous counsel
> for the Treasury, on whose behalf an official
> shorthand of the proceedings is being taken.[137]

Day three was due to start at noon but long before that a large crowd had gathered in the court. At eleven-forty, Albert arrived in a dark lounge suit, wearing a gold ring on the third finger the right hand. In his black tie was a diamond pin. He took the same seat he had occupied the day before, below the dock alongside Josiah Henry Hanlin, his brother-in-law. Hanlin was a well-known Swansea man and the principal partner in J H Hanlin & Co, coal exporters and agents. They both worked at the Clyne Valley Colliery. Also supporting Albert was his friend Andrew Paton, a well-known golf and billiard player, described by the *Cambrian Daily Leader* as Albert's 'intimate personal friend'.[138]

Eric's mother, who had not attended the day before because of an 'indisposition' arrived with Claude and Mrs Hanson, the wife of her solicitor. Dressed in black she wore, as on the Friday, a black hat with large ostrich feathers. In the cramped room, she and Mrs Hanson sat facing the witness box with Claude sitting behind her.

THE HAIRDRESSER

Auguste Malfaison, a fashionable manicurist and hairdresser,[139] was called to give evidence as to Eric's general state of mind. Eric had visited Malfaison's shop once a week, he said, to have his hands manicured and hair dressed. While Malfaison usually saw to him personally, only occasionally would he go to the flat.

Muir asked if Malfaison was the only one who did Eric's manicure and the hairdresser said yes, as Eric objected to a lady. Even though his daughter did all the manicuring at the shop, Eric would not let her touch him and he told Malfaison, 'what a pity your family are not nice boys instead of girls.'[140]

In fact, Eric had very little to do with women generally. He had no female friends that are known of but he was fond of his grandmother and his old governess, Mary Geneste.

Although Eric would only allow Malfaison to do his nails, he did permit the assistant to do his hair. On the day following the August overdose, Eric sent for the assistant to wave and curl his hair and dye it golden. Later Malfaison arrived and Eric asked him to wait until the assistant finished, so Malfaison went and sat in the dining room. Eric joined him there while the assistant did Nurse Rice's hair in the bedroom.

Malfaison testified that Eric was dressed in a blue silk gown and wore white lady's satin shoes with very high heels and was having difficulties standing so he took off the shoes. Eric spoke to Malfaison in fluent French, telling the hairdresser how he had been crying a lot lately. They had only been speaking for a short while when Eric felt faint and Malfaison had to hold him up and call for the nurse.

Between them they moved Eric to the lavatory and held him as he vomited several times, possibly the lingering results of the emetic given to him the day before to counter the overdose. They then carried him into the bedroom but had to lay him on the floor as they could not hold him long enough to reach the bed. Malfaison asked the nurse to fetch some Eau de Cologne and a smelling bottle and they bathed Eric's face and forehead, but he seemed to be breathing badly. After about an hour they managed to get him to come round but he continued to lie on the floor. Despite this, Eric still wanted Malfaison to do his nails and the hairdresser did the best he could while Eric cried nearly the whole time. Nurse Rice took Malfaison aside and asked him to hide the golden dye as she feared Eric might drink it.

Malfaison stayed with Eric for two hours, during which time the young man related how unhappy he was. Eric said that he had been crying a lot in recent days and had been very ill. When asked at the inquest if he knew the cause of his unhappiness, Malfaison said that he could not remember but he had told Eric he had a nice place to live and should be happy. Given that he could remember so much about that afternoon when his client collapsed, it seems odd that Malfaison claims he could not remember what they discussed. A possible explanation is that Eric did talk about something to do with his relationship with Albert and Malfaison simply did not want to repeat it.

The foreman of the jury asked, 'What was your opinion of the state of his intellect?'

'Oh, he was very weak-minded, sir.' At the first inquest the hairdresser had said, 'In my opinion Mr Trevanion was not responsible for his actions, he frequently cried, and seemed much depressed.'[141]

Coroner Benson asked if Malfaison meant he believed Eric to be generally weak-minded or just on that occasion. Malfaison replied, 'By his manner he was very weak-minded.'

The Coroner continued, 'Did he not insist on having his own way?'

'Not particularly. He was very weak-minded. He was in a drowsy state continually.'

'Did he say anything to you about taking drugs?'

'Yes, at my place at King's Road, he told me in French he had been taken Veronal and he said that he was a Catholic. I told him it was very wrong of him as a Catholic to take such things.'

Malfaison seems to have appeared as a witness only to testify about Eric's 'weak' state of mind and continual drug habit, so his testimony was short. It is interesting to note, however, that this testimony again refers to Eric being in a 'drowsy state continually' which implies he was regularly taking some drug, but the Veronal figures do not add up and there is no evidence of other drugs. If Eric had taken only one dose the night before, then had alcohol the following day it may well have affected him in this way.

THE PICTURE FRAME MAKER

Next into the witness box was Charles Ham, described as a picture frame maker,[142] but who was also assisting in general decorations at the flat. He had known Eric for about five years and had been to his Brighton home on several occasions. Ham was at the flat all day on 7 September. Two days later on the 9th, the day of the overdose, Eric had risen about 10.30am and Ham saw him intermittently as Eric supervised Ham in gilding chairs in the morning and hanging curtains in the afternoon. Eric, he said, seemed very well in the morning and was cheerful all day long and was delighted with the pictures. 'He appeared quite happy, and in the evening time while I was sewing some rings on some curtains he was laughing at the way I used a needle and thread.'[143]

He later added that Eric felt compelled to lie down in the afternoon as he was feeling tired.

Eric and Albert had dinner together from between 8 and 8.15pm and Ham saw them once after dinner at 10.15pm:

> About 10 o'clock I wanted to go away so went into the corridor when deceased came out to me. He said "Well Charles you look like patience on a monument". I replied "Yes sir, I am ready to go, I am finished". He then smiled and said "I suppose you want a cheque", to which I replied "I should esteem it a great favour". Deceased said "Certainly, come into the dining room, by the way how much is it?" I replied "I cannot tell you exactly what it is up to night, but you have the first account", to which he replied "Have I?" Roe was in an adjoining room, and he called out "Of course you have you fool, it is here, it is £19". Deceased then said to me "Well Charles when do you return to London". I said "I am too late to night, I will go first train in the morning" to which he replied "Very well immediately you get back send me your account in full, and I will send you a cheque.[144]

Ham left the flat at 10.20pm noting that Eric was 'sober, and cheerful and quite himself.' When asked if he appeared suicidal, Ham replied, 'I am strongly of the opinion from the deceased's general cheerful manner, and the evident satisfaction he had at the way the flat looked, and from his arranging for me to go down the following Wednesday that when I left him he had no thought of committing suicide.' Ham had agreed to return the following week with a range of water colours for Eric to select from.

When it came to Eric's alcohol intake, Ham said, 'It did not strike me that he had had much considering the number of times I saw him that day.'

'Did you see him take any drink?'

'He had one during the afternoon.'

He had not taken any particular notice of the time but estimated it was around 3.30-4pm when the glass was brought in on a tray with some Vichy water 'or something' according to Joiner. Ham then recalled that he had heard Eric ask for a glass of whisky or something in the morning about 11.30.

The Coroner asked if Eric was sober when he left the flat about 10.20, to which Ham replied, 'Undoubtedly.'

'Was he cheerful at that time?'

'Very cheerful indeed.'

Palmer, for Albert, asked, 'Do I understand that his condition was different in the afternoon to what it was in the morning?'

'Yes.'

'What was the difference?'

'The difference was that he went to bed in the afternoon. He usually laid on the couch.' Eric was not dressed but as Ham hung up the curtains in the bedroom Eric chatted to him from the bed.

'Did you come to the conclusion that he had taken something?'

'No.'

Hanson, for Mrs Trevanion, then asked if Eric had mentioned taking anything to make him sleep at night. Ham said no.

The foreman of the jury now asked the question he had asked of most witnesses, 'What was your opinion of the state of his intellect?'

'Perfectly bright. He would laugh and talk and joke.'

'Did you ever see him not sober?'

Ham hesitated for some time before replying, 'There are

stages of not being sober,' but this statement was not followed up by anyone in the court.

The foreman continued, 'Was he effeminate in his dress and manners?'

'Undoubtedly, very effeminate.'

'Did he ever confide to you any of his troubles?'

'No, sir.'

Ham is clear in his testimony that Eric was 'very cheerful' throughout his time there, which jars with Albert's account that Eric was angry and moody. Would Eric deliberately have tried to mask his feelings in front of the contractor? He had been openly emotional, even tearful, in front of people he had known for a much shorter time. However, there may be another explanation for Ham's testimony: there is a letter held at ESRO that he had written to the Coroner's office, expressing his unhappiness over reimbursed expenses, claiming they did not fully account for his losses while attending the inquest. At the end of the letter he writes, 'I did not want to have anything to do with the case, and should not have had only I was in the flat so late at night.' Could Ham have deliberately played down his testimony to avoid further involvement in the case?

THE BUTLER

W.T. JOINER
(BUTLER)

William Thomas Joiner was the resident butler in the flat; his wife Mary was the housekeeper; and they lived-in with their baby daughter. However, he was not a butler at all -he had no training and had been a foreman packer for twenty years. It was Mary who acquired the job as she knew the Trevanion family and had known Eric for about two years. The connection must have been quite close, for when their daughter was born, Eric was godfather and he would often happily sit playing with the baby in the flat.[145] About a year earlier, in the August, Mary and Joiner had looked after Eric in rooms at the Geneste's while he went on a motoring tour with Albert.

Joiner confirmed to Muir that he had been engaged by both Eric and Albert, but then corrected himself, saying it was Eric alone who had engaged him in London as Albert was not there at the time.

Joiner told the inquest that he had arrived at Grand Avenue Mansions on Saturday 3 August two weeks before Eric moved in. The flat had not been furnished; but the carpet was down and the furniture came shortly afterwards.

He was handed a plan of the flat which was on two floors[146] and was asked if it represented the position of the rooms in the flat, to which Joiner agreed it did.

On the upper floor was a drawing room, a dressing room and a dining room adjacent to a large bedroom. Next to that was a den or smoking room whose walls, carpets, curtains and lamps were all

110

in shades of red. Along the corridor was a servant's room with a single bed where the nurse sometimes slept and, finally, a box room and kitchen attached to the servant's quarters, where the Joiners lived with their baby. In all, four rooms were furnished as bedrooms. Below the dining room on the lower floor was a visitor's bedroom with a double bed.

The entire flat was lavishly decorated: in the dining room was a table of black oak and on the walls hung oil paintings, some by George Romney,[12] of past Trevanions (Eric's apparent indifference to his father did not seem to extend towards his paternal ancestors). At the head of the table was a black oak chair with faces of women carved on the arms. This had apparently been presented to Eric by a high dignitary of the Roman Catholic Church (not the Pope, as a neighbour thought).[147] Elsewhere in the dining room was a gilded bureau, 8ft in height (about 2.4 metres) containing a fascinating array of secret drawers. One large case was devoted to curios picked up by Eric on his travels and there was old china of rare beauty.[148] In Eric and Albert's bedroom, the silk on the bed harmonised with the tints in the old tapestry curtains. On the wall hung the Da Vinci painting of the Madonna, said to be worth a fortune.

As they were still in the process of moving in when Eric died, the servant's room where the nurse slept was still full of odds and ends, as it had been used by Ham to unpack the pictures.

On the left-hand side of the plan, Muir pointed out the drawing room, which Joiner said was never used. When asked how it was furnished Joiner seemed evasive, saying, 'Everything as it should be.'

He struggled to answer whether it was furnished as a bedroom or a drawing room, finally confirming that it was a drawing room. Muir went on 'Then, off the drawing room there is a room called a dressing room?'

Again, Joiner evasively answered, 'There is a room.'

'Was it furnished?'

'Yes; that was Mr Roe's dressing room.'

When asked who occupied the main bedroom on the upper floor, Joiner said it was Eric and Albert together.

---

[12] Romney was a fashionable painter of the late eighteen century painting many portraits of leading society members such as Emma Hamilton the mistress of Lord Nelson.

'The bedroom and the bed together?'

'Yes.'

'Always?'

'Yes, sir.'

Muir seemed to be emphasising that Eric and Albert shared a room, emphasising that there were three rooms furnished as bedrooms, until corrected by Joiner who said four if his room was counted.

Joiner confirmed that he and Mary had moved in on 3 August, followed by Eric on the 17th. However, Eric must have visited earlier as he purchased Veronal in Brighton on 15th. Joiner says he did not meet Albert for the first time until Sunday 18th and could not remember the date when Albert moved in. As he stood in the witness box, Joiner suddenly produced a notebook.

An alarmed Muir asked what the book was and when it had been written. Joiner admitted that he had only used it since he was subpoenaed to appear at the inquest. Muir asked to see it and Joiner handed it over.

Examining the small black covered pocket book, Muir repeated the question of when exactly he had made it up. 'Recently,' answered Joiner, 'within the last day or two.'

As Muir leafed through it, Joiner corrected himself on when he had met Albert, 'The first time I saw Mr Roe,' he said, 'was on the Sunday following us going in. It was on the 4th that he came to the flat.' Albert, he said, had come by himself to see if things were progressing correctly.

When Muir asked how he had introduced himself, Joiner did not answer directly but said that his wife had met him previously. Before he could continue, Muir was suddenly distracted by something in the notebook. He had noticed that there were some notes in blue pencil at both ends of the book and asked when these had been made. Joiner said within the last day or two, with others in black pencil 'recently'.

Muir drew attention to the entry that had caught his eye, 'Baby christened June 16' and challenged Joiner that that this entry could not have been written in the last few days. But Joiner said it was only a matter of reference and he had been writing things down as they came into his mind.

Muir seemed unconvinced that parts of the notebook had been written recently and obviously thought that the note about the christening had been made earlier, despite Joiner being adamant that it had not. The notebook was deemed unimportant and they moved on.

Joiner then testified that his wife managed the business of the flat, such as ordering meals and such. When Muir asked him from whom she received instructions, he answered, 'I expect it would be from Mr Roe.'

'Who generally gave the orders to your wife?'

'She used to do as she wanted. She used her discretion.' However, Joiner then backtracked, claiming it was Eric who usually gave direct orders, less so from Albert.

'He kept in the background?' suggested Muir.

'Not exactly in the background. We looked upon Mr Trevanion as our master,' but he admitted it was Albert who gave them money to pay the accounts which would imply that Albert was indeed using some of the money to do exactly what Eric said he would do.

When asked about the relationship between the two men, Joiner said Eric treated Albert 'as a kind of secretary or someone put there in a kind of responsible position to look after his well-being.' This contravenes almost everyone else's descriptions of Albert being 'the same' as Eric and acting as a companion, not a servant.

'What secretarial work did Roe have to do?'

'I have known him have correspondence to answer. He has been at work for a considerable time in "The Den".'

Muir asked if Eric went out much and Joiner said no.

'When he went out did he go out alone?'

'Never alone, I don't remember him going out alone. He has been out with Mr Roe and with Dr Baines, but always in the motor car. He never walked.'

The hammered toe had been corrected only a month earlier and Eric was still recovering, but he still wore high-heeled shoes which probably exacerbated the pain.

'When Mr Roe was away who was his companion?'

'I have seen Dr Baines and one of two others who have gone

with him in the motor, but it has only been for a very short distance.' And when Albert was there, Eric only went out with him.

Joiner also confirmed that he had never heard Albert speak harshly to Eric, 'Mr Roe always spoke to him kindly.'

Muir pushed, 'Mr Roe never had occasion to be cross with him, had he?

'No.'

'Was Mr Trevanion always sober?'

'I can't say not always.'

'Did Mr Roe put any restrictions upon his drink?'

'Yes, I think he did. Mr Trevanion used to pour out a glass and swallow the drink down quickly when Mr Roe was about, as if he was doing it unbeknown to Mr Roe.' This in itself is telling, as it appears Eric had something to fear if he was surreptitiously drinking behind Albert's back.

'He was afraid Mr Roe would catch him?'

'Yes.'

'Generally, did he seem afraid of Mr Roe?'

'Not afraid exactly'. Another telling answer, indicating there was some adverse reaction. Joiner then added, 'but as if Mr Roe had got control over him in some direction or another.'

'Did Mr Roe behave as if he had some control over him?'

'No, he used to show his firmness when Mr Trevanion got a little irritable. I have seen Mr Roe put his foot down.'

'What words did he use?'

'Words to the effect of bringing Mr Trevanion under subjection.'

'Did Mr Trevanion always come under subjections on these occasions?'

'Yes, sir.'

'Any difficulty on the part of Mr Roe in bringing him under subjection?'

'No.'

This reiterates the point that if Eric could so easily be brought 'under subjection', there may well have been something for him to fear.

Muir then turned to the incident when Eric had taken an overdose on 24 August. Albert had been away but Mary Geneste and her mother were staying at the flat.

About 3pm Eric locked himself in his bedroom and Geneste had banged on the door several times calling to him. Hearing no answer, she called Joiner to break open the door - he in turn called the Mansion's porter and together they broke into the room. Eric was awake, lying on top of the bed in his dressing gown and promptly ordered the porter to leave. Shortly afterwards, Joiner testified, Eric became unconscious.

Joiner's earlier statement seems confused, as he first says Eric quickly became unconscious but then changes his answer, saying Eric was 'chewing a piece of paper' and that he made an emetic but Eric refused to take it.[149] He was also confused about how he had notified Dr Baines. At the first inquest he said he had telephoned Baines but at the second, his testimony was that he had sent Willmore, the chauffeur, as he was waiting nearby to take the Genestes out. Now said he could not remember which.

Joiner's inability to remember whether he phoned the doctor or sent the chauffeur is symptomatic of his whole appearance in court. Throughout his time in the witness box, he seemed very uncertain of his testimony, confused and changed his mind often even after making notes.

Muir asked if the emetic that Joiner and his wife administered was successful but Joiner said no, as Eric threw it away on the floor just before he became unconscious. As Baines had not arrived, a second doctor was called in, a Dr Eccles, the Hove police surgeon.

Muir asked if it were true that Dr Eccles told Eric that if he refused to take the emetic he would use a stomach pump. Joiner could not remember, he thought something was said about a stomach pump but did not remember it being used. Then he said that as far as he could remember, Eric did take the emetic and it made him vomit; but then completely contradicted himself by saying he had left the room soon after Dr Eccles arrived.

In his earlier statement to the police, Joiner was clearer, saying that Dr Eccles told Eric that if he still refused to take an emetic, they would use a stomach pump, so Eric took the dose which made him vomit. Joiner said he could not account for why he had said things in the police statement and it was concluded that Dr Eccles never threatened his patient. The doctor himself was never called to confirm or deny what had happened.

Nurse Rice, Joiner continued, came over the same evening and took Eric away in the car, (his earlier statement said it was Geneste and her mother who had taken him) but Eric returned later that evening alone looking very ill. Joiner telephoned Dr Baines, who came back with Nurse Rice on the 25th and the Genestes came to the flat but Eric refused to see them.

The following day Albert returned and a few days later both men went to London. Eric returned alone as Albert had gone to Swansea to see his mother who had been taken ill. Albert was not to return to the flat until the fateful day of 9 September.

That morning Mary Joiner took Eric his tea, but he did not drink it. Breakfast was taken in but he ignored that as well and when they took him his lunch of fried whiting, he left it untouched. Dr Baines called in the afternoon and had tea with him but Eric ate only a small portion of an egg - his total intake of food all day.

He did have several drinks in the morning: 'drops of sherry' according to Joiner, however the butler could not remember if Eric had taken anything in the afternoon. In any event, he seemed perfectly sober. With reference to Ham's statement about Eric lying down in the afternoon, Joiner said he often did this as he was 'far from strong'.

Albert arrived about 8pm that evening and dinner was served shortly afterwards. Eric ate hardly anything and while he had a drink at dinner, Joiner could not remember if it was hock or champagne.

'Mr Roe was in the room with him … and Mr Roe would regulate what he had to drink?' asked Muir.

'Probably he would, sir.'

After dinner Joiner served them coffee in the den. He described this as a pot with 'sufficient coffee' for two cups with hot milk and sugar. He said that the next time he saw Eric was about 9pm in the bedroom, as far as he could remember, perhaps a little later. When Joiner arrived, Eric was alone and told him, 'I am going to bed now; bring me small bottle of hock'. Joiner got the wine and asked if he should draw the cork and Eric told him to do so, and to pour some of it out. As he was pouring it into a tumbler by the side of the bed, Albert entered the room and Joiner left.

Throughout the inquest many questions were asked about

what Eric wore and this subject was again returned to when Joiner was asked to describe Eric's dress.

'What night things did he wear?'

'A kimono and a silk night shirt. That was what he dressed himself in. In the flat he never fully dressed himself.'

'A long night shirt? Would it be right to say it was like a woman's night shirt?'

'I could not say that it was. Perhaps it was out of the ordinary.'

Muir returned to the question of the wine that Joiner had taken in to Eric. Joiner confirmed that it was only a half bottle and that once he had poured it, he went to sit in the kitchen for a while, before going to bed a little after eleven. He hadn't fully undressed when Albert called to him, 'Are you in bed?' and when Joiner replied no, he was told, 'bring some mustard and water as quickly as possible, as Mr Trevanion has taken an overdose.'

Joiner got the mustard and water and rushed to Eric's bedroom, where his employer was lying on his back on the bed quite unconscious. He had removed the kimono and was dressed only in his night shirt.

Muir asked what had happened to the hock bottle but while he agreed that he had emptied the entire half bottle into the tumbler and left the bottle in the room, he didn't know what had become of it. Joiner also didn't know if the hock had been drunk, his attention being on trying to revive Eric.

Muir wanted to know if he had he ever seen Eric take Veronal and Joiner said never, in fact the only person who ever seems to have witnessed the act was Albert.

Joiner was aware that Eric was taking something, as he testified that, on one or two occasions during Albert's absence, Eric had told him, 'I am going to bed. I am going to take a sleeping draught.' He would tell Joiner not to call him until a certain time, usually later than when he normally got up, so he could sleep it out. However, on the 8 September Eric did not mention he was going to take the drug - although in later testimony, Joiner, who was continually switching his evidence, admitted that Eric did not always tell him when he was going to take a sleeping draught.

He did not even know where Eric kept it: 'I have never seen any,' he said, 'or rather, that is a falsehood when I say that. The first time I saw a Veronal cachet was at the time of the inquest when they were put on the table for inspection.' If his wife was finding drugs lying around the flat to the point where she discussed it with Albert, would she really have not mentioned it to her husband? How was it that he never saw any? He may not have known the name of the drug but his testimony does seem disingenuous.

On those occasions when Joiner had been given instructions to wake Eric after taking a sleeping draught, he sometimes 'had a job to rouse him; he seemed to be in a heavy sleep.'

Muir turned his attention to the telephone, which was by the front door. 'Did Mr Roe say when he came to your bedroom whether he had telephoned?'

'Yes, I think he did, sir.'

'Did Mr Roe say, "Mr Eric has taken an overdose. The doctor says he must have mustard and water. Bring it quickly?"' Joiner confirmed that those were Albert's words.

'Did Mr Roe go over to the fireplace?'

'I cannot recall that to mind.'

'Then, after, did he throw something into the fire?'

'No, sir, I never noticed it.'

It seems Muir was basing his questions on an earlier statement of Joiner's, which he read out:

> Mr Roe came in and said, "Mr Eric has taken an overdose. The doctor says he must have mustard and water. Bring it quick," and Mr Roe went over to the fireplace and threw something into the fire. I then followed him into the bedroom with the mustard and water.

The paper Muir was reading from was most likely the statement Joiner made to the police after Mrs Trevanion had convinced them to reopen the case, copies of which have not been retained. He did not mention seeing Albert throw something in the fire at the first inquest but as he said it to both Mrs Trevanion and to the police it should not be dismissed.

'Is not that what took place?' asked Muir.

'I don't remember seeing Mr Roe throw anything into the fireplace.'

118

'Did you say so?'

'I don't remember making the statement.'

'Never mind whether you made the statement or not. Is it not the fact that he threw something into the fire?'

'I cannot say. I never saw it.'

Hanson, on behalf of Mrs Trevanion, also pursued this line of inquiry by pointing out that the statement was made and signed just two weeks after the first inquest, 'Isn't it more likely,' he asked, 'that what you said a fortnight after the death of the deceased is correct than what you said some months after?'

Joiner replied, 'Yes.'

'And do you accept that,' said Hanson holding up his copy of the typewritten sheet, 'as a correct statement?'

'I accept it,' replied Joiner, 'It must be correct.' However, he still repudiated the evidence.

The discussion then turned to how long Joiner and Albert had been in Eric's bedroom before Dr Baines arrived. Joiner said it had been around half an hour, during which both men had been trying to administer the emetic of mustard and water in an attempt to make Eric vomit but without success.

Muir wanted to know if Dr Baines had shown any interest in the proceedings. 'When the doctor came,' he asked Joiner, 'did he ask you whether you had succeeded in administering the emetic?'

'I could not say whether Dr Baines asked the question.'

'Did you or Mr Roe tell the doctor whether you last succeeded?'

'I don't know, but we tried.'

'Was Mr Roe dressed ... fully dressed?'

'Yes, sir.'

From the time that Joiner left, as Albert entered the bedroom, to when he was called to help administer the emetic, an hour had passed and Muir wanted to know if Joiner had any idea as to what had transpired during that hour. 'Did Albert,' he asked, 'ever tell you how he spent that hour?'

'No, sir.'

At this point, perhaps to establish Eric's state of mind, Muir asked, 'Did Mr Trevanion seem quite cheerful when you poured the hock out for him?'

'I did not notice anything.'

119

'Neither unusually cheerful nor unusually depressed?'

'He seemed as if he was anxious to get to bed.'

'Was Mr Trevanion in his right mind or not?'

The evasive Joiner replied, 'As far as we were able to judge; he was eccentric, very nervous, but very cute indeed - most cute.'

Muir switched back to the subject of Eric's personal appearance, 'Was he in the habit of dyeing his hair?'

'I only saw it on one occasion.'

'Did he wear any rings?'

'Yes, on his finger - a plain gold ring on the ring finger of the left hand.' Interestingly, newspaper reports differ on what Joiner actually said: the *Cambrian Daily Leader* wrote that Joiner said 'yes, on his finger' whilst the *Daily Mirror* reported 'yes, on his wedding finger.' The official documents in ESRO say he 'wore a plain gold ring on the ring finger of the left hand - it was like a wedding ring.'

Nevertheless, Muir immediately pounced on the point, 'Like a wedding ring?'

'Yes,' replied Joiner, but no further efforts were made to understand why Eric wore what appeared to be a wedding ring.

'Any bangles?'

'Yes, on his arm.'

'Did he paint his face at all?'

'He had a kind of preparation which he put on at times, but I don't know what it consisted of I am sure.'

In his police statement Joiner also said, 'I have seen Mr. Trevanion cry on one or two occasions. I could not say what he cried about. He never said why. He did not cry either in the afternoon or the evening on Monday'. This would be consistent with other testimony that Eric was excited about seeing Albert but something must have occurred between them to make him, according to Albert, depressed and angry.

Palmer, representing Albert, then cross-examined Joiner who agreed that Albert and Eric were the best of friends and were greatly attached to each other. Palmer even tried to play down Joiner's statement of the 'subjection' of Eric. 'When you say that Mr Roe put him in subjection,' he asked, 'do you mean that he used to remonstrate with him?'

'Yes.'

'Did he say to him sometimes: "Be a man?"'

'I cannot swear to those words but something to that effect.'

To Palmer's next questions, Joiner said he hadn't attached any importance to Albert and Eric sleeping in the same bed because he saw Albert as a kind of guardian to Eric. He had himself had slept 'in the bedroom' on two occasions when Albert was away. In fact, he said, Eric would not sleep by himself and always wished to have someone around as he was continually in a nervous state. Joiner, by his own admission, had only known Eric since he had moved into the flat and his statement that Eric 'would not sleep by himself' is patently not true. They had been in the flat for twenty-three days and during that time Joiner slept with Eric twice. Albert arrived on the 18th but only stayed a few days and was not present when Eric took the overdose on 24 August. The Genestes arrived on the 19th and were present for the overdose but they left on the 25th. According to Joiner, 'Miss Amy Geneste' spent one night 'in' the bedroom. He had known the Genestes since he and his wife had looked after Eric's rooms and Mary and her mother had stayed at the flat during the August overdose, so it seems odd that he should get Mary's name wrong. He may have meant Ada Hawkins the nurse, or perhaps the transcriber made an error. In any event, Albert does not seem to have returned until 9 September which leaves sixteen days when Eric slept alone. Prior to moving into the flat, there is no evidence that Eric continually needed someone to share his bed, only occasionally when he was emotionally wrought.

Nobody, either for the prosecution or defence, asked if the butler had slept in the same bed as Eric. Surely, if the defence wanted to prove that Eric often shared a bed for companionship and so play down Albert sleeping with Eric, then they would have stressed that Joiner slept in the bed but the subject was never followed up and only 'in the bedroom' was ever said.

Questions turned back to Albert's influence over Eric and Joiner was asked, 'Have you heard Mr Roe frequently try to get Mr Trevanion to go out?'

'Yes.'

'Mr Roe used to go out himself?' Joiner agreed that Albert would go out for long walks.

Hanson, for Eric's mother, produced a statement signed by Joiner a fortnight after Eric's death in which he said in reference to his pouring out the hock, 'At that time Mr Roe was in the bedroom and I left them together.'

'Isn't that statement, made a fortnight after the occurrence much more likely to be correct than what you remember now?'

Joiner hesitated but then agreed it was.

'Do you accept that as being a correct statement?'

'I expect I must do that.'

Albert's own testimony puts him in the room with the butler but he says he left because he did not want to chide Eric in front of staff. This is another indication of Joiner's apparently confused and contradictory evidence.

'When you took the wine in, Mr Trevanion was quite well, and spoke to you?'

'Yes.'

'You agree that he had been very cheerful at dinner time?'

'You could not say he was very cheerful.'

Hanson started to read from Joiner's previous statement, 'Mr Trevanion ate hardly anything at dinner, but seemed quite cheerful.'

'I expect that is true.'

The foreman of the jury interjected, 'What was your opinion as to the state of the intellect of the deceased?'

'He was a very intellectual gentleman but he was peculiar and very eccentric. He was very nervous, and very high strung.'

'Were his dress and manners more like a female than a male?'

'Yes.'

In the official coroner's reports held at ESRO, there are numerous underlining and notes made in pencil. A rare underlining in red pen reads 'in fact more like a female than a male.'

'Did he try to pass himself off as a female?'

'No, I could not say that.'

'Have you ever seen any gambling going on at the flat?'

'No, I have seen cards, but I have only seen money passed at one game.'

Another juryman asked, 'Did Mr Trevanion appear to be under the thumb of Mr Roe?'

'No, I should say that Mr Roe had a certain amount of influence over him.'

'He always obeyed Mr Roe?'

'Yes.'

'Do you think he was meditating suicide that evening?'

'No.'

He added that after the August overdose he was not of the opinion that Eric tried to commit suicide but that Miss Geneste thought he had.

The court then adjourned for lunch.

One thing that is clear from Joiner's testimony is the extent to which Albert controlled Eric. The rest, however, is contradictory and unreliable, with Joiner admitting that what he said in his police statements must be true but then recanting them at the inquest. It was left to his wife to show that there was a very good reason for his unreliability.

ERIC'S APPEARANCE

Much was made at the inquest of Eric's appearance. Newspapers across the world are littered with examples of working-class people who cross-dressed and cross-lived and who were arrested simply for wearing clothes of the opposite sex but most of these stories concerned women. There was enormous fascination with those females who rejected their position as second-class citizens and 'masqueraded' as men, either for a day or a life-time. While such cross-dressing was generally disapproved of by society, there was a reluctant understanding of why women would desire a rise in social standing. For men, however, it was different. Man was the dominant species and to surrender that position for the lowly place of a woman was looked on in horror and bewilderment.

For those who were transgender or homosexual, the only way to meet others was often by advertising oneself using clothes and/or accessories. Some used codes, such as Oscar Wilde and his circle wearing green carnations, and in more modern times, men displayed coloured handkerchiefs in their back pockets; lesbians wore thumb rings; and, in the USA during WWII, a red tie. Bleached or 'blonded' hair could be a code, particularly in the USA, which led to Bruce Kenilworth entitling his 1933 gay novel *Goldie*.

While these codes were intended to denote sexual orientation, they did not necessarily include cross-dressing or effeminacy. One of the difficulties of examining the past is the limitations of the information available. Eric's use of powders; vanity case; waved and dyed hair; women's shoes; nightclothes like a woman's; and a dress-like kimono implies more than codes. His methods of dressing may imply transgender.

On the other hand, throughout history, the effeminate homosexual was a standard way of advertising one's sexuality and it may be that Eric falls into this category. The dominant characteristics of dressing effeminately were those aspects believed to be close to femininity, such as an attention to one's clothes, hair, makeup, walk and nails. For many years, a key entry into the underworld of gay clubs was the ability to recognise another gay man because of his effeminacy.

There was a great divide in how men could achieve this. Presenting a feminine aspect was restricted to those brave enough or simply rich enough not to care. Those like Eric and the Marquis of Anglesey could rely on their fortunes to protect them and be marked as eccentric but if a working-class man walked the streets with hair permed, face powdered, and wearing high-heel shoes, they could be and were arrested on an assumption of 'degeneracy' or similar charge. The assumption was that they were prostitutes looking for male clients. As well as arrest they also risked physical attack from passers-by.

This 'camp' image, although common, did not dominate gay men's behaviour, However, the stereotype persisted well into the late twentieth century embodied by characters such as John Inman's Mr Humphries from TV's *Are You Being Served*. Inman was credited as being 'probably responsible for raising the profile of the homosexual male to its highest level since the heyday of Oscar Wilde,'[150] yet this image of the camp man was often loathed by other gay men; and some activist groups campaigned against Inman and his portrayal.

Despite this overt feminisation, relatively few wore women's clothing or cross-dressed except in secure private environments. They were much more likely to use a single item of feminine or unconventional clothing to signify their identity.'[151] Most were not transgender but used clothes as signals.

The effeminate man is different from the queer aesthete or

effete gay man such as Oscar Wilde. Those who became popular shortly after Eric's death, were nicknamed the 'Brideshead Generation' after Sebastian Flyte from Evelyn Waugh's *Brideshead Revisited*.

'Non-effeminate men by comparison were not supposed to take a great deal of interest in clothes. The rhetoric of men's fashion takes the form of a set of denials that include the following propositions: that there is no men's fashion; that men dress for fit and comfortable, rather than for style; that women dress men and buy clothes for men; that men who dress up are peculiar (one way or another); that men do not notice clothes.'[152] The 'peculiar' implying homosexuality, instead these men dressed conservatively usually in suit and tie.

There is no evidence that Eric ever cross-dressed as a woman, so describing him as trans would be difficult, although not out of the realms of possibility. It is more likely that he was an effeminate homosexual but it was precisely this description that was so troubling during the inquest. To identify him as such would raise too many uncomfortable questions, not least of what to do with Albert.

THE HOUSEKEEPER

Mary Joiner was not in court when her husband gave evidence but came into the witness box after him. She was a reluctant witness, refusing to sign her police statement as she did not want to be brought into the case.[153]

She was asked to describe her interactions with Eric the day he went into the coma. She told the inquest that she had taken him breakfast around 8.30am but had trouble rousing him and that he appeared very drowsy. She went back to collect the breakfast things at 9am and did persuade him to take a little of the tea but he would not eat anything. Around 11am she took him some beef tea but did not say whether he drank it or not. She also testified that at some point in the morning Eric came into the kitchen and sat chatting to her but then left. Later she made his lunch and took it to him but yet again he would not eat anything.

At 4pm Eric had a meal but ate just an egg and a little dry toast with some tea.

Mary saw him several times during the afternoon, when he was 'not very cheerful' and again after dinner when she was carrying Albert's portmanteau through the dining room. He was sitting at the table and appeared fine.

'Was he very cheerful?' she was asked.

'He was cheerful. Towards the evening he seemed to be very lively, he seemed to regain his usual manner, and was witty, and was passing jokes as we were arranging the curtains of his bedroom.'

Perhaps his cheery demeanour was a result of Albert's return after spending two weeks away.

Palmer asked if Eric and Albert were good friends and she confirmed they were excellent friends. She had known Eric, she told the inquest, for about two years, having first met him at Miss Geneste's. Later Eric engaged her and her husband to live and work at the flat.

'He said Mr Roe would be a co-tenant at the flat, and that he was sure I should like Mr Roe as much as I liked him.'

She acknowledged that Eric often said he was going to take a sleeping draught but her only experience of their effect was on one occasion when she had trouble rousing him, so concluded that he must have taken something.

When asked if she had ever found morphine, Mary replied that she had found some little tablets but hadn't known what they were, so threw them in the waste bin. Albert claimed he had told her to dispose of drugs but she said had no recollection of those instructions and that she had 'done it for the boy's sake.'

Mary Joiner, like her husband, was contradictory in her evidence, having previously stated she didn't know Eric was taking drugs; then saying she had worked it out for herself; finally stating that she had 'constantly' spoken to Eric about his drug taking and that it made her nervous. She testified that he once replied, 'Mrs Joiner, it is no good you saying anything to me, because I must have them' and told her he knew more about them than she did.

Mary confirmed that Eric had been preparing the flat and that the only bedroom to have been finished was the one Eric and Albert slept in. When Miss Geneste came to stay, Mary made up a single bed for her but the room was still in a state and the pictures were stacked up in it. Nurse Rice gave testimony that she had stayed in the guest bedroom, so it was obviously habitable despite the clutter.

On the night of the fatal overdose, Mary explained that she had served a full dinner and confirmed Albert had eaten everything but Eric had nothing.[154] She prepared the coffee and then went through to the dining room about half past nine where Eric was sitting alone at the table. She remonstrated with him about sitting in the chilly room as he was so lightly clad. When he put out his hand, she took it and it was stone cold.

She went to bed about 10.45 after leaving her husband in the kitchen to have his habitual smoke before going to bed; and there Mary Joiner's testimony ended, although she was to be recalled later when more worrying aspects began to emerge.

ERIC'S MOTHER SPEAKS

Mrs Trevanion was then called to the stand. She rose from her seat next to her son, Claude, and walked to a chair placed for her below the witness box by the side of her solicitor. She was dressed in a mourning costume of black silk; a hat with nodding black plumes; and a dark feather boa round her neck, accentuating the pallor of her face and the silver of her hair. She appeared self-possessed, calm and as she drew off her glove to take the Testament, her ring-encircled fingers were as steady as her voice as she took the oath. More than once she glanced across the court to Albert who sat with folded arms.

Muir asked her to confirm that she did not benefit in any way from her son's will, which she did, adding that 'he was my son. It was my duty to do what I have done to learn how he died.'

She told the court that Eric had left home about six years previously, when he was about twenty-one and a half years old, to go and live with Miss Geneste. The last time she had seen him was two days after he had left a nursing home, where he had undergone an operation upon his toe. She said he had not suffered from insomnia when he lived with her and claimed his addiction to morphine began after he had been treated by a doctor on board the *Orotava*. She told him the strain was too great if he was taking morphine and so he moved out to stay with the Genestes. Shortly after, he went to Ceylon with his brother and when he returned, she found he was addicted to drugs and it was she who insisted he go to the nursing home in December 1910 for a cure.

In the files in the East Sussex Records Office, there is a police statement made by Amy Mahony which was never used in the inquest. Mahony was a matron of the nursing home[155] where Eric had stayed twice, the first being the rest cure just before Christmas 1910. The second was for the operation on his hammer toe, when he was operated on by Dr Sandifer and remained for two weeks. Albert visited Eric 'every day when he was in town and sometimes twice a day. Mrs Trevanion … came once.'

While at the nursing home on the first occasion, Mahony said she believed she had witnessed his will but had trouble recalling, as she had witnessed wills of three different occupiers of the same room.

Sometime after leaving the nursing home, Mrs Trevanion said that Eric and Albert had driven up to see her. Eric came into the house by himself, leaving Albert in the car, and stayed for about an hour and a half. This was the first time she had seen Albert in the six years after she had met him on the *Orotava*.

During the visit at her house, Eric explained that he had employed Albert. When Mrs Trevanion asked what he was paying him in salary and Eric replied 'nothing'. She replied 'Nonsense; neither Mr Roe nor anybody else would work for nothing. He has nothing himself.' This indicates that she knew at least a little about Albert's background. Eric admitted that he had given some money and his mother told him he was very foolish, adding, 'When Mr Roe wants more he will make you give it to him, and it will only lead to more trouble.' Eric replied, 'Then he won't get it.'

He told her about the flat in Hove and when she asked if anyone was going with him, he replied Albert was. She asked if there was anyone else and he said no.

Muir wanted to know if she had expressed an opinion of

these arrangements and she replied, 'I told him I thought it was very wrong. Mr Roe knows nothing at all about your health. I think you ought to have one of the Misses Geneste's to live with you; you are far too delicate to live alone.'

Instead Eric suggested she and the Genestes could come and stay with him. As he was leaving, she also asked him to think about what he was doing and he said he would, adding that they were motoring down to Wales, so they made plans for her to visit him in September at the Brighton flat. When he left, Mrs Trevanion insisted they were on good terms.

She did not hear from Eric until an incident when a young unnamed lady who was staying with her wrote to Eric but the letter was returned. Mrs Trevanion asked her to write again, this time via Eric's solicitor, and a telegram came back 'Will answer your letter later.' There was no name on the telegram and 'I was of opinion that my son had not sent it himself. I heard nothing further from my son.

On 10 September at 3.50pm, the telephone rang and Mrs Trevanion asked the same unnamed lady to answer it. The call was from Mr Quincy from Eric's solicitors, who had decided to call her, to say that Eric was seriously ill and not expected to live.

Mrs Trevanion caught the 6.30pm train to Brighton, arriving at 7pm. She had sent a telegram from Charing Cross to ask for a car meet her. Albert and her youngest son, Claude, collected her from the station but she didn't say anything to Albert until she reached the flat.

When she entered her son's bedroom, newspaper reports described Mrs Trevanion as saying, 'I at once saw my son was dying' but the archives at the East Sussex Records Office are more detailed, and show that she asked the doctor to let her look in Eric's eyes and having done so 'expressed my opinion that he was dying.' She asked, 'Why was I not sent for? Mr Quincy rang me up on his own responsibility,' and when Albert challenged this, she retorted, 'I believe Mr Quincy, and I do not believe you. My son had been unconscious sixteen hours.'[156]

The point had been made that the Eric's solicitors had been notified before his mother and, to explore this, Mrs Trevanion was questioned over Albert's attitude towards Eric's estate.

About 1am in the morning Dr Baines joined her in the

bedroom and expressed the opinion that Eric was slightly better, to which she replied, 'He will never be better.' As she said this, Albert, who was also present, appeared 'very uneasy.' She left the room and went to sit in the dining room. Albert followed, asking her to 'promise one thing faithfully, that if Eric pulls round before he recovers consciousness, you will leave the flat and take the boys with you without having let him see you, he must be left to me to pull him through his convalescence.' If Albert did say this, then it contradicts what he told others: that if Eric recovered, he wanted nothing more to do with him.

Mrs Trevanion replied, 'so far as I can see Eric will never recover and I certainly should not think of complying with your request.'

According to Mrs Trevanion, Albert then told her that everything was in his name, 'the flat and the furniture, all the heirlooms, and the money in the bank is in my name and it was our joint income that had been keeping up the flat.' She replied, 'Joint income, you have no joint income, what was all this done for? It must have been temporary insanity on Eric's part.' Albert continued to relate 'which of the things in the flat he was going to sell, and which he was going to keep, and assumed a general air of proprietorship. I asked if he did not think he was a bit previous as I was not likely to take this sort of thing sitting down.' When she asked why he was doing this he replied, 'I had this done so that in the event of anything happening and you or the boys making yourselves disagreeable, I could turn you out of the flat.'

'I have been told to go,' Mrs Trevanion retorted, 'but have not gone, and do not intend going unless I take Eric's body with me.'

'Are you sure it was before your son's death?' Muir asked.

'Yes, it was a few hours after I arrived.'

When asked if she had also spoken to Dr Baines, Mrs Trevanion replied that yes, he had told her, 'Have nothing touched in this room; lock the door and keep the key in your pocket' as there had to be an inquest. She said that Albert, who was standing close by, objected, saying he could not see why there should be an investigation, 'he died from an overdose of Veronal,' he said, 'why do you want an inquest?'

'We only have your word for that,' she responded, 'for I have seen him under morphia and Veronal, but I have never seen him like this before.'

Mrs Trevanion then retired to the spare room where she spent the rest of the night. Around 11am the following morning, there was a knock on the door. It was Albert, who wanted the key to Eric's room saying, 'You have no right to the key'[157] claiming that 'I have got some valuable papers in there and I thought you might read them.' Rather than give it to him, she went with him and opened the door herself.

Albert initially stood at the foot of the bed looking down at the body while Mrs Trevanion stood by the dressing table, on which were a few telegrams held together by a pin, sent by Albert and detailing his return. When he joined her at the table and went to take the pin out, she said, 'Please do not touch these things. Dr Baines said that nothing in the room was to be touched.'

According to Mrs Trevanion, Albert seemed to be looking for something on the dressing table, but then he left and she followed him out, carefully locking the door and putting the key back in her pocket.

Albert said he was tired and was going to lie down so she told him he could use the spare room and she would go to the dining room. There she sat alone for several minutes before deciding that she would go and see what Albert had been looking for on the dressing table, and locked herself into the bedroom. On the table, she found a man's handkerchief lying by a pincushion. It was too large to have been used by her son. She lifted it up and found underneath an empty cachet which had been opened as if by a pin or a knife between the two lips, it was empty.

One of the reasons that cachets had been developed was to avoid having to take tablets made of bitter drugs, such as Veronal. They could be taken one at a time with some liquid and so swallowed whole with no taste before dissolving slowly in the stomach. Opening the cachets and emptying out the grains meant they needed to be put into strong tasting liquids like coffee or wine to disguise the bitterness but absorption was faster without the cachet shell.

When Mrs Trevanion went to a medicine cupboard in Eric's bedroom, she found a box bearing the name of Gibson the chemists, which contained eight cachets. Between May and

September, Eric bought nine boxes of which only this one remained so the others must have been thrown out. It is feasible, particularly given that one of the cachets was described by Marshall as being 'different', that either Eric or someone else tipped the remaining few cachets into each new box. If true, then why was it the Gibson's box that was found and not Douthwaite's? The last Gibson box was bought on the 2 September but Douthwaite's box arrived from London on the 6th just two days before the overdose. Where was Douthwaite's box? Another anomaly, never considered at the inquest, is the wrapping of the Veronal. Cachets would often be placed in glass tubes or waxed paper to protect them so where was this wrapping? Nobody provides any testimony about disposing of phials or paper even though the main argument at the inquest was that cachets had been put into the wine.

Mrs Trevanion returned the Gibson box to the cupboard, having first placed the empty cachet in it; she could not put them in her room as Albert was sleeping there. It was these samples which were sent for analysis, the empty one accounting for the 0.1 grains. She telephoned Dr. Baines to say she had found the cachets and he instructed her to leave them in the cupboard but after Albert had left her room, she retrieved the box and put it in her suitcase. The following day she returned the box to the cupboard and it was later produced during the first inquest.

Afterwards, according to her, Albert asked her what she had done with the cachets and if she had them. She said she did not (Inspector Ward had given them to Claude), but Albert did not believe her.[158]

If what Mrs Trevanion says is true, then why was Albert interested in the cachets, particularly if the first inquest had ruled death by misadventure? It is not known when the samples were sent for analysis but was Albert's question a catalyst for Claude to send them? In addition, if the cachets had been opened and poured into the wine, where were all the empty shells? If this was deliberate murder, it would have been extremely difficult to force someone to swallow twenty-odd cachets but much easier to get them to drink half a bottle of wine. If the empty shells had been left lying around, it would have been immediately apparent to the doctors just how much Eric had taken and they may have altered their treatment of him. Empty shells would also have raised questions at the first inquest as to how Eric could have taken so much, and perhaps the verdict of death by misadventure would not have been given.

No evidence of external violence, such as bruises from being held, had been found on the body but there seems to have been no examination at the time of Eric's death as to the state of his clothes. Contrast this with the trial of Eric Mareo, where his dead wife's nightgown was examined and found to be covered down the front with the milk she was supposed to have drunk.

Despite the fact that Charles Mathews had written to Coroner Benson before the second inquest, stating that the new evidence was 'directly implicating the friend', Mathews never made it clear what evidence he considered implicated Albert.

In the period between Eric's death and the funeral on the 14 September, Mrs Trevanion spoke to the Joiners, saying she thought it most extraordinary that nothing had been done to save her son and asking why had she not been called earlier? Summing up her conversation with Joiner, she included his preparation of the mustard and water emetic in the kitchen and Albert coming into the room and throwing something into the fire.

Palmer, representing Albert, got up and asked her sternly if she had mentioned anything about this at the first inquest and she replied, 'I did not think I did,' but after some hesitation added, 'I believe I did but it is the coroner's mistake in leaving it out of my evidence.'

Palmer followed up, 'You did not attach any importance to it?'

'Yes, I did,' she said, 'I did not consider he died from Veronal by his own hand, and Mr Roe jumped up at the first inquest and said, "Does Mrs Trevanion accuse me of murdering her son?"'. As she said this, Albert looked up and smiled.[159]

'It is strange,' Palmer continued, 'there is no report of this.' Palmer was either creating a smokescreen or simply being disingenuous as her comments had been widely reported in newspapers at the time of the first inquest.

'I said I did not think he had died from Veronal poisoning,' continued Mrs Trevanion.

'Are you satisfied now that he died from Veronal?'

'Yes,' she said with a set face, 'but I am not satisfied that he took it by his own hand.'

Palmer asked her if it were true as she claimed, that Eric had suffered from insomnia since he was twenty-one and that he had several doctors. She replied she had not said such a thing and Palmer retorted 'Well the Coroner would not have taken it down if you had not.'

Mrs Trevanion continued to deny it, 'The Coroner does not say I said that.'

'Oh yes he does.'

'Then all I can say is that Mr Benson must have made a mistake.'

'To your knowledge, has he taken Veronal for years?'

'No.'

'Again, I will read from the depositions, "I knew he took Veronal for years".'

'No.'

Palmer was becoming frustrated, 'I am reading the answers you gave at the first inquest. "I knew he took Veronal for years".'

'No, I knew he took morphia for years.'

'Did you implore him to give it up?'

'I did.'

Palmer was using Mrs Trevanion's statement at the first inquest and the copy in the archives at the East Sussex Records Office confirms her statement, 'I knew he took Veronal for years' and that she had implored him to give it up but he would not. At the end of her statement, she said he had been taking it for six years and 'never would give it up. He seemed to lose all self-control when he wanted it. Apart from that he was mentally all right, but he had no control over himself when he had taken some.'

Perhaps she had genuinely forgotten what she had said five months previously or perhaps she was lying but it may also be a confusion of what he was taking and when. Eric did have two morphine scares and one near fatal overdose and although Dr Sandifer said he was taking both morphine and Veronal, he had only known Eric for four years. Mrs Trevanion was really the only person who knew what he was taking prior to 1906. Curiously, neither of Eric's brothers were asked, or offered, to give testimony about either his drug use or his life.

It was Eric's confession to his mother that he could not and would not give up morphine that caused her refusal to have him living with her, as the strain was too great and it caused her such anxiety. He was, she said, 'very excitable' and could not sleep when he was excited. She mentioned an incident at Woodhall Spa, Lincolnshire when Eric was unconscious for two hours but did not say when.

'Who was to have him if you would not?' Palmer asked.

'He must go into the rooms and have somebody to look after him.'

'Did you ever try to get any doctors to take him?'

'No,' although she admitted she did try and get doctors to cure him.

The foreman of the jury asked if, when Eric lived at home, he was 'peculiar'. Mrs Trevanion replied, 'In his habits and dress he was rather effeminate, but his mind was perfectly sound. He was really clever.'

When discussing his religion, she claimed that Eric was a Protestant but that he would tell people he was a Roman Catholic because he knew she did not care for them. This rather arrogant claim can be discounted as Eric's interest in Catholicism seems a bit more than simply wishing to aggravate his mother. He had valuable religious artefacts in his flat and had told the hairdresser that he was Catholic.

Palmer tried to make her to admit Albert knew nothing about the will but she insisted that Albert had told her everything the night before Eric died.

Mrs Trevanion's evidence was wound up with a reinforcement of her suspicions about the cause of her son's death. She had been present when the body was exhumed; had officially identified it and had pinned a little brooch in the jacket of Eric's pyjamas as he lay in his coffin. The brooch was gold in the form of an umbrella of diamonds with a pearl handle (not the gun metal reported in some papers) and it was her own personal brooch. 'I asked the undertakers to allow me to be for a minute alone with my dead son,' she said, 'and then I pinned it on. I intended to have his body exhumed and I thought I should be able to identify him by that … I could not bear the idea of cremation and besides, I did not know what he had died from.'[160]

Hints as to the nature of Mrs Trevanion's character come through in her testimony. She had not wanted Eric living with her because it caused *her* such anxiety; Eric's express wish as documented with his solicitor was to be cremated, which his mother overruled. Whilst it can be accepted that she intended to have the body exhumed due to her suspicions, she gives herself away by stating that *she* could not bear him to be cremated and believed he only spoke of Catholicism to annoy her. All this may go some way to explaining why Eric found his mother domineering.

THE VERONAL EXPERT RECALLED

As Dr Willcox was still in attendance, Palmer took the opportunity to ask some more questions about Veronal. Before he could begin, the foreman of the jury asked if they could taste some Veronal and Dr Willcox supplied a crystal of the poison and the foreman cautiously tasted it. There is no record of his reaction.

Willcox said it would take two and a quarter pints of water to dissolve 150 grains of Veronal with constant stirring. It would be impossible to dissolve it all in half a bottle of hock. Muir suggested Dr Willcox show them and so he took a paper and poured about 120 grains into a tumbler of water. He stirred it with the blade of his penknife and then held up the milky solution which grew clearer but retained a white froth on top. It would not dissolve but by constantly stirring it was kept suspended in the water; it would be very gritty to drink.

As we now know, Willcox's figures cannot be relied on but despite that, the fact remains there were still 75.8 grains in Eric's body and as some would have leached out in the twenty-eight days before the exhumation the actual dose would have been higher.

Willcox believed that it would be very difficult for one person to force another to take twenty cachets although they were not difficult to take voluntarily. As long as they were moistened, they could be swallowed like oysters, some said. Dr Sandifer said '20 cachets could be taken quite easily in a minute or two, and by dipping the cachets in water he could swallow them as easily as he could take bread and milk.'

Willcox also said that a tea-cup of boiling coffee would have sufficed to dissolve 150 grains so they could not be seen. However, as people cannot drink boiling liquids, three-quarters of a pint of coffee at a palatable temperature would be needed to dissolve this amount.

As for the dose, Willcox stated that while some people could take larger doses than others, fifty grains would be fatal in most cases although others could recover from sixty grains if they were medically treated.

The Coroner then told everyone that the next witness would take a long time and as it was now late the court would be adjourned for two days, due to his other commitments.[161]

One of the things not discussed about Veronal at the inquest, and something Willcox does not write about it until a few years later, is the side-effects of the drug. Long term usage of Veronal included a range of symptoms, many of which Eric presented. Dr Helen Young did a study of the available literature on Veronal poisoning, published in 1927, in which she cites the case of a healthy, mentally sound woman who had undergone an operation for the relief of asthma. She was prescribed Veronal to manage post-operative infections, which she then took for four years. Twelve months before her death she began to exhibit various symptoms and these present some interesting comparisons with Eric's illnesses including:

- headaches (Eric often complained of headaches and Albert, and others said Eric was often in pain);
- nausea (Eric had a very low appetite, and it is possible that when Auguste Malfaison, the hairdresser, witnessed him being sick that this was a side-effect);
- depression (many people attested to Eric being depressed);
- ataxic gait with dragging of the feet and difficulty in walking upstairs (there is consistent evidence of Eric's refusal to walk anywhere and his gait was described as 'tottering' not helped by the high heels he loved to wear, although his walking was also influenced by the hammered toe);
- and a knowledge of what Veronal could do but the inability to see how it was harming them (Eric continually stated he knew the dangers of the drug but did not apply them to himself).[162]

Young's analysis lends weight to the argument that Eric was

suffering long-term side-effects of taking Veronal. Willcox in his papers stated that many cases of long-term usage did result in suicide as a result of the increased depression. What is not made clear in Young's paper is the amount needed over what period to bring on all these symptoms, so whilst they may apply to Eric there is also the possibility they did not.

8

DAY 4 – THURSDAY 30 JANUARY

By day four, conversation in Hove and Brighton was about nothing except the case. With no knowledge about the long-term side-effects of Veronal, people could not see why a seemingly healthy and cheerful man, who was busily decorating his flat, would take his own life. What was the nature of the two men's friendship and what was in the note passed to the Coroner by the nurse? It was hoped that these things would soon be made clear when the star witness spoke: Albert himself.

Even before the doors opened, a huge crowd surrounded the building trying to get in, then fought to get the best seats, desperate to hear the latest sensational revelations.

Albert arrived early and took the seat he had always occupied, accompanied by his brother-in-law, Mr Hanlon of the Clyne Valley Colliery Co, and his friend, Andrew Paton. The Coroner sat precisely at 12 noon, flanked by Inspector Ward of Scotland Yard and Detective Inspector Parsons who was in charge of the case locally.

Before they started, Palmer asked if he could bring in one or two witnesses before Albert: Mr Bridges of Eric's solicitors and executors of his will: and the chauffeur, Conrad Willmore.

The Coroner seemed unconvinced, 'You consider it necessary for the inquiry?'

Palmer replied that he did. Everyone would now have to wait for Albert's testimony.

MR BRIDGES – THE SOLICITOR'S CLERK

Joseph William Bridges entered the box and told Palmer he was a solicitor's clerk at Mackrell, Maton, Godlee and Quincy. He related how he had received a telephone message from Albert on 10 September about 1.25pm saying that Eric was very ill. He left immediately, arriving in Brighton about half past three. In the flat were Dr Baines, Albert, Nurse Ada Hawkins and Mr and Mrs Joiner. At this time, Eric was unconscious.

Palmer asked Bridges to confirm that Eric was not on good terms with his family, which he did. He then asked why the clerk had taken the decision to see how ill Eric was before notifying the family. Bridges explained that when the severity of the situation was apparent, he called Quincy who then called Mrs Trevanion, who presumably called her other sons.

Claude Trevanion arrived around 4.45 and Cecil Trevanion around 5.15. Shortly after this Dr Sandifer arrived and about ten minutes later, despite there being numerous other rooms in the flat, they all stayed in the sick room to take tea, although Claude had whisky and soda and he could not remember if Cecil had anything.

Having received a telegram from Mrs Trevanion notifying them of her arrival, Albert and Claude left at 6pm to collect her. Cecil Trevanion suggested he and Bridges tidy the room so, after everyone else left, they cleared all the tea things, a tumbler the doctor had used (it is not clear if this was the same tumbler Joiner had put Eric's wine in) and what Bridges believed was the original hock bottle. They placed everything in the hall, but Bridges didn't know who removed them from there, presumable Mary Joiner.

When asked about the tumbler, Bridges said that there was only one which was on a table placed against the bed at which Nurse Hawkins was sitting. On it were her notebooks, thermometer and some other things including, he believed, some smelling salts but he couldn't quite recall. If Nurse Hawkins' notebooks were ever examined, the evidence in them was not included; if they were not examined, why not?

Another small table was at the foot of the bed and it was on this that the tea things had been placed. Several newspapers were lying about and a lavatory basin was by the side of the bed.

There was also a dressing table against the window on the other side of the bed. Muir, for the prosecution, seemed fixated on this table and asked Bridges over and over again about where it was and what was on it despite Bridges repeating that he could not recall. Muir did not accept this and he said he would keep asking the question until he got an answer.

The frustrated Bridges replied, 'I cannot be sure it was a

dressing table, and I cannot be sure it was not.'

When asked if there was anything on it, he said a small jewel or trinket case which Albert had shown him. All Bridges could remember was that the box was about three inches high; about three to four inches deep; and about five to six inches wide. It was lined or padded with cotton wool or something of that nature and appeared to be empty. When Muir criticised his powers of observation, the stung Bridges retorted that he had no reason to recall the details.

'Even though Roe had drawn your attention to it?' Muir argued.

'It was the cachet that had been pointed out,' Bridges responded, 'not the box or any other contents.'

Albert had pointed out the cachet to him during a discussion with the doctors about how many cachets Eric might have taken and where he must have got them from. Bridges said he had never heard of the drug before and did not understand the conversation, so when Dr Baines mentioned Veronal, he asked what it was, wanting to know so he could report back to his boss, Mr Quincy. Albert took him over to the table, picked up the jewel case and opened it as Dr Baines sat watching from a chair, appearing very tired and worn out. Albert then showed the cachet to Dr Sandifer, although Sandifer had said nothing about this in his evidence.

Inside the jewel case, stuck to the inside of the lid, was a cachet which appeared to be whole but as Bridges did not touch it, he said he could not be sure. He had never seen anything like the cachet and he had not handled it. It was left there after Albert had shown it to him.

Albert told Bridges that, realising how ill Eric was, he had looked around the room to see what drugs he had taken. On lifting the lid of the case, he saw the cachet attached to it and assumed it had been overlooked by Eric.

'In the same way,' asked Muir, 'that a lozenge or anything else would stick to a lid of a box or anything else by being moistened, or being of a sticky substance, it would stick to the lid, is that what you say?'

'Yes, that is what I imagine.'

Muir did not explain his apparent fixation on this single cachet. Perhaps, as Bridges thought the box was empty, Muir may have believed it was where Eric kept the drug and so those cachets were used in the overdose, not the ones in the Gibson box Mrs Trevanion found in the cupboard. Or, perhaps there was another reason: he may have been trying to show that Eric was not secretive about where he kept the drugs, as the box was in the open; or he thought the empty cachets had been put back in the box because they still had not been accounted for.

If, as everyone was contending, Eric took the grains in liquid then where were the empty shells? It seems unlikely that Eric would take an overdose and then clear up after himself, so either someone else disposed of them or Eric did not dissolve the cachets at all and swallowed them whole. Was it the shells Albert threw into the fire?

The number of empty cachets is also unclear. Mrs Trevanion had found one under the handkerchief on the table and this was sent for analysis, but it was the only one. It seems unlikely that the cachet was moved from the case to the table so it was probably a different one. Mrs Trevanion was not aware of the one in the jewel case and Albert was not aware of the one under the handkerchief.

The more Muir dug, the more Bridges' evidence becomes confused, initially saying that only he and Albert knew about the single cachet, then adding that Dr Sandifer knew until finally including Dr Baines into the mix. In fairness, little attention had previously been paid to this one cachet so it is understandable that Bridges could not remember the event five months later. The confusion continued, however, when Bridges went on to state that Dr Baines was asleep in a chair, despite the fact he had included him in the conversation between Albert and Dr Sandifer. Muir's frustration with who had discussed the cachet and who had not, was evident and once again he asked for clarification.

Bridges changed his story, omitting the discussion by those in the room and now saying that he had asked what drug Eric had taken as he had wanted to tell Mr Quincy over the telephone and Dr Baines replied Veronal. Only then did Albert show him the cachet but Baines was some ten feet (three metres) away and did not see it.

Muir then asked about the hock bottle.

As far as Bridges could remember, it was on the table with the tumbler, although earlier he had said the tumbler was the only item there and everything remained untouched until he and Cecil removed it. He also said it was 'lying' on the table but it could easily have been knocked over in the efforts to revive Eric.

He supposed that the hock bottle was about a pint in size.

'I don't want you,' said Muir, 'to suppose anything. I want to know whether you remember what size it was?'

'No, not further than that.'

'You cannot tell whether it was a half-bottle or a whole bottle?'

'No, I don't know enough about hock bottles. I know a hock bottle when I see it.'

'By the colour or the shape?'

'And by the label.'

'Can you remember the colour of this bottle?'

'Black as far as I know, or very dark.'

There followed a great deal of confusion about how Bridges' testimony had come about. It seems that the day before he appeared in court, Bridges had been reading about the inquest in the papers and suddenly remembered the bottle and the cachet. He informed his employer, Mr Godlee, who wrote his recollection down and read it back to Bridges who then signed the document. Apparently, he had told Godlee that he had removed the bottle with the tea things but Godlee had said it was not important and not to include it. Muir was incredulous that Bridges had not written or signed his own testimony and said he wanted Bridges to remain in town until Cecil had given evidence.

Palmer then rose simply to confirm that Bridges' firm represented both Claude and Cecil and Bridges said that was true.

CONRAD WILLMORE - THE CHAUFFEUR

Conrad Willmore lived at 4 Black Lion Street, about a ten-minute walk from Eric and Albert's flat although he had since moved back to London and only returned to Brighton for the inquest.

With a recommendation from the Automobile Association, Willmore had been engaged by Eric around 16 April 1912 while the two men were still living at 6 St Stephen's Crescent in London. He did not meet Albert until some twelve to fourteen days later.

Eric owned two cars and a third body which was

interchangeable with both cars. He had bought a Rolls Royce on the 3 June and the other car was already there when Willmore arrived. On one occasion, Eric had written out a cheque for £700 in part payment for the Rolls and sent the chauffeur to deliver the cheque personally to Mr Royce in Pontin Street. When they moved to Brighton, both cars were moved from London and were housed at the Brighton and Sussex Garage, part of the Grand Hotel. At the time of the second inquest, Willmore was still looking after both cars under a letter of authority from the executors given to him the day after Eric died. Asked under whose powers the authority had been issued, Willmore said Albert's and nobody else. In fact, he was still being paid by Albert.

Although Eric had employed him, it was Albert who spoke to Willmore in one of the bedrooms one afternoon; why they had been talking in a bedroom was not explained. Albert told the chauffeur that he was to consider himself in the joint employ of both Eric and Albert. When Albert was away, Willmore would drive Eric about a great deal, particularly up and down to London to visit the Genestes, or bring the couple back and forth to the flat.

After Eric had the operation on his toe, Willmore drove them both down to Devon. On the return journey, Albert left them at Ilfracombe and Eric remained at the Ilfracombe Hotel for the night. The chauffeur, who appeared to double as a valet, was laying out Eric's dress clothes one evening when Eric asked if he would have any objections to sleeping with him, saying that he felt nervous and lonely when Albert was away. Willmore says he did indeed share his bed that night but saw nothing improper in that. When asked how often he had slept in Eric's bed, Willmore stated this had taken place on only four other occasions, once in Exeter, two nights in Bath, and once in Brighton when Eric knocked on his door at 11.40pm asking him to share the bed as he was afraid.

Palmer asked if he thought it was improper and Willmore said 'No, knowing the boy as I did, he was always very nervous when he was alone.'

Asked if he had ever seen him worse for drink, Willmore said yes, on several occasions and he knew he took drugs.

Were Albert and Eric on good terms or bad, he was asked? Willmore said they were always on the best of terms when he saw them and Eric always spoke highly of Albert. Asked if he had witnessed Albert ever stopping Eric from drinking, Willmore replied that on two or three occasions when they had been out for an afternoon run in the car. Eric had a habit of putting up at hotels for refreshments and Willmore had heard Albert say 'You have had quite enough, old man. You don't want any more of that.'

On a few other occasions, Wilmore had acquired brandy for Eric, who had asked him not to tell Albert. He bought two large bottles of Hennessey and one half bottle of Martell Three Star, taking them to Eric when he was staying in the nursing home recovering from operation on his foot. Eric instructed the chauffeur not to tell the nursing staff that he was bringing in the drink, so Wilmore smuggled it under a mackintosh. He knew it was wrong but Eric was his employer and he wanted to keep his job. Muir asked that, despite referring to Albert as 'the boss', he did not tell him anything and the chauffeur admitted that was so.

Willmore said he had driven Eric around a great deal while Albert was away and had stopped at various chemists' shops, but he does not say when or where so these could have been the orders from Douthwaite or Gibson. He did add that on other occasions they 'pulled up' at a chemist and Eric had gone in, but he was quite adamant that he 'did not order any drugs from any chemists himself, and he could not say what was in parcels he collected from the chemists.

According to Willmore, Eric only told him once that he was taking drugs. This was at the London flat in the middle of May 1912 when Willmore had seen Eric cleaning a syringe. Out of curiosity he asked Eric what a man could stand in regard to taking drugs and how much morphia would kill a man. Eric said he did not know about morphia as he was impervious to it but that he had taken 120 grains of Veronal which had not harmed him. Willmore had never heard of Veronal, so did not know if this was a large or small dose but did not ask and they never spoke of it again.

Willmore had frequently seen Eric with boxes from chemists and he always carried a small dressing case in which he had a collection of powders and puffs.

Willmore drove Eric to take lunch at the Grand Hotel and testified that when his employer got back into the car, he was obviously the worse for drink; the daughter of the hotel owner told

Willmore that Eric had consumed the best part of a large bottle of port. Seeing the state that he was in, Willmore persuaded Eric to ride in the front of the car so he could get some fresh air.

Willmore explained that on the Friday following this episode, Joiner the butler asked him to fetch Dr Hobhouse, as Eric had taken another overdose of Veronal. The chauffeur could not find Hobhouse so fetched Dr Eccles instead. He added that Albert was away.

Willmore went on to explain that another overdose followed on 31 August. He had been driving his employer to visit Dr Baines but on the way Eric changed his mind and told him to take him to the Genestes. On the way back, with the Genestes in the car, he had looked in the back and seen Eric collapsed with his head on Mary's chest and Mrs Geneste holding his legs in her lap. He pulled up at a hotel in Tonbridge and asked for a room, where he carried the unconscious Eric. Placing him onto a bed, Willmore loosened his clothes and gave Eric an emetic of salt and brandy, forcing his teeth apart with his pocket knife. Eric immediately vomited a thick brown fluid down his shirt although elsewhere he says a reddish-brown fluid. Willmore later told Dr. Baines about the colouring and was told it was consistent with Veronal poisoning. However, in court Dr Willcox disagreed as he had seen many more cases of Veronal poisoning than Baines, having dealt with six cases in the previous six months alone. Coroner Benson said he too had dealt with a number of cases and had never heard of this type of colouring, so the foreman of the jury asked what would cause a reddish vomit. Willcox replied that straining caused by vomiting might have induced a little blood but he had never heard of it in any other context before. Interestingly, in the Eric Mareo trial, Freda Stark testified that when Thelma Mareo was suffering from Veronal poisoning, 'there was some brown saliva that had run down her face.'

Back at Tonbridge, Eric had recovered about ten to fifteen minutes after Willmore had administered the salt and brandy but was hysterical. They all had to remain in the hotel room for another half hour to allow Eric to recover and Willmore gave him a glass of brandy. On their return to Brighton, the chauffeur kept Eric in the front of the car with him and then carried him into the lift and up to the flat.

When the chauffeur put him on the bed, Eric asked him to call Albert at '257 Swansea Docks' and Willmore subsequently did so but only spoke to Albert's brother. He asked for Albert to return as soon as possible and sent two further telegrams.

The following day, Eric remained in bed all day and on Monday, 2 September, he gave Willmore a cheque for £25 to get cash from the Grand Hotel, presumably to pay for the Veronal he bought from Gibson that same day. Albert was due to arrive on the 7.45pm train from Victoria and Willmore went to collect him.

On the Wednesday, the chauffeur took Albert and Eric to the Grosvenor Hotel in London, telephoning the following morning for orders. He spoke to Eric who said that Albert had received a letter from his mother saying she was very ill and Willmore was to take him to the station to catch the 11.30 train.

After he dropped Albert off at Paddington, it was believed by the prosecution that the chauffeur stopped at Douthwaite to collect a parcel and on his return gave it to the hotel porter.

In keeping with Willmore's testimony, this supposed visit would have to have taken place on 5 September but this does not conform to Douthwaite's evidence. Muir picked up on this, asking if he had also gone on the 4th but Willmore said he had not. According to Douthwaite's account books, Eric himself placed the order and, given that Eric never went anywhere by himself, he could not have gone to Douthwaite's alone, yet the chauffeur was adamant he had not driven to the chemist on the 4th and on the occasion he had gone, he had collected a parcel.

Douthwaite was equally adamant that he had supplied no other drugs after the 4th so Willmore could not have picked them up. Willmore told the inquest that he had never driven Eric to any other chemist in London; did not know what was in the parcel; and had never ordered drugs on Eric's behalf, yet elsewhere he said he often drove Eric to chemists but did not give any names. Given that Douthwaite gave his testimony from his order books, and Willmore was relying on his memory, the most obvious explanation is that the chauffeur's recollection was at fault.

After Willmore had apparently dropped off the parcel on the 5th, Eric told him he would no longer be required, as he was having some friends in to dinner. This is a rare mention of Eric having friends. Witnesses rarely mentioned any names and other than Willmore, nobody spoke of people visiting Eric or him visiting them. Given how much testimony was heard regarding Albert's control over Eric, it seems surprising that the prosecution and Mrs Trevanion did not produce people to speak on Eric's behalf, but none was called. There was always the possibility that if they were also homosexual, Eric's friends might not wish to draw attention to themselves.

On 6 September, Willmore drove Eric back to Brighton and neither went out again until he took Albert and Claude to pick up Mrs Trevanion on the 10th.

Turning away from the drugs, Willmore was asked in court about Eric and Albert's relationship. He knew, he said, that Albert had tried to take Eric out for drives and had heard Albert trying to persuade him to go out when it was a nice afternoon. On several occasions, the chauffeur had himself persuaded Eric to go out but other times the offer was refused. However, in his earlier testimony, Willmore had said that he drove Eric about a great deal when Albert was away, so either Eric wanted his friend to himself when he was at the flat, or he did not want to go out with Albert.

'From the first to the last, was Mr Roe always extremely kind?' asked Muir.

'I have never seen him otherwise. He was firm, but very kindly.'

When asked if Eric had ever spoken firmly to Albert, he admitted that he did when under the influence of drink. He would become morbid and miserable, said Willmore, and then it was impossible to do anything with him. He admitted he exceeded his position on occasion but found that if he was firm with Eric, the young man would eventually give way, particularly if he saw it was for his own good.

Muir asked why everybody referred to Eric as 'the boy' and Willmore replied, 'Amongst ourselves, the servants, we used to call him "the boy" owing to his being so young.'

'How did you speak of Mr Roe?'

'Sometimes as "the old man" and sometimes as "the boss".' The court laughed at the latter.

'And did you find that he had control over Mr Trevanion?'

'He had a great influence over Mr Trevanion in every way.'

Muir wanted to know when Albert's influence over Eric was

at its greatest and Willmore explained that it was when he was drunk, or in his 'miserable condition'. He also asked how often Albert was away but the chauffeur could not remember the exact number of times. He told the court that usually these absences were 'a long weekend' from Wednesday to Monday about once or twice a month but usually no longer than that. He added that when Albert was away, Eric was miserable.

Despite Albert telling Willmore that he was also his boss, he never told the chauffeur how to contact him. Willmore knew that Albert went to Swansea because of the train he caught but nothing was ever mentioned about where or why he was going. It was not until after Eric collapsed at Tonbridge that he was given Albert's address.

Hanson, representing Mrs Trevanion, asked if he recalled driving Eric and Albert to Mrs Trevanion's house the previous June or July. Willmore replied that he had only taken Eric and that Albert had not been there, denying Mrs Trevanion's claim that Albert had waited in the car. Hanson pressed him, asking if he was sure. Willmore said he was and remembered the address at 43 Argyll Street, Kensington but could not remember the date.

Muir then asked Willmore about the vanity case that Eric kept in one of the pockets in the car. It was, said the chauffeur, more like a lady's jewel-case, the top had a looking glass and it opened in two halves hinged together. In it was a collection of boxes of powders, puffs, and paints, 'that kind of thing' said Willmore. Eric was very noticeable, he continued, going about with dyed hair, a painted face, bangles on his wrists and high heeled shoes. He did not notice, he said when asked, if Eric was wearing a wedding ring.

The chauffeur had seen Albert two days after Eric had died, when he had gone to the flat for his orders and a 'very cut up' Albert asked if he would like to see Eric in his coffin.

Although Albert had kept on the flat in Brighton, the chauffeur had moved to London. Muir asked him to confirm that he was still being paid by Albert and when the last payment had been made. The chauffeur hesitated, then replied, 'On the Saturday after the Monday this case first appeared in the papers the second time.' However, despite Willmore having seen Albert every day for the last fortnight, they had not spoken in all that time, or at least since the payment was made. Hanson was incredulous and asked, 'You see your joint employer here for a whole week, and you have not spoken to him?' Which the chauffeur agreed was correct and an equally amazed foreman asked Willmore to confirm the date when the last payment was made. Willmore calculated that it was the Saturday before the second inquest was announced in the newspapers. As the inquest was announced on 14 January, the previous Saturday would be 11 January, which means that, since Eric's death on 11 September, Willmore had remained in Albert's employ for four months. Willmore never mentions seeing or driving Albert around during that time instead saying the cars were 'being used by Mr Roe only.' Why would someone keep an employee for four months and never use them?

The last point the jurors wanted to clarify was Eric's weight. Willmore, when he described carrying Eric into the lift and up to the flat, had stated he had no 'difficulty carrying him as he was light as a feather … As far as I could give a rough estimate, he was about 7st 8lbs.'

The foreman of the jury then asked if they could have the pathologist's estimate of the weight for comparison. Muir reminded them that they had that already but the foreman said he did not remember. Muir consulted his notes and quoted the weight given by Dr Willcox as between ten and eleven stone (around 150 lbs, the average male weight calculated in 2009 was around 180lbs).

The court then adjourned for lunch.

It was obvious why Palmer, representing Albert, wanted to bring in Bridges and Willmore as extra witnesses. Bridges was meant to reinforce the split between Eric and his family and show that nothing untoward had happened to the hock bottle. Muir, however, wanted to show how confused Bridges' testimony was and how the drug still had not been properly accounted for. Willmore was intended to show a history of Eric's instability with his repeated overdoses and that as he had also slept in the same bed as Eric, Albert doing so was not unusual.

WHY ALBERT?

Eric was an extremely wealthy man from a privileged background yet preferred the company of a working-class man. This was not unusual. Edward Carpenter, the man who had written the ground breaking work *Love's Coming of Age* (1896), the first UK non-medical book to explore gender, sex and relationships, had also written extensively on homosexuality. He was the first person to advocate that homosexuals be given 'their fitting place and sphere of usefulness in the general scheme of society.'[163] He was himself in a relationship with a working-class man and wrote, 'It is noticeable how often Uranians[13] of good position and breeding are drawn to rougher types, as of manual workers, and frequently very permanent alliances grow up in this way, which although not publicly acknowledged have a decided influence on social institutions, customs and political tendencies.'[164]

Numerous other men 'of good position', such as Oscar Wilde, also had these types of relationships and at the turn of the century, works by Walt Whitman, John Addington Symonds, Edward Carpenter and others highlighted the attraction of middle and upper-class homosexuals to working-class men. There are two reasons suggested for this; one was a means of avoiding the dangers of being 'outed' in the relatively small circles of middle- and upper-class societies; the other that 'in the first quarter of the twentieth century a "real" form of working-class masculinity was seen as sexually attractive'.[165] This attraction to a manly, muscular *'real* man' is sometimes today insultingly referred to as playing with 'rough trade'.

Despite Carpenter's *The Intermediate Sex* being available from 1908 and many other works concerning homosexuality which Eric with his fortune could easily have acquired, neither he nor Albert appears to have been big readers, nor do they seem to have associated with any circles or known homosexuals, keeping themselves very much to themselves.

---

[13] Homosexuals

ALBERT EDWARD ROE – 'THE BOSS'

Finally, the time had come for the witness everyone was waiting for: Albert himself.

A murmur went around the court as he stood and the Coroner reassured him, saying, 'You are not bound to give evidence unless you desire to do so, and anything you say will be taken down in writing, and may possibly be given in evidence against you. You understand?' Albert said he did and that he wished to give evidence - it was to take nearly three hours. It is noticeable that the Coroner did not warn any other witness that their testimony may be taken down and used in evidence, emphasising the precarious position Albert was in - one wrong word and he could be arrested.

He gave his name as Albert Edward Roe, residing at 10 Grand Avenue Mansions, the flat he had lived in with Eric. As he spoke the *Daily Express* noted his appearance:

> He was neatly, almost fashionably dressed. His dark reefer suit was well cut and in his dark blue tie, under a wing collar, gleamed a large diamond pin. His black, wavy hair was trimly parted in the middle, and his square-cut, bronzed, clean-shaven face showed determination in each line.
>
> On his wrist was a watch bracelet, and on the third finger of his left hand was a plain gold circle, while on the other hand he wore a heavy gold signet ring. Across his waistcoat was stretched a gold watch-chain, which he displayed as he spread out his arms in a leisurely fashion on the rail of the witness-box.
>
> He did not once raise his voice or show any sign of passion. In a low, rather musical voice, at times

slurring into a somewhat languid drawl, he answered all questions in a ready, self-possessed way. His speech was that of an educated man, save that occasionally in the quickness of his replies he dropped an aspirate or the final letter of a word.

He told without flinching of the last night together in the flat.[166]

This description by the *Daily Express* is notable for its condescension: Albert is 'almost fashionably dressed' with an emphasis on all his jewellery; they remind readers of his lowly background; his 'slurring' into a 'languid drawl'; and dropping letters in his speech. He is also still wearing a wedding-ring. It is not known if this was the same ring he wore with Eric but as his marriage was still some time away, there was no reason to wear one at this time.

Albert began by summarising when and how the two men had met which we now know was riddled in errors or lies.

After his recovery from blood poisoning, Albert returned from London to Swansea (although in other evidence he said he recuperated at Aberystwyth) and worked there for nine months. During this time, according to him, he only visited Eric on four or five occasions when he would spend the week. Once, while on a motoring tour through Wales with his friend, Hugo Mongomery, Eric picked up Albert and drove him to London. Albert's testimony up to this point is of a very casual friendship when the two men hardly spending any time together.

In November 1910, Albert received a letter from Eric, who was in Paris, telling him he was very ill and asking Albert to collect him and take him home. Eric told Albert he thought he had been 'going on too strong' by staying out late at nights and taking drugs. When they met, Albert told him he was very foolish to trifle with his already delicate constitution. He took Eric back to the Geneste's house but his mother sent him to the nursing home for a rest cure in December.

This indicates that two years before Eric died, he was motoring with friends; travelling to Paris; and generally getting about without Albert.

While they were in Paris, according to Albert, Eric told him he 'was the only one who would put himself out to do anything for him'. Albert testified that Eric 'asked me if I could see my way clear to stay with him permanently'. Eric also asked what Albert was earning and then offered to double his £100 salary plus expenses to act as his 'companion'.

Albert, according to his own testimony, was not initially taken with the idea, telling Eric he was perfectly happy where he was in Swansea, but Eric would not take no for an answer. After some consideration, he finally agreed as long as Eric's solicitors were happy with the arrangement and a contract was drawn up. After leaving Eric at the Geneste's, Albert returned to Swansea but came back on 15 December when Eric confirmed he had been to the solicitors and everything was arranged.

Albert claimed that he returned to Swansea the 'following Sunday' to hand in his notice which would make it 22 December However, he then said he returned to London on 21 December to take up his new duties.

Whatever the precise sequence of events, as Eric's health was still frail, it was decided he and his new 'companion' should go on a world tour. They set off to Egypt, accompanied by Hugo Montgomery, the man Eric had been with on a driving tour of Wales, stopping on the way in Paris, where Eric became ill and began breathing very heavily.

Albert spoke to Hugo, who 'was in the room with him' and said, 'Good God, what has the man been taking?' Albert replied, 'I suppose it is those damn drugs again!' 'I asked Mr Montgomery what drug the deceased had been taking, and he replied that the deceased usually took Veronal. I then learnt that Veronal had been his favourite drug.'

From this testimony, Hugo Montgomery appears to know Eric better than Albert did, so why wasn't he asked to give evidence? It leaves us with no way of knowing if this story is true.

Once Eric had recovered, they carried on to Marseilles and Cairo and then up the Nile to Assouan (Aswan). Albert claims Eric was very ill again in Egypt due to taking excessive drugs, even though he used every means to try and stop him. While there, Eric bought some very expensive things and Albert arranged to ship them back to the UK, stressing he was acting as a secretary. At this

154

time, according to Albert, Eric became concerned about people's perceptions of his companion's social status so, not wanting him to appear 'less than him', he offered to settle £10,000 on him but stop his salary. Again, Albert objects saying it was such a lot of money and repeats that he was happy as he was. 'Eventually' he claims, he gave way and again said only if it was done through solicitors. By any standards this is an extraordinary statement. Albert has portrayed himself as essentially a servant to a man he did not know that well but expects everyone to take his word that Eric wanted to raise a servant to a social position equal to his own.

Albert's own testimony demonstrates his dominance. Eric had been in the habit of dyeing his hair and Albert told him he would have to 'drop' it or drop him and 'as a result of my influence over him he discontinued it.' The desire to modify Eric's appearance is understandable, as he looked and behaved in an effeminate manner which would have brought unwelcome attention in public.

While they were in the south of Italy, Eric had said he wanted to go to Japan. When asked why, he said he wanted to get out 'of the atmosphere of his relations', reinforcing Albert's claims that Eric was at odds with his family.

As they continued their journey, they went from Naples to Rome and back to Naples, going from there to Sicily, then England via Florence, Milan, and the Italian Lakes. For about five or six weeks while they were in the south of Italy, Albert claims that Eric discontinued his use of drugs, proudly writing to Mary Geneste stating that he had not had drugs for a time. It did not last long and before long, Eric's 'health was bad, and we returned via Rome and Naples, and arrived in London on the 6 April 1911.'

On arriving in England, Eric, according to Albert, was feeling much better and when at Victoria Station he weighed 9st 3lbs dressed though he did not say how he knew this and why he would be weighed at Victoria Station.

Both men returned to Eric's rooms at Mary Geneste's, Albert adding, 'He was always of a very nervous disposition, and insisted upon my sleeping with him. At first I slept on the couch. I would sometimes wake up between 3 and 4am and would find him reading. He told me (he) could not sleep as he was so nervous.

Eventually he asked me if I would sleep with him, and I slept with him. I treated him as a younger brother. There was no impropriety between us whatever.'

In his role as secretary or companion, (both are given by Albert as his paid position), he tried to modify Eric's appearance. 'The deceased wore a lot of jewellery. I told him I would not allow him to wear it. In order to take away the temptation to wear the jewellery he gave them to me and told me to put them in the Bank in my own name. I did this, and they have not been moved by me.'

There are hints here of Albert's temperament, 'I would not allow him'. In the ESRO transcripts, the word 'allow' is underlined. However, again, the emphasis is all on Eric's actions; it is Eric who gives up the jewels and who asks for them to be put in Albert's bank.

The two men had returned on 6 April and went to the solicitor's on 20 April in order for Eric to transfer £5,000 into Albert's account as part payment of the £10,000 settlement. Eric, however, went into the office alone, having sent Albert away. They returned in the second week of May when Albert was 'informed' that the Consols had been transferred to him. He promptly sold them and 'bought more stock', presumably the Swansea shares.

According to the evidence of the bank clerk, Eric was living beyond his means and could not really afford to be transferring large amounts out of his account. A significant part of his estate was tied up in property and while he received rent, it would only have been paid quarterly. Albert claimed ignorance about Eric's financial affairs until one day late in May at the solicitor's office, he overheard Lumb telling Eric about his extravagences. Albert calculated the trip to Egypt had cost around £1,400 and he also knew that Eric had helped out his brother by giving him a cheque for £500. However, this concern for Eric's money was not sufficient to offer to return the £5,000 Eric had given him.

In May 1912, Eric decided he would move out the Geneste's. He wanted to enjoy his furniture which was stored in Pantechinon[14] and so decided to move to Brighton and asked Albert to be a joint tenant. In his usual self-effacing way, Albert

---

[14] The Pantechnicon was a company in Belgravia, London which stored furniture and had large vans of the same name which would transport furniture and goods.

said he did not want any more responsibilities but Eric pointed out that now he had the £400 a year, he could afford it. If Albert would pay the £175 a year rent, he would pay everything else. The flat would be in joint names so that Albert could have a say 'who should come into the flat'.

'Whom did he fear?' asked Palmer.

'His family.'

Again, Albert claimed that he had insisted that Eric get clearance from the solicitors before the flat was put in their joint names and in return he said he was 'continually' at the flat checking on things; something not borne out by other testimony and the dates he was there.

In June, Eric bought a new car, presumably the Rolls Royce for which the chauffeur was sent to deliver a cheque. It was registered in both their names in order, according to Albert, to prevent any interference from Eric's brothers or anybody else. Albert had heard that Eric's brother had used his first car without permission and damaged it to a cost of £60 as well as leaving a debt for petrol of £27 10s. Albert doesn't say which brother had used it but given both had enormous fortunes, they could easily have affordedto pay Eric back. Albert doesn't provide a date for this event and it may be that it was related to the letter he received from Claude on 11 December 1911 which annoyed Eric so much. Neither brother provided any evidence as to whether this story was true or not.

Returning to the subject of the flat, Albert claimed that he insisted on having twin beds but Eric refused as he wanted a washstand and a wardrobe built on one side and a dressing table on the other so that the room would be cramped if they had two beds. Despite all the talk of Albert's dominance over Eric, on this occasion he claimed Eric's decision was final. Apparently to appease Albert, Eric said he would get the widest bed he could find and so bought one at five foot that today would be considered a small double.

Questions at the inquest turned to Eric's drink and drug habits and Albert started by saying that when Eric went into the nursing home for the toe operation, he had he stayed with him until the operation had been performed. During his recovery in the home,

Nurse Mahomy complained to Albert that someone had taken brandy in for him (the chauffeur admitted it was him) and that he had been taking Veronal (presumably some he had taken there himself).

Before Albert could continue, the inquest came to a close for the weekend and Albert returned to Swansea to spend time with his family.

9

DAY 5 – TUESDAY 4 FEBRUARY

ALBERT AGAIN

At the start of day five, Albert was asked about Eric's drug taking habits and what he had done to control the intake of his friend.

On or around 10 July, Albert says he was in bed when Eric left the room and went to the lavatory taking a newspaper with him to read. He had been gone for some time and Albert went to the stairs and called out. Eric replied, 'All right, I won't be a minute' and Albert went back to bed. Minutes later Eric fell 'into the door' with a knife in his hand and cut the telephone wire. He then fell into a chair 'in a stupefied, collapsed condition' and dropped a hypodermic needle.

Albert rushed over to him asking what was wrong but could get no 'satisfactory' answer. He hurried upstairs and called the Genestes who came down immediately. Mary ran for a doctor while Albert administered hot coffee. A doctor, he does not say who, arrived and asked for a medical history, telling Albert to keep giving the coffee while he used an artificial respirator on Eric. Dr Sandifer then arrived and also said to keep up the artificial respiration and sent for a nurse. He asked Albert to go to a chemist and get oxygen and so he went to Clarke's in Richmond Road. In the meantime, Dr Sandifer had gone home and returned with a stomach pump.

Returning with the oxygen, Albert and the Genestes continued the artificial respiration until the morning with Dr Sandifer using the pump all night at regular intervals of forty minutes. Eventually Eric recovered despite, said Sandifer, nearly dying.

Afterwards, Albert had asked him why he had cut the telephone wire but Eric had no recollections of doing so. Albert told Dr Sandifer he suspected morphine was the drug Eric had used as he had seen the syringe so they asked Eric where he kept it. Eric replied that it was in the bathroom but they searched and could not find any. Eventually they found the store in a disused umbrella stand in the bathroom which consisted of four or five tubes in a box. Other reports claim Albert said 'he told me he kept the tubes in an old disused umbrella and stick stand' and that there were twenty-two tubes in two boxes.[167]

After the doctor had left, Albert said Eric seemed amused and he asked him why. 'The doctor thinks he's got the lot' smiled Eric and Albert reprimanded him as he had given the doctor his word that he would not take morphia again. During the following day, Albert searched the flat again and eventually found two boxes each contained twenty tubes in Eric's safe and he removed them.

After Eric recovered from the morphine overdose, the two men went on a motor trip to Cornwall. During the journey, Albert reprimanded Eric about using Veronal and asked him not to take any more, especially so soon after the morphia incident as it would be dangerous. He repeatedly quizzed Eric if he had brought any with him and was assured that there was none but when they arrived in Newquay, Albert found ten cachets hidden in a playing card box. Eric 'begged' Albert not to throw the drugs away, so he kept the box and gave the cachets to Eric one by one. (It should be noted that Albert had told others he found the cachets in the playing card box at the flat, not in Newquay[168]).

Despite the recent overdose, Albert testified that Eric seemed cheerful on their Cornish trip, which supports the evidence of others that he was usually cheerful when Albert was with him.

'He even went bathing in the sea, didn't he?' Muir asked.

'He was very fond of paddling,' Albert said dismissively, 'You would hardly call it swimming.'

The *Daily Express* noted that Muir's 'forceful and calm' questions did not shake Albert in any detail. 'He fixed his dark eyes on counsel, and hardly took them off once, answering quietly, but with a slight note of irritation at time when certain suggestions were made.'[169]

Albert left Eric in Ilfracombe with the chauffeur and went to Swansea, returning shortly afterwards to meet in London where they motored down to the Grand Hotel in Brighton. There Eric suffered from rheumatism and Albert asked the hotel staff for a doctor, which was how they came to meet Dr Baines. Albert accompanied Eric to the doctor's but did not go in with him.

In August 1912, the two men moved into the Brighton flat,

engaging Mr and Mrs Joiner to live with them. For the next few weeks they were all busy sorting out the flat, buying supplies and arranging for furniture to be shipped from London in a pantechnicon.

Once settled in, Albert joined the County Cricket Club and went to every match he could; he attempted to get Eric to accompany him and even bought a double ticket membership, but Eric rarely went. In addition, Albert would go for long walks every morning but Eric was seldom lively before lunch time and stayed indoors.

Albert testified that, about a month before his death, Eric was drinking a great deal, except when busy decorating the flat, when he seemed to forget about the drinking. Eric was also taking drugs and Mrs Joiner mentioned to him that she had seen them lying around so Albert told her throw away anything she found.

'Was it a common occurrence to find drugs lying about?' asked Palmer.

'Quite,' said Albert and related how he had repeatedly thrown away morphine, Veronal, aspirin and bromide, and was continually remonstrating with Eric about the drugs. Bromide, usually potassium bromide, was an over the counter medicine used as a sedative or to combat headaches, now primarily used in veterinary medicine (and according to myth used during WWI to curb the sexual drive of soldiers). Bromide has a half-life in the body of twelve days. As there were twenty-seven days between Eric's death and the exhumation, any bromide he had taken is unlikely to have shown up in the analysis had he taken any.

Persuading Eric to give up drugs was not easy, according to Albert. He was not someone you could drive, he had to be coaxed and Albert admitted that he would only be able to keep Eric away from drugs by repeatedly threatening to leave him.

About the middle of August 1912, Albert suggested they both go abroad. A friend of his, Dr Sandifer's partner, Dr Hugh Phillips, was working as a ship's surgeon on one of the Allan liners going to Canada. Eric was very enthusiastic about the trip and told Albert he wanted to go even if it meant going alone. As Eric did not seem to need him, Albert decided to forego the voyage and instead made arrangements to go home to Swansea for a week or ten days. About a week later, he had gone to Devon on holiday when he received a message from his brother that Willmore the chauffeur had telephoned, asking him to return at once. Eric's trip had fallen through, claimed Albert, because the boat had been full.

This is another of Albert's stories which does not quite have the ring of truth. The ship's name is unknown so it cannot be determined if the voyage actually took place but it is interesting that Dr Hugh Phillips was Dr Sandifer's partner. Did Sandifer become Eric's doctor before or after Eric was a friend of Phillips? Another point of interest uncovered in the statements held at the East Sussex Records Office is that Douthwaite cites a H. R. P. who was the signatory on Eric's prescriptions. It seems likely that the initials stand for Hugh Phillips and he may have signed the prescriptions in the absence of Sandifer. This also shows that Eric must have had two prescriptions, the French one and the one signed by Phillips.

Albert's claim that Eric was happy to go on the voyage alone is also suspicious because everyone testified that during the year prior to his death, Eric never travelled on his own; never walked anywhere; and was absolutely miserable when Albert was away from him. Willmore, the chauffeur, had been driving Eric to London when they had to stop at Tunbridge because Eric had overdosed. Had Albert, who was already distancing himself from their relationship, simply gone on his own holiday and this was Eric's attempt to frighten him back? Albert was spending more time in Swansea than in Brighton and, although the first morphine overdose in July 1911 was possibly an accident, all subsequent overdoses were in periods when Albert was spending more and more time away from Eric.

Albert had remonstrated with Eric over the incidents, 'I told him it was very rough,' he said, apparently thinking mainly of himself, 'I could not be away for a little while without things of this kind happening.' He was, according to him, essentially Eric's servant and receiving a substantial pay so why would he object to being at the beck and call of his employer?

By 4 September, Eric had recovered and said he wanted to go to London for an evening out. Willmore drove them both to Daly's theatre that evening[15], staying the night at the Grosvenor Hotel. Albert's mother was then taken ill and Eric 'told me I had better run home for the week-end'. He ordered the chauffeur to take him

---

[15]Probably the operetta *Gypsy Love* which was playing at the time

to Paddington but before leaving, Albert told Eric 'to be a good boy.' Eric told him not to worry as Mr Lumb was coming for lunch and he was meeting friends for dinner although Albert does not name the friends. He next returned to Brighton on the 9 September, the fateful day.

When Albert got to the flat about 7.50pm, Eric was standing alone in the dining room (elsewhere he says sitting but these may be journalistic errors). He was wearing a Japanese silk kimono, seemed depressed and a little drowsy and Albert asked if he was going to dress for dinner. Eric said no, he was too tired as he had been hanging curtains and pictures all day. The butler brought dinner about 8.10 and Eric seemed, according to him, very angry and unwell throughout the meal, eating nothing but drinking half a bottle of hock. Albert had whisky and soda and a full dinner but he did not try to persuade Eric to eat as the young man had told him he'd had a good tea. This is contrary to Mary Joiner's evidence when she said that Eric had hardly eaten anything throughout the day and that Eric was very cheerful because Albert had returned after two weeks away.

According to all other evidence, on the day Eric was reasonably cheerful and certainly nobody mentioned him being angry. Perhaps the two men had a row, possibly over Albert's decision to leave Eric and get married.

About 9pm, they adjourned to the 'den', where Albert used to do a little writing and smoking. Some ten minutes later, Joiner brought in coffee and laid it on the couch. Albert poured the coffee into cups, about the size of afternoon tea-cups but Eric only drank part of his and he continued to be very depressed and uncommunicative. Shortly after this, Eric wanted more wine but Albert told him he could not have any. Explaining why Eric had to ask him, Albert said, 'he always looked to me to speak to him when I thought he had had enough, and this I was in the habit of doing; and the deceased generally obeyed me. Sometimes I experienced a difficulty in making him submissive. On this occasion I did not make any effort to restrain him from having the hock. At dinner he had a little hors d'oeuvre consisting of a little cucumber and oil and tomato.'

Albert's words are telling, once more reinforcing that his actions were as a result of Eric's decisions but also reinforcing how much control he had over his friend.

Eric, who according to Albert was still annoyed, accused him of taking advantage of the authority given to curtail his drinking, something Albert denied. Eric got into 'a huff' and left the room. Believing he would eventually come around, Albert left him alone and twenty minutes later Eric returned, although still very sullen and dejected.

At around 10.15pm, Ham, the picture framer, called to say that Eric still had an outstanding bill.

'Have I?' Eric replied vaguely.

Albert interrupted them saying, 'Of course you have, Eric. Here it is, you fool.'

Albert replied saying, 'It is no pleasure for me to lecture to you, I want something more to live with than the furniture in the house! This is no place for me to come back and find you like this.'

Eric replied, 'Oh, very well!' and left, again seemingly in a sulk.

Not thinking any more of it, Albert went on reading for about a quarter of an hour before deciding to go to bed around 11pm. Joiner was opening a bottle of wine and as Albert did not wish to speak to 'the boy' in front of Joiner, he left both of them and went back into the den. The reason for not wanting to speak in front of Joiner, said Albert, was that he wanted to remonstrate with Eric for ordering the wine after he had told him not to.

Mrs Trevanion testified that Joiner had told her 'I had seen him only a quarter of an hour before standing by the table and I poured him out a glass of wine and Mr Roe was standing by Mr Eric, I left them both in the room together.' Something he later denied.

Muir asked if Albert had ever said anything harsh to Eric in front of Joiner, but Albert said he used to talk to Mrs Joiner more than her husband and he didn't remember ever telling Eric off in front of either of them. What was it, Muir asked, that made Albert so nervous about castigating Eric in front of Joiner? Albert replied that as Eric was a friend, he wouldn't do that in front of a servant. Asked why he didn't go back after the butler had left and stop Eric drinking the wine, Albert said, 'I thought he was taking it, and he might as well have it, as it might make him sleep.'

About a quarter of an hour later, Albert went back into the bedroom. Joiner had cleared away all the coffee items and Eric was in bed but 'did not look very well and did not answer me when

I spoke ... he looked very queer, as if he had taken drugs or something similar. I asked him how he felt'. Eric said he didn't feel right and thought he had taken an overdose.

The use of the word 'thought' is curious. If he had been intending suicide, it would make more sense if he said 'I have taken an overdose' or similar. If he had taken an accidental overdose, he could hardly have failed to notice he was taking such a large amount. Even allowing for Willcox's mistakes, it would still have needed a minimum of ten cachets, far more than he normally took. Alternatively, if he had taken one dose already and had become befuddled and took a second, he may then have 'thought' he had overdosed.

'I asked him if he was quite sure,' said Albert, 'as I did not want to give unnecessary trouble and he said "Yes"'. In the original statement held at the East Sussex Records Office, Albert is recorded as saying, 'Don't be silly' when Eric told him of the overdose, but this reply does not appear anywhere else.

Around 11.20, Albert called Dr Baines who said he would be around immediately but, in the meantime, he instructed Albert to give Eric an emetic of mustard and water.

Albert went into the housekeeper's quarters, knocked at the door and told Joiner who exclaimed, 'Good God! What again?' and they both went into the kitchen to prepare the emetic. Albert had been gone for about ten minutes and got back to the bedroom about 11.30 to find Eric unconscious.

Palmer asked if there was any truth in what Mrs Trevanion said in that he threw something into the fire and Albert replied, 'No, sir; not a particle.' He also he said did not go near either the bottle or the glass.

Joiner forced his fingers between Eric's teeth while Albert tried to pour the mustard and water down his throat. They must have got a little down, perhaps a couple of tea-spoonfuls, because Eric gurgled once, as though he had swallowed but they could get him to take no more. Albert then got the feather which he used to clean his cigarette holder and put that down Eric's throat, trying to force him to vomit. In the meantime, Dr Baines had arrived and asked them to stop as he thought they might choke the boy. Albert was sent to get hot water in which Baines dissolved a small strychnine pellet (a very strong poison which could be injected straight into a vein) and he injected Eric but to no effect. All night, insisted Albert, he did everything he could to assist Doctor Baines and told him it was a pity he had to stand there and do nothing for the boy, but Baines replied, 'I'm doing everything I dare do.'

In the morning, Baines telephoned for Nurse Hawkins. Albert suggested calling a second doctor so Baines summoned a Dr Hobhouse who arrived but made no alterations to what Baines had done. Albert then told Baines he would be more satisfied if Eric's doctor from London came down and so phoned Dr Sandifer, who arrived that afternoon. He too agreed with what Baines had done. Now Albert made another phone call, not to the family, but to Eric's solicitors and Mr Bridges also joined them at the flat.

When asked what he personally knew about drugs, Albert replied that he had never bought Veronal or any other drug apart from aspirin when he had a headache except for some opium three years earlier when he had been ill with blood poisoning. Albert admitted he knew Eric took Veronal to make him sleep but insisted, 'I have repeatedly warned this fellow about taking Veronal,' adding, 'I did not know that the deceased had a lot of Veronal in the flat.' Yet the next statement he makes is that Eric 'left the cachets everywhere. We would find them all over the place; sometimes loose, and sometimes in boxes.'

Asked why he had wanted to search the bedroom about 10am the following morning (or 11am according to Mrs Trevanion), Albert explained he had wanted to know what Eric had taken and said the incident took place 'more than two days' after Eric was first taken ill and not as Mrs Trevanion said, on the second night of Eric's illness. He looked in the cupboard and on the dressing table but didn't find anything before adding that in reality he hadn't looked that hard. The only cachet he had found was the one in the trinket box which he had shown to Bridges the day before and in which there were also four aspirins. Bridges, however, thought there was nothing in the box. Albert said he could not remember if it was the nurse or the doctor who found the cachet sticking to the lid, yet he had told Bridges that he found it.

Muir asked if he was aware of the cachet found on a silver tray on the dressing table, Albert replied that there was never a silver tray on the dressing table but Muir persisted, suggesting the nurse had held it up saying, 'This looks like one?'

'I don't remember, sir,' said Albert, but added that he did show her a bottle of aspirin.

Muir then claimed that Dr Baines had said the cachet held by the nurse looked like Veronal, but he did not know what happened to it afterwards.

If the cachet had been picked up by the nurse, why was it covered with a man's handkerchief when Mrs Trevanion found it the following day?

'Do you know anything about the handkerchief?' Palmer asked and Albert replied 'Nothing whatever.'

'Did you look about to see if you could find any empty boxes?'

'Yes,'

'Did you find any?'

'No.'

There may not have been any empty boxes but Mrs Trevanion had found the Gibson box in the cupboard containing eight cachets, something Albert seems to have missed, despite his statement that he had looked in the cupboard.

'Was the deceased in the habit of keeping these cachets in the trinket box?'

'I used to find them all over the place,' said Albert.

'How would he take the cachets?'

'He would take them up between his fingers one at a time, put them into the drink - generally Vichy water and swallow it, and then drink more water afterwards.' This explanation matches Willcox's evidence that in order to swallow the cachets, they needed to be moistened first. Albert then said that Eric normally took two at most.

Palmer asked him how concerned he had been about Eric before the overdose and Albert replied that he had been very concerned. In fact, he had spoken to Dr Sandifer telling him 'that the family would have to get someone else to help with the responsibility of looking after him, as I had had enough.'

'That was the third time he had an overdose?' Palmer said.

'The third time I was there,' answered Albert, 'six times altogether.'

This, however, was not true unless there were two overdoses which nobody else had mentioned. There are only four attested incidents: the one involving morphine in 1911; two in the month before Eric died; and the one that killed him. Interestingly all but the morphine overdose occurred around the time Albert decided to get married and leave for good.

Attention then turned to what had happened between Albert and Mrs Trevanion with regard to Eric's funeral. 'The question,' said Albert, 'was raised as to who should be asked to the funeral. They thought I might know with whom Eric was friendly. They did not know the people. I thought the only two people would be the Bishop of London and a lady named Mrs Burleigh.' It's not known who Mrs Burleigh was, in the testimony she is referred to as Mrs Barlow, but what is noticeable is that Albert mentions 'the only two people' he could think of despite a much more obvious friend, Dr Rees.

Eric had stayed at Carmarthen several times with Rees and another doctor called Denzil Harries.[170] Mary Geneste mentions Rees in her evidence when she outlined Eric's time boarding with her, saying that Rees stayed for one night, sleeping in Eric's room with him. She stated that Eric had been on a short motoring tour with the doctor in 1907 just before going to live with her; and he was listed as a passenger alongside Eric and Charles Montgomery on the *Agadir* sailing to Spain on 27 January 1909. He was also the executor of Eric's will and, given their obvious friendship, he would have been an ideal person to speak about the relationship between the two men and why everything had been left to Albert.

Dr Rees had been appointed medical officer for Cardiganshire in 1911 and lived with his widowed mother at Plasnewydd, Llanwrda. He did not attend Eric's funeral and was not called to speak about their friendship at the inquest. A letter in the East Sussex Records Office dated 21 January 1913 from Charles Mathews, the Public Prosecutor, to Coroner Benson, states that instructions were given to Chief Inspector Ward to deliver a subpoena on Rees. A second letter dated 20 January again demonstrates that Mathews did want Rees present in court right from the start but he was never called and is curiously absent throughout. Perhaps linking such a prominent man with a case that had undertones of homosexuality was considered too great a reputational risk.

Rees suffered from a number of health problems and died aged forty-two in 1917 having never married.[171] How Eric had met the Welsh doctor is unclear but they both travelled a great deal and so possibly they met on one of Eric's trips. Rees may have known Albert. The area where he practiced included Aberystwyth where Albert spent much time and where Albert had in one version, gone to recuperate after his nine-month illness in Swansea.

The other doctor, Denzil Harries a married and prominent figure in Carmarthen, also did not attend Eric's funeral or attend the inquest.

In the discussions with Mrs Trevanion as to who should be invited to the funeral, Albert mentioned an aunt, Ellen Sophia Cooper, the woman who had approached him in 1907 asking for his help to wean Eric off drugs and drink. Claude agreed their aunt should be invited but his mother seemed to take offence replying, 'Aunt Ellen will have nothing to do with it,' and objected to Claude mentioning her name. Why she thought Aunt Ellen did not wish to be involved was not explained but it points to a change in her attitude during the five years since she asked Albert for help. Eric does seem to have retained affection for her however, as in his final will he left her a diamond necklace. Nothing is known about Mrs Trevanion's relationships with her six siblings; perhaps they had little to do with her due to the adverse publicity over her messy divorce and re-marriage, or perhaps they steered clear of Albert and Eric's 'close' relationship or Eric's drug use. It is noteworthy that no other family member besides his mother and two brothers attended Eric's funeral.

'There were high words about it,' continued Albert, 'and I felt compelled to remonstrate with Mrs Trevanion about her behaviour. The words I used were, 'If you have no respect among yourselves, have a little for the boy who lies next door.' Mrs Trevanion then said, 'I should not be surprised if he turns us out,' and I pointed out that I was joint tenant of the flat and they were my guests',[172] conveniently ignoring it was Eric's money he was using to fund his tenancy.

Relations between them seemed to thaw somewhat and Albert agreed that Mrs Trevanion was very friendly towards him at this time. After the funeral they travelled back in her 'Victoria' (other reports say it was in the same train carriage) but there was a 'slight difference' at the funeral resulting in Cecil refusing to lunch with them.[173]

When asked if he felt he had done enough for Eric, Albert replied, 'I have done everything that one man could do for another; as much as I would do for my own brother.'

'When the £10,000 was given to you, did you arrange to make a will leaving £8,400 back to the estate?' asked Palmer.

'Yes, and the remainder to my mother.'

'You only left yourself £1,600, the rest to go back to him?'

'Yes.'

There is no evidence to prove this was true. No solicitor confirmed such an arrangement and whilst Miss Geneste mentions it, she does not say when she knew about it. No written evidence of such an arrangement was ever supplied and considering Albert's attitude towards the Trevanions afterwards when he refused to relinquish any of the money he had been left, it seems hard to believe.

Albert was asked to describe Eric when he first knew him and Albert confirmed 'the boy' was twenty-one. At that time, he did not dye his hair, or paint his face, or wear extraordinary clothes, although he did favour rather high heeled boots. 'Beyond that there was nothing extraordinary. He was very delicate and thin.' Albert recalled the time around Christmas 1908 when he was laid up with blood poisoning in Swansea and Eric had visited him. At that time, he said Eric did not dye his hair and did not start doing so or painting his face until about April or May 1911 when he had come to London 'once or twice' to visit his friend. Yet a member of staff at the hotel where Eric was staying in Swansea told the local newspaper they were 'surprised to see the quantity of powders, puffs and cosmetics he had lying about. It was just like a small chemist's shop'.

Albert said Eric had given up painting his face and dyeing his hair while they were in the south of Italy early in 1912 and had not resumed it again to his knowledge, which makes him very unobservant as the hairdresser stated that he had been to the flat every week waving and dyeing Eric's hair. His hair was a natural sandy colour, Albert said but Muir pointed out that Dr Sandifer had called it a light brown and Albert agreed that it could be called both. He then tried to explain away his statement by saying that Eric resumed dyeing his hair with peroxide after they had come back from the trip and 'told me at one time he was using henna to bring the natural colour back. He told me it had gone lighter about July 1912.' It continued to get lighter to a different colour, a glaring straw colour, which could hardly be called natural.

'Did you take him to the Kursaal,[16] Muir asked, 'and he was so extraordinary a figure that anyone would notice?'

'Yes, sir, he was … only because of his extreme height and delicacy.'

'And his manner of wearing his clothes and the kind of clothes he wore?'

'There was nothing wrong about the clothes. He used to wear a double-breasted jacket, and a flannel suit.'

'Generally high heeled shoes … painted face?'

'I do not say it was painted.'

Asked if Eric's nightshirt was like a woman's? Albert denied it, 'No, sir,' he said, 'he never used night things like a woman's. He wore a plain silk night shirt. The only thing on it was a decorated collar, the same as is worn on a suit of pyjamas.' He could not remember when Eric started wearing the night shirt but he would wear either this or pyjamas.

Albert confirmed that Eric also wore a 'slave bangle' and another armlet but said the only time they could be seen was when playing billiards as he had his cuffs tucked up. However, both the butler and the chauffeur attested that Eric wore bangles, the chauffeur saying, 'He was very noticeable as he went about with dyed hair, painted face and bangles on his wrists' which implies the bangles were visible.

Albert also said Eric wore diamond rings, sometimes a marquise ring[17] and sometimes a large stone ring but also a plain ring which he said he had been wearing for a long time. However, this did not explain why he was wearing it on his wedding finger.

A large amount of jewellery had been left to Eric by his grandfather, including a necklace, rings and seals. Albert had locked them up in a vault at his bank. 'When I first went with him,' Albert explained, 'he wanted to take the whole lot out and wear them at different hotels but I thought it ridiculous. I have seen him wearing large rings but no heavy bangles.' As he had objected so strongly to them, Eric had apparently said, in that case Albert

16 The Kursaal was one of the world's first purpose-built amusement parks situated in Southend-on-Sea, Essex.

17 A marquise ring, an ornate pointed oval usually of precious gems such as diamonds, was originally commissioned by Louis XV of France to represented the lips of his mistress, Madame de Pompadour, and generally worn by courtiers. By 1912 it had become a classic engagement ring.

might as well lock them up to prevent the temptation to use them.

'If he had not worn them what was the necessity of locking them up in the bank?' asked Muir.

'I cannot answer that, sir.'

There was an extensive number of valuables in the flat. There was a safe in the flat because Albert says he found a quantity of drugs in it. Why then did Eric not put the jewellery in it so he could use his jewellery when he wanted, instead of having to ask Albert to get them out of the bank for him?

Muir taunted Albert, 'What was the object you had in going about with this man with the high-heeled shoes and painted face, and sleeping in the same room with him?'

Albert snapped back, 'That was not my job.'

'What,' said Muir, 'was your job?'

'Attending to a delicate man.'

Muir pointed out that he had no medical training to look after such a delicate man and Albert agreed.

He confirmed that he did sleep in the same room as Eric but claimed he had not known it was to be part of his duties when he signed on as a companion despite Mary Geneste saying they shared a bed at her place.

'And you were quite satisfied with it?' Muir asked about the job.

'Quite. I was grateful for it.'

'Did you like the job?'

'I liked the boy.'

'Did you like the job of travelling about with this extraordinary youth?'

'I didn't much like it. He was a person whom anybody would notice. I liked the deceased, and I did not like dislike the job of travelling with him.' In this, Albert confirms Eric was a tall, eccentrically dressed man who would automatically attract attention. If Albert was trying to keep his sexuality hidden, this was not the way to do it.

Muir paused before sardonically adding, 'But you took it?... for £200 a year and your expenses, I suppose?'

'Yes, sir.'

'When did you begin to sleep in the same bed with him as a regular thing?'

'It depends upon the arrangements at the hotels. Sometimes

there would be twin beds, and sometimes we could not get them.'

Muir carefully set up his next questions to trap Albert, 'Whenever you could get them, did you ask for them?'

'We asked for twin beds.'

'Do you say it was only when you could not get twin beds that you had one bed?'

'Yes, sir.'

'Was one of the hotels you stayed at the Paris Hotel at Lugano?' Muir asked and when Albert confirmed they were there, Muir added, 'were you shown a room with two beds in it, and did you not say you wanted a little matrimonielle?'[18]

'I did not,' bristled Albert.

'Did Trevanion?'

'I don't know about Trevanion. I did not.'

'Was the deceased partial to female society?' Muir asked.

'I don't think I could say he was particularly partial. There was one lady in particular he liked,' said Albert but mentioned no names.

When asked if Eric went to Ceylon with him, Albert said, 'Yes. He came on another trip with us, each trip occupying three and a half months on the average.' However, no passenger lists can be found to confirm these trips.

Muir switched tack and began to question Albert about money.

'Did you sometimes make Trevanion give up his money to you? ... Did you at Lugano take two £5 notes from him?' How Muir obtained this information was not disclosed. The only other person who could have known what happened on that trip was Hugo Montgomery and while he was not called as a witness the police may have interviewed him.

'Not that I know of, unless it was to pay a bill.'

'You took two £5 notes from him and put them in your own pocket to take care of?'

'I might have done,' said Albert, 'sometimes he used to offer it to me to look after for him.' 'Eric was,' said Albert, 'apt to be careless'.

Muir asked for clarification about the transferred money, 'and it was not by making a settlement, but by actually handing over to

---

[18] Marriage bed

you certain investments... which were yours to do whatever you please with?' asked Muir.

'Yes, sir.'

'And nobody could exercise any control over them?'

'No, sir.'

'And if the boy died in your lifetime that was yours.'

'Yes, sir.'

'What was to happen with regard to the £10,000 in the event of your leaving him?'

'I assume I should have retained it.'

Muir then began to build up a line of questioning to shed light on why Eric may possibly have wished to commit suicide. 'You threatened several times to leave him?' he asked.

'Yes, I did.'

'Did you ever contemplate leaving him?'

'No, sir, not really.'

This was not true: Albert had already arranged to get married before Eric died. Muir picked up on this and taunted him, 'Supposed, for example, you had wanted to get married? You would not have felt bound to sacrifice your life to him for £10,000?'

'No, sir, I pointed that out to him and he told me that if ever I wished to marry I should give him long notice.' In the official inquest transcripts, the line 'in the event of my getting married' is underlined in red and in that version he said he felt compelled to give back the £10,000.

'Did you ever give him any notice?'

'Some time in August.'

Putting aside the accidental morphine overdose a year previously, all three of Eric's subsequent overdoses took place in August when Albert was persistently absent. He says he told Eric around mid-August that he was leaving to get married, just over three weeks before Eric died.

'When was marriage contemplated?' Muir asked.

'There was no fixed time.'

'What is the lady's age?'

'Thirty-one or thirty-two, I am not sure.' Albert was thirty-five.

'No reason at all except your engagement to Mr Trevanion why it should be put off?'

'None at all, sir.'

Albert said he had contemplated marriage sometime in early August and Muir asked him if it would be reasonable to assume that Eric would therefore need a new companion. As Albert organised so much of Eric's life by taking care of his money and jewellery, wouldn't he need to make provisions for the new companion to do the same? Albert answered vaguely that he didn't know; a lie, as it was later revealed that Albert had already made arrangements for Eric to be taken care of.

Perhaps the stress of the inquest was beginning to affect Albert, as he then made a strange rambling comment, 'If he found or thought he had done anything great for him I suppose he would have acted in the same manner.'

Muir asked what the great thing was that Albert had done for Eric, but he replied that it was obviously Eric who thought what he had done was great, not himself. He personally didn't think he had done anything out of the ordinary. Muir responded that if he hadn't done anything 'so great' then wouldn't Eric want to show the same generosity to the next companion and so need his money back? He kept pressing for an answer on how Eric was to be cared for after Albert had gone; an answer he obviously knew and was trying to get the man in the dock to admit but Albert would not be drawn.

Muir then turned his attention to the will.

On 20 October 1912, just over a month after Eric had died, a writ was issued in favour of Mr William Rees of Swansea, regarding the will being enacted. In the action, Rees is referred to as Mr, not Dr, and his address is listed as Swansea, not his official addresses in Aberystwyth or Llanwrda, although the reason for this is not made clear. Listing Swansea may have been a mistake by the journalists but it is curious that this is also Albert's home town. Albert did not take part in the action but had given his consent, while Eric's brothers, mother and father, Hugh Arundell Trevanion, were registering claims to stop the will being enacted.

Eric's estate consisted of real estate that brought a revenue of £140 a year; investments of £34,000; but also debts: bills to various tradesmen of £21,000; an overdraft on the London, County and Westminster Bank of £2,300; and various mortgages of £2,100. As part of the estate, Eric also had shares in estates in Carmarthenshire, Cornwall and abroad, and investments in a

South Wales enterprise that was not named. The executors were Mr Maton from Eric's solicitors, of whom Lumb gave evidence at the inquest, and Mr/Dr Rees.

The action had been brought forward because there was a need to take care of the valuable furniture and pictures in the flat at Brighton and the executors wanted sufficient money to pay the estate duties. They asked for Henry William Holland, a chartered accountant who had done work for the Trevanion family, to oversee the payments and there was no objection to his appointment. The executors proposed to sell some of the investments to pay the overdraft as all the free cash was in Albert's account.

The court granted that monies should be released to pay bills and take care of the flat[174] but as soon as the new inquiry had been granted, Eric's mother filed a caveat to prevent Albert being given anything until the inquest had finished. Various newspapers attempted to get copies but it could not be confirmed as Somerset House would not release it. However, some in the media did manage to see the will and did report on it.

According to the *Daily Mail*, Eric's will gave £1,500 to doctors and servants but 'the residue absolutely to my friend Albert Edward Roe, now of 30, Green hill-street, Swansea, who is to live with me at Grand-avenue-mansions, Hove.'[175] In the event of Albert predeceasing him, the money would be divided between hospitals. The executors were Mr William Rees of Llanwrda (his mother's address) and Mr L.S. Maton who were both to receive £300 for their troubles. Eric's relatives were not mentioned in the will. A year previously, Eric's estate had been worth about £100,000 but by the time of his death it had been reduced to between £40-50,000.[176] It was claimed that overtures had been made by Eric's family to reach a compromise over the will but this had been refused by Albert.[177]

At the inquest, Albert denied knowing that Eric had made a will in his favour, 'He talked about lots of things, but never told me definitely he had made a will,' claiming he didn't know about it until after the funeral. However, solicitor Lumb said that as far as he knew Albert *was* aware of the will. Miss Geneste also testified that she had spoken with Albert the day after Eric died, specifically because Mrs Trevanion had told her about the will. The question is how did Eric's mother know? It would not have been discussed by the solicitors so early on and unless Eric himself told her there was no other way of knowing except if it is true that on the night of Eric's death, Albert had told her that her son had left her out of his will.

Albert said he had not spoken to Mrs Trevanion about the will, claiming he would leave it to the lawyers to sort out and it was only after he had the details some time later that he communicated with Mary Geneste. This contradicts her statement that they discussed it the day after Eric's death.

Albert claimed that when he did finally speak to the lawyer they were 'discussing the boy and the trouble we were expecting about the will. I said I was sorry he had made me residuary legatee, as I was a chap that had not been used to a lot of money and did not want it.' Yet he had taken responsibility for the £10,000.

'Was a compromise offered about the will?' Muir asked.

'No, sir, I could not compromise,' replied Albert, 'if things were arranged all right I would be quite willing to meet them, but I was not going to bind myself to any compromise.' If Albert was, as he claimed, a reluctant legatee and didn't want the money, why didn'the want to sort a compromise out as soon as possible? It was now five months since Eric died and he and the family still hadn't reached an agreement.

Turning to the night Eric died, Albert confirmed that at dinner Eric had drunk half a bottle of wine.

'That of course was with your consent?' said Muir pressing the point about Albert's level of control.

'He always looked to me to stop him when he had had enough,' replied Albert, once again putting the responsibility for his actions firmly on Eric.

'And you were in the habit of doing so?'

'Yes, sir, by his wish.'

Albert must have realised how his answers were coming across as he added that Eric didn't always do as he said, in fact generally speaking he did not.

'Did you have any difficulty of making him submissive?' Muir persisted.

'At times, sir', adding that it was not often, despite others testifying that Eric always did what Albert said.

'After the dose of morphia that occurred in London, we have heard one of the witnesses say that Mr Eric Trevanion did it to frighten you. Have you any idea why?'

'I think I may have been a bit firm and severe with him for something he had done, and he may have tried to give me a shock,' but Albert didn't expand on this and no-one asked what he had done to upset Eric.

During dinner Albert said he had not made any efforts to stop Eric from drinking the half bottle of wine and that the young man had eaten a small hors d'oeuvre of cucumber, oil and tomato. This, despite his earlier testimony in which he said Eric had eaten nothing at all.

Hanson, acting for Mrs Trevanion, then rose and cross-examined Albert about Eric's time in the nursing home. Albert said he went to visit Eric 'for three or four days', not making clear if he meant together or, as Amy Mahony said, days when he was in town.

Hanson asked Albert if knew Eric's mother had visited him whilst he was laid up and Albert admitted he didn't.

'Did you know that twice, a short time before, he had dined with his mother,' Hanson continued, 'and went to the theatre? Did you know that he had visited his mother in Argyle-road in June?'

Albert said he hadn't known about the dinner or the theatre but that he did know about the visit in June and admitted to being in the car. Willmore, the chauffeur had been asked twice if Albert was there and on both occasions he denied it, but perhaps it was just a case of the chauffeur's bad memory.

Turning to the day Eric was taken ill, Palmer asked, 'Though he was obviously on the point of death you did not think it advisable to send for his people?'

'I knew that differences had existed between them.'

He was asked if these difficulties existed in 1906-8, in the early parts of their friendship. Albert replied, 'I don't know. I had not seen much of the boy.' Given how much Albert was at sea in this early period he was probably being truthful.

Further questions were asked about Eric's relationship with Claude and whether Eric had behaved badly towards him. Albert replied, 'I can't say that he behaved well, considering he was in bad health. He behaved ordinarily.' Why Eric had behaved badly towards his brother was not discussed.

Hanson then produced a letter addressed to Mrs Trevanion which Albert admitted was in his handwriting. In it he wrote that Claude was most devoted to Eric but when asked about this, Albert claimed, 'he was at that time.' Trying to push Albert further, Hanson pointed out that he had told the jury a minute ago that he was not.

Hanson produced another letter from Eric written from Rome on 26 April 1907 in which he commenced, 'My dear mother,' and went on to describe his sightseeing before speaking of family affairs, saying he naturally took an interest in these matters.

'He is the son who was supposed to have been at enmity with his mother, what do you say to that?' asked Hanson.

Albert did not reply.

Another letter from Egypt started, 'My dear mother' and ended, 'with best love from your affectionate son, Eric.' Hanson continued, 'And this letter is from this son, who was supposed always to be at variance with her, and you told us he was at enmity with his mother.'

'I did.'

'And at the same time that he was telling you this he was writing affectionate letters to his mother?'

'I told you what he had told me.' Albert said and claimed Eric had told him about the family enmity when he had been ill in Swansea.

Albert seemed to struggle to recall how long he had been in Swansea during this illness, finally saying that he had gone home in 1908 and was laid up in bed from November until September 1909 when he went to Aberystwyth to recuperate despite claiming elsewhere that he went to London with Eric.

Continuing to read from the series of letters, Hanson quoted from one dated 1908, where Mrs Trevanion asked Eric if he would stay with her for a while. Albert denied knowing anything about this, so Hanson asked how he would account for such letters if there was such supposed animosity between Eric and his mother. Albert did not reply.

'Your only impression was that he was at enmity with her,' Hanson said to Albert, 'Is that the excuse you make for not writing her when he was nearly dead?'

'I did not want to call upon people unnecessarily.'

'Why unnecessarily?'

'I left it to the discretion of those who knew the family better than I did to call them.'

'And rather than send a telegram to Mrs Trevanion you preferred to leave it to them and let him die?'

'Oh no, sir, I did not say that.'

'Do you know what he went to his mother's house for in July?' pressed Hanson.

'No.'

'Did he tell you that his mother advised him that he was foolish in treating you as he did?'

'No.'

'And that you would probably be asking for more very soon?'

'No.'

Most of the narrative concerning Eric's relationships with his mother and brothers came from Albert; it was he who had consistently portrayed an estrangement which may not have been true if the family are to be believed. There had been two incidents when Eric had disinherited his brothers but he was constantly altering his will and the brothers had since become friends. It is possible that Eric may have exaggerated his family difficulties to Albert, portraying himself as alone in the world to foster sympathy and to get his friend to stay with him. Or it may be, as was suggested elsewhere, Albert had deliberately driven a wedge between them.

Hanson produced a copy of the evidence that Albert had given at the last inquest. This showed that Albert had said that Eric had been fine on the night of his death before suddenly telling him that he had taken an overdose.

'He was perfectly rational one moment,' asked Hanson, 'but then suddenly became unconscious?'

No, replied Albert, Eric was rational enough to talk to him and rather than suddenly becoming unconscious he suddenly said he had taken an overdose.

Albert calculated that from the moment Eric confessed to the overdose to when he became unconscious was about half an hour. 'I noticed nothing until he told me,' he said, 'perhaps when I looked at him I asked how he felt.'

This is not in keeping with Albert's earlier statement, when he said that on entering the room, Eric 'did not look very well and did not answer me when I spoke ... he looked very queer, as if he had taken drugs or something similar. I asked him how he felt'.

Hanson was still worrying over the details of how long it had taken Eric to lose consciousness, 'I want to point out this,' he said, 'you went to the telephone, received instructions, and made the emetic, probably all in five minutes, but when you tried to administer it, he was so far gone in those five minutes that he could only take two tablespoonsful; so that the transition period from being able to talk rationally and unconsciousness was five minutes?'

'Oh, no,' said Albert, because according to his calculations, it was closer to thirteen minutes although Hanson argued it was more like ten.

Willcox had stated that the deep sleep caused by an overdose of Veronal would usually occur within an hour or more of taking the drug, depending on whether the stomach was full or not. An empty stomach would accelerate unconsciousness and both Mrs Joiner and Albert had said that Eric had hardly eaten anything that day. Therefore, Albert's claim that the coma began about half an hour after Eric admitted taking the overdose is feasible.

Hanson turned to the conversation Albert had with Mrs Trevanion and whether he told her she did not have a right to be in the flat? Albert admitted the conversation saying he thought she was abusing the privilege of staying.

'You don't agree as to telling her that her son had left everything to you?'

'No, no.'

Hanson asked if he had often spoken of the £10,000 that was supposedly 'forced' upon him and Albert admitted that he had. He had said that the only reason he had accepted it was because the solicitors had applied 'the last ton of pressure' to force him and he would not have agreed until the solicitors were fully aware of the transaction.

Albert once again claimed he did not know Eric had made a will or that he had been going to the solicitors every few weeks to change it. He said that all he knew was Eric was fond of going to the solicitors but did not know what it was about.

He agreed that he did request to go into Eric's room after he had died. Mrs Trevanion said she found a cachet on the dressing-table with a handkerchief over it but Albert thought she must have been mistaken, and it might have been the same one he had seen in the trinket box.

Hanson was sarcastic in his reply, 'It might have walked from where you saw it and got under the handkerchief?'

Albert did not reply.

When asked why he wanted to look around the room, Albert denied he had looked for other Veronal and said he had been thinking of what he could do for the boy.

'But he was dead,' snapped Hanson, 'what could you do for him but bury him? If it is true that the cachet had been obviously opened, have you any idea why the deceased should have done it?'

'I do not know. I said I found it pinched, as if it had been pinched in closing the cachet.'

Hanson took no notice of Albert's suggestion that the cachet was merely 'pinched' by the edge of the box, apparently convinced that the powder inside had been emptied out. 'Have you any idea,' he asked, 'why he should have wanted to extract the powder?'

'I do not know.'

'It would have been quite easy to open the cachet?'

'Yes, just pinch it.'

Albert continued, 'I looked in the cupboard used as a medicine cupboard, but did not see any in it' but then added, 'I did not make a thorough search.'

Although there is no mention in the newspaper accounts, there must have been some question about this as Albert went on to say, 'I do not doubt her story as to the finding of the 8 cachets in the medicine cupboard.' Was Albert implying Mrs Trevanion could have placed them there? There would be no purpose to this.

Throughout the inquest, Hanson seemed to be the only person concerned about apparent discrepancies with how the Veronal was taken. According to Albert's testimony, Eric had swallowed the cachets, which would explain why there were no shells, but why were there opened cachets, if Eric did not normally take them this way? Was Hanson suggesting that Albert had used some force to get Eric to drink more Veronal in the wine?

Palmer, representing Albert, then cross-examined his client about the letters Hanson had produced and asked about the family being on bad terms. He asked if Albert knew if Eric was wealthy and if Eric had ever told him how he got his wealth. Albert replied, 'He said that I had a mother and that he had not.'

Turning to the overdose, Palmer asked, 'You thought that as soon as he knew he had taken an overdose he was anxious to send for the doctor … so you didn't think he wanted to kill himself?' Albert agreed that he did not think Eric had been suicidal.

'Did you receive a letter from Mr Cecil Trevanion, commencing "Dear Roe," and suggesting that you should go and see him?' Albert agreed that he had and Palmer read from the letter, which referred to Albert discussing an amicable settlement of Eric's estate. Cecil had the authority to act for 'The pater and Claude' and trusted they could come to terms. Albert said that he had sent the letter to his solicitors and as far as he was concerned that was where matter lay.

Once the lawyers had finished their questioning, the foreman of the jury asked about Albert's qualifications. He told them he had an honorary certificate as a master mariner; had passed four examinations in Swansea and Cardiff; but he did not have his discharge papers with him. He told the jury that his character was always good. The foreman asked, 'If I were to make the same inquiries at Lloyd's should I get the same answer?'

'Yes.'

'At times,' wrote the *Daily Express*, 'Mr Roe leaned his head wearily on his hand as though tired of the whole inquiry, and after he had been two hours and three-quarters under examination he smiled when told he might leave the box.'[178]

There Albert's testimony came to an end. He had spent nearly three hours convincing the jury that he was a kind, caring companion who had done only the best for a drug-addicted 'boy' who had thrust upon him unwelcome responsibilities: sharing a bed and taking charge of money, jewellery and the like. Nevertheless, he was certainly not going to surrender any of Eric's money or possessions to the family.

At some point, according to Albert's witness statement made to the police, he rang Douthwaite wanting to know if they had supplied Eric with any Veronal and been told they had supplied twelve cachets on the 4th. Albert claimed he knew nothing of this purchase. Douthwaite's evidence differs from Albert's: according to the chemist he was called by an unidentified man who asked what Eric had ordered. Douthwaite complied and told him what he had supplied. The man then said 'I suppose you know he is dead?' Douthwaite replied, 'No, I do not' and the conversation ended.[179] Why Albert wanted the information he does not make clear.

NURSE HAWKINS

Nurse Hawkins was briefly recalled to confirm that she had been at the flat since 8.30 on the morning that Eric died. She told the court that she had put the room straight when she arrived but she could not remember if the bottle of hock was still there; nor could she remember the handkerchief covering the opened cachet. None of her notebooks filled out on the day were included in evidence.

CHARLES CECIL TREVANION

Equally brief was the testimony of Eric's brother, Cecil, who stated that he had lived in Ceylon but had moved back to London some time in 1911.

Cecil was living mainly in Ceylon and suffering from his own losses. His wife Sybil, whom he had married in 1908, died just four months before Eric and he had been left to bring up their son Hugh on his own. It is not known when Eric gave him the £500 but it may have been around this time.

He had not originally been intended as a witness and in a letter by Charles Mathews to Coroner Benson dated 23 January 1913, Mathews had stated 'Cecil Trevanion … does not appear to be a necessary.'

Cecil confirmed that once he had learned how seriously ill Eric was, he had left London at 5pm and had reached the flat around 6pm on 10 September, the same day his mother had arrived. With asked about clearing up the room, he had very little to add and couldn't remember exact details about either the tea things or the hock bottle.

Hanson produced another letter dated 23 July 1912 which Cecil had received from Eric saying, 'My dear Cecil, I shall be delighted to be Godfather to your baby. Am sending cheque for baby for fifty pounds. Your loving brother Eric.'[180] This was seven months after Cecil had sent the letter which had annoyed Eric so much. It appears the animosity which had existed in September

1911, when Eric had cut both his brothers out of his will, had abated and by early 1912 he was getting on well with his mother and his brothers. Due to his being abroad, Cecil hadn't seen Eric very much but since moving back he had seen more of him, something it would seem Albert was unaware of.

The court was then adjourned until the following Thursday, when the judge would sum up.

In the meantime, the *Cambrian Daily Leader* had found out what Nurse Rice had written in the note she had passed to the Coroner but chose not to publish it, writing 'while they concern the deceased himself, they have absolutely no connection with the cause of death, and that was why the Coroner did not reveal them.'[181] The content, however, was entirely dependent on interpretation.

10

DAY 6 – FRIDAY 7 FEBRUARY

As day six dawned, new measures had been put in place by the police to prevent a recurrence of the unseemly scenes that had occurred at the last sitting. There had been an 'ugly rush' by the public, mainly women, to get into the court. The Coroner was overheard to remark that it was disgusting behaviour and journalists noted many of the women watching the inquest had brought their own lunch so as not to lose their places.[182] The *Cambrian Daily Leader* also commented that the court had been besieged with anonymous letters claiming all sorts of things but none had been published.[183] However, some can be found in the ESRO and several are very revealing.

Speculation had been rife about new witnesses and Hanson, the solicitor for the family, had been seen arriving in Swansea on the evening of the 5 February. On the morning of the 6th, he had a long interview with Detective Inspector Roberts at the Guild Hall.[184] The 'famous' Detective Inspector Ward of Scotland Yard had also been in Swansea, trying to keep a low profile due to the notoriety of the case, booking into his hotel as Mr Blank, commercial traveller. The *Leader*, trying to find out what they were looking for in Swansea, was merely told to 'wait and see.'

It seemed that there were now three new witnesses to be brought from Swansea. They were Mrs Derrick of Sketty Road, to whom Albert was engaged to be married; Tom Davies, a commissioning agent and T. Dunning, a commercial traveller, with perhaps V. Hugo of Brynmill also joining them.

According to Tom Davies, who gave an interview to the *Leader*, two Swansea Detectives Barry and Hayes, operating on the instructions of Inspector Ward of Scotland Yard had called early at his house in Craddock Street and informed him that he was required at Hove. They took Davies to Dunning's house in a taxi and from there to the Central Police Station where both were told that they had to leave by the 5am train on Tuesday morning. Mrs Derrick was also told to go to Hove.

Shortly before 2pm on the Tuesday, all three were in court and being instructed by Detective Inspector Parsons. A quarter of an hour later, Mrs Derrick, who was smartly attired in a blue costume entered the court accompanied by her legal advisor, Mr S. Andrew, who also spoke briefly to the Detective Inspector.

Albert arrived a few minutes later with his brother-in-law, Hanlon and Andrew Paton, all having travelled from Swansea the previous morning. Mrs Trevanion and Mrs Hanson entered, soon followed by Claude. Detective Inspector Ward arrived some minutes later, the two male witnesses were introduced to him and he asked them to step into a private room.

The Coroner then entered the court. Taking his seat, he said, 'Gentlemen of the jury, I was quite under the belief that this would have been the last occasion upon which I should have to call your names. Since coming here I am informed that there are other witnesses which it is desirable to call, and which cannot be done today. I hope there will be some evidence taken today, so that your time may not be entirely wasted, but it will be impossible to finish. Therefore, it is proposed that we shall adjourn until Thursday or Friday to see if it will be possible to finish then. It may be necessary to again adjourn, but I cannot say any more.'

Benson seemed to be under the impression that no witnesses were present, despite the fact that Davies and Dunning were in a room with Detective Inspector Ward. Therefore, the foreman of the jury asked if they could put two or three questions to Albert who then entered the box with the 'same quiet air of confidence that characterised him on the previous occasion.'[185]

The foreman asked if it was true that Albert had found Eric a wreck at Paris in March 1911 and did he know what Eric had been doing to make himself such a wreck?

Albert explained he did not know for certain, 'All I gathered was that he used to do a lot of roller-skating, and from what he told me he had been going too strong.'

The foreman was sceptical, 'as a man of the world, do you mean to tell me that skating would make a wreck of a man?'

'I did not say so. It is what I gathered - that he was going too strongly. I gather he had too much to drink.'

The foreman then asked an interesting question, 'Have you ever threatened the deceased with exposure?'

'In what way?' said Albert.

'In any sort of way as to cause him to be depressed?'

'No.'

'Was the deceased, to your knowledge, addicted to any immoral practices whatever?'

'None, sir.'

The foreman's question of exposure is interesting but not one that Albert would have answered in the affirmative because if he had been suspected of driving Eric to suicide, it could have ended badly for him. Nor could he answer yes to the second question as homosexuality was illegal and not to report such a crime could also have caused trouble for Albert. If he confessed to knowing Eric had 'immoral' habits then suspicion would have fallen on him and he could have been arrested.

Had this been a case involving a heterosexual couple, Albert would have been asked if he had sex with the other person, particularly given that they often shared a bed but despite a number of questions about Eric's 'immoral practices', nobody ever asked Albert if he had any.

The use of the word 'addiction' is also illustrative of the time. Much work had been done in an attempt to understand sexuality by the sexologists of the late nineteenth and early twentieth centuries but the general understanding at this time was that people were 'addicted' to certain practices. Despite much work being carried out by sexologists at that time and many of their findings being made public, newspaper coverage did not attempt to draw on this corpus of work to understand 'immoral practices.'

As this line of questioning was not pursued any further, Palmer took the opportunity to mention he had contacted the Royal Mail Steam Packet Co about Albert's character. They confirmed that Albert had been in service from April 1906 to 22 October 1909 and reports from his commanding officers on the various vessels he had served were all entirely satisfactory.[186]

NURSE RICE AGAIN

As the new witnesses did not appear to be forthcoming, Nurse Rice was also asked back to confirm a few details.

'When you were nursing him in August,' Hanson, representing the Trevanion family, asked, 'did he express to you any wish if he were ill again as to your attending him again?'

'Yes, he asked me if I would come back if he was taken ill again at any time.' And she promised him she would if it were possible.

Rice said that about a week after Eric's death, she had called on Dr Baines to ask why she had not been sent for the morning he had been taken ill. Baines told her he had forgotten her telephone number, or that he hadn't got it with him, and so he had asked Nurse Hawkins to attend.[187] They chatted further about the situation and the doctor told her that Albert had retained him to take sole charge of Eric for £1,000 a year.[188]

This was a bombshell.

Palmer immediately jumped up objecting that this was hearsay and Baines had not been asked about it. Hanson said he had not known about the conversation either.

Palmer commented that it was a very piecemeal way of giving evidence and unfair to those who had to watch out for the interests of persons concerned. The Coroner said he agreed in principle with him but added that if the evidence appeared in any way material to the trial, he could not justify excluding it. He did not want to leave any reason to suggest that the second inquiry was insufficient or that he had shut out any evidence, particularly as the first inquiry had been criticised. Palmer continued to argue that hearsay evidence could not be called legal evidence and whilst the Coroner agreed it might not be admissible in ordinary courts, at his inquiry he did not think he should exclude it.

Palmer sarcastically retorted that he must therefore rely on Hanson to as to what questions he put and Hanson snapped back, 'If my friend does not want to hear a conversation that is alleged to have taken place between Mr Roe and Dr Baines, let him say so … the only question I was going to ask this witness was as to a conversation that Dr Baines is alleged to have had with Mr Roe.'

'But Dr Baines has never been asked about it.'

'Are you afraid?' taunted Hanson.

'I am afraid of nothing,' Palmer thundered, 'and you have no right to put that to me, except that this inquiry will never finish. That is what I object to.'

Hanson then said he would leave it up to Coroner Benson to decide whether he could ask Nurse Rice the question but Benson was worried about making the decision because, although he had looked at the proof for a moment or two before he came into court, he had not gone through it very carefully. Hanson offered a compromise: if the witness did say anything which was not strictly evidence, Benson could instruct the jury accordingly.

'There is so much that might be evidence in this court that would not be evidence in another court that I cannot exclude it,' Benson reasoned, 'I quite agree that it is most desirable this inquiry should not be prolonged more than is necessary, but I must bear in mind the fact that Mr Hanson is representing the relatives.'

'I am here to help the jury arrive at a proper decision,' offered Hanson and added, 'If any one does not want the jury to arrive at a proper decision, let him say so.'

Palmer immediately bristled, 'If that is a challenge to me, I am here for the same reason.'

The Coroner cut them both short saying, 'We are all here to get at the truth.'

Finally, the Coroner decided that if Hanson thought it should be included then they would include it. Muir, for the Public Prosecution added, 'I think it will be most unsatisfactory if any evidence that can be of any use or is at all relevant is shut out.'

Having now gained permission to continue, Hanson asked the nurse to repeat the allegation that Baines was going to be on a retainer of £1,000 a year and that Albert was going to be Eric's guardian. She said that Baines was given the choice to either live in the flat or in his own house but Baines, who was sitting on the bench, vigorously shook his head.[189]

Nurse Rice had no recollection of any discussions about Albert getting married and could not remember passing any comment about the arrangement when Benson told her.

After Eric's death, she had sent a registered letter to Eric's mother, explaining that she had nursed Eric three weeks before his death and would like to see some members of the family. She received a reply from the solicitors for the executors saying, 'Your registered letter addressed to Mr H. E. Trevanion has been handed to us, as solicitors for the executors. We do not quite understand the object of your letter, but if you would like to see us we should be pleased to see you.'

Palmer dryly observed that she had addressed the letter to a dead man and therefore nobody had the right to open it, but Hanson brushed off his objection, 'I do not complain about that.'

'What are you complaining of?' Palmer said with sarcasm.

'I am complaining about the solicitor keeping the letter,' replied Hanson. Nurse Rice had gone to the flat after Eric's death to see Mrs Trevanion but could not get in so she addressed a letter to Eric's old London flat and from there it was passed to the solicitors. Mrs Trevanion had not been made aware of it and so could not make an informed decision as to whether she wanted to see the nurse.

'Are we going to try the solicitors for that?' Palmer sneered.

'I wish you would not interrupt me,' Hanson told him, 'It is not a bit funny. Anyone with half an eye could see why the letter was kept. The letter was carefully kept away from Mrs Trevanion and the members of the family. The solicitors are not acting for the family at all.'

Palmer said nothing and so Hanson turned back to Nurse Rice, 'About three days before Christmas, did you meet Mrs Joiner?'

The nurse said she had and related their conversation. Mary Joiner had told her that Albert would not have the nurse sent for and that the Trevanions' lawyers were 'after her' -presumably for her testimony - Albert apparently saying that £50 would buy a woman like Rice any day. 'Mrs Joiner said his conversation about Nurse Rice was most disgusting,' the nurse told the court, 'She said she had never heard such disgusting language in all her life.'

Rice told Mary Joiner not to be so complacent, that 'probably now that Mr Roe had got the money he would turn them out,' but Mary Joiner replied, 'that they were not going unless they got a good lump sum, or unless they were well paid – some such phrase as that.'

When Hanson had finished with his questions, Palmer rose to ask when she had first made this statement about the conversation with Mary Joiner. Rice replied that it was just the day before. She had not spoken to anyone from the Director of Public Prosecution's office and when she was put in the box on the last occasion, she did not make the statement because, 'No one asked me.'

The Coroner seemed shocked and asked if he understood that 'you to say you had never made a statement to anyone before you were called on the last occasion?'

'No,' she said, 'Only to Inspector Parsons,' after she had written the letter.

Benson asked if she had written the letter because she had information she had wanted to give. She replied that she had just wanted to speak to the boy's mother. When she had spoken to Inspector Parsons, she had told him what she knew.

Benson was confused, 'But what you have told us today only occurred to you yesterday?'

'Some of it I told to Inspector Parsons', Rice replied, 'About the conversation with Mrs Joiner ... and Dr Baines ... going to have charge of the patient for £1,000 a year ... then Dr Baines was very interested in keeping the young man alive.' To which the court laughed and Nurse Rice added, 'Yes, he was very sorry he died.'

Muir asked what she remembered Dr Baines saying about Eric. 'He said he was going to have Mr Trevanion for £1,000 a year, and he was not going to take on any more new patients, but was going to retain a few of his old patients.'

'Who was going to pay him the money?'

'Mr Roe.'

She did not know what position Albert would be taking in Eric's life although Dr Baines implied that Albert would be some sort of guardian.

'How was Mr Roe to get the £1,000 a year?'

'He already had control of the patient's money,' adding that all her previous fees had been paid by Albert.

According to her understanding, Eric was going to live either in the flat or at Dr Baines' house but she didn't know where Albert was going to live. She understood Albert wouldn't be necessary but she didn't know what he was going to do - only that he was to retain the use of the motor car.

Muir pressed home the point, 'Mr Roe was not going to be there?'

'No.'

'Was it suggested why Mr Roe was not going to be there?'

'I think it was inferred he was going to be married.'

'How did you get that idea?'

'The question of marriage was talked about. Mr Roe was engaged to a widow. Dr Baines said there was a young woman whom he was constantly going to see down in Swansea, and he was going to be married to her.'

Albert must have known Mrs Derrick for several months before he proposed to her but only Dr Baines seems to have been aware of the relationship. Given how open Eric was about his unhappiness, he never mentions a woman in Albert's life so it is possible he never knew about her until the engagement announcement. This could explain why he took two overdoses in the month before his death. Either he really was attempting suicide or he was trying to shock Albert into returning to him. It would also support arguments elsewhere that the doctor and Albert were closer than they let on.

'Did Dr Baines say whether he was going to have any further employment with Mr Roe?' 'No'

'Was anything said in this case about a trump card?'

'Yes. He said he was going to give evidence for Roe and help him get the money. He said being a doctor, he 'had Roe's trump card', as he was with the deceased when he died.'[190]

'When did this conversation take place?'

'About a week after the boy's death.'

'The first inquest was over.'

'Yes, but I did not go there.'

'In what proceedings was it that Dr Baines's evidence would be a trump card?'

'I suppose in reference to gaining the money.'

Mr Godlee, who had attended all the proceedings on behalf of the solicitors, was asked to confirm that they had received a letter. He did so, saying that it had been addressed to Eric on the outside but to Mrs Trevanion on the letter itself. Godlee said that at his office they believed the writer had the impression that Eric was married, so had not passed it on and did not understand what the letter writer meant. Nurse Rice probably made a simple mistake in addressing the letter but she never replied to the solicitor's letter nor did she meet with them.

There the testimony of Nurse Rice ended. In the meantime, the three Swansea witnesses had been interviewed by the Public Prosecutor and it was decided their evidence was not relevant, so they were not going to be included. However, when the inquiry was to be resumed, there was the prospect of other Swansea evidence being called. The inquiry was then adjourned until the Friday.[191]

The testimony of Nurse Rice was quite extraordinary if it is to be believed. Albert had made arrangements for Eric to be 'looked after' by Dr Baines for a fee of around £1,000 a year. In which case, it is quite understandable for him to be upset that Eric had died. Albert would be freed of all responsibilities, able to get married and keep the £10,000 which he had possession of, not to mention the lease on the flat and all Eric's possessions. Is it possible he told Eric this? Was the delicate and depressed young man driven to suicide at the idea of Albert leaving him and of committing him to the care of someone else? Albert believed Eric had been cut off from his family, unaware that Eric was seeing them behind his back, but did he implant in Eric's mind the thought that Albert could legally sign him into medical care?

Dr Baines would have to be called back but before that could happen, the court adjourned for three days.

There followed a rustle of excitement as Dr Baines was recalled.

DR BAINES RECALLED

'I think you were present in court at the last sitting when Nurse Rice gave some evidence?' Muir asked and Baines agreed. 'Do you wish to make any statement about it?'

'In what way?' asked Baines.

'Do you wish to make any statement in answer?'

'Yes.'

'Do you wish to deny it? I think it only right to give you the fullest opportunity of saying whether the statements she made are true or not.'

'Some were true and some were not true,' Baines answered.

"Well, shall I just take you through her statements? Muir took him through what Nurse Rice had said about him taking charge of Eric for £1,000 a year and that Albert was to be guardian.

'The conversation was with Mr Roe when the boy lay ill,' explained Baines, 'Mr Roe said he could not take any further responsibility. The strain was too great for him.' They had spoken sometime in the middle of the night as Eric lay ill on the 9th. Baines had advised Albert to get a medical man to take charge of him and Albert asked, 'Will you take it on?' I said, 'Yes, but I shall want a big sum. You see, it was a troublesome case and caused great anxiety, and I named a thousand pounds.'

'That was all that passed?' asked Muir.

Baines thought for a while before replying, 'Then Mr Roe said, "I think he will agree to that," meaning of course the boy. That is all that passed between us.'

Palmer rose and asked, 'I want to ask you about this conversation, Dr Baines. As I understand it, this conversation took place when the deceased was suffering from the last overdose … and Mr Roe at that time was naturally very much upset, and he said he really could not undertake the responsibility for him any longer.' Baines agreed, but to Palmer's next question about living in the flat or his house, he said it was never discussed. Palmer asked if Baines was intending to retire with the £1,000 and he said no, he could not afford to give up his practice, at least not his old patients. He also denied that Albert had said anything about becoming Eric's guardian only saying, 'I cannot stand the strain any longer.' They had not discussed how or by whom the money was to be paid.

If this was such as casual a conversation as Baines implied and no details had been made, why did he tell Nurse Rice a week after Eric died? She specifically uses the word 'retained' inferring something which had already been agreed and she obviously had not made the story up as Baines confirmed most of it.

'Was the nurse very angry with Mr Roe?' Palmer asked.

'Exceedingly angry,' said Baines.

'Because she was not called in on the last occasion?'

'Yes.'

'I think the calling in of the nurse was left entirely to you?'

'Practically so.'

'And Nurse Hawkins was sent for then?'

'I believe so, but I cannot tell you the name.'

Baines stated that he had not known Eric wanted Nurse Rice back if he was taken ill again and denied knowing there was an arrangement.

'Why did you say you had forgotten her telephone number?'

'I don't know I'm sure' replied the ever-vague Baines. He insisted that he had simply telephoned the nursing home, as private nurses were not always home and he didn't know which nurse was coming.

'Did the nurse say what she would do for Mr Roe?'

'Must I say?'Baines asked. When Palmer insisted, he replied, 'She said she would "make it hot" for him.' He then made disconnected statements denying that he was 'the trump card' and adding that Eric had told him he had left everything to Albert, 'I said he should have left some to the family, at least the pictures. He said he would sooner burn them.'

Hanson asked when this conversation had taken place but Baines could not remember if it was Sunday 8 September, the day before Eric went into the coma, or the Sunday before that. It might be thought that having endured the trauma of Eric's coma, Baines would have remembered if he'd just seen the young man the day before. Besides, it could not have been the previous week as that would make it 1 September, the day after the Tunbridge incident, and the chauffeur testified that Eric remained in bed all day on that Sunday.

Therefore, on Sunday 8 September, Eric had called Baines in the morning asking him come to the flat as he 'seemed ill' and, as he sounded depressed, Baines said he would drive over later and have tea with him. When he arrived, Eric was in bed having tea and several workmen were about the flat so they went into the dining room. Baines says 'I complained then about his crying' so Eric asked him to go on a drive and they went to Chichester that afternoon, (the chauffeur does not mention this). 'I believe it was the only time I went out in the car with him.' Albert was not there and Baines supposed he was in Swansea.

'Can you remember how the conversation led up to his telling you how he had left everything to Mr Roe?'

'No.' Baines said, and added that he did not know if Albert was aware either. He insisted that he had not told Albert or anyone else, as that would be a breach of confidence.

196

'At any rate, he did not seem to make any secret about it. He spoke to you quite openly?'

'He spoke to me as his medical man.'

'Quite openly … did he bind you over to secrecy?... Or say that he did not want anybody to know?'

'No,' said Baines.

Returning to Nurse Rice's claims, Baines admitted that he did have a conversation with her after the inquest but could not remember when it was. He confirmed that there was a suggestion for him to look after Eric for £1,000 a year but denied anything else was said.

'What she did say was that she could not understand why I took Mr Roe's part because she said Mr Roe said that money would buy any woman, and he used bad language, and I said, "Nurse, you must not believe all you hear. I never do." She had assumed that because I did not agree with her, I must have been siding with Roe.' Baines did not believe that Albert would say that any woman could be bought with money and when Muir asked him to pledge his reputation on that, Baines said, 'Yes, because I told her I did not care two pence which side won, and I don't.'

'Was anything said about the will being disputed at this conversation with Nurse Rice?' Baines replied that he expected it was and he agreed they did discuss his being called to give evidence in support of the will. He also confirmed that on the evening of Eric's death, 'I saw Mrs Trevanion and Mr Cecil Trevanion, Mrs Trevanion told me that her son had left everything to Mr Roe.'[192] This meant that Mrs Trevanion's version of events was true as the only way she could have known about the will was if Albert had told her.

Muir tried to push Baines that a doctor who was the last to treat Eric would be in a position to be a 'trump card' but Baines didn't agree.

Hanson asked if he had room to accommodate a patient at his house. Baines admitted he had a spare room but when asked about the size of the house he replied, 'I cannot tell you.' Hanson was confused, 'How do you mean? Surely you know the size of your own house?'

'There is a dining room, consulting room, and a drawing room, - that's three - and a double drawing room… five bedrooms

'– I think.' As before when he was on the stand, Baines' nervousness made his statements appear foolish.

The foreman of the jury asked if Eric had ever complained to him about Albert and Baines said he had not. He also denied that any money had passed between him and Albert, presumably with reference to him taking permanent care of Eric.

Baines was not a reliable witness, his vague and evasive answers made him look suspicious but if the £1,000 retainer is to be believed then he would not have benefitted from Eric's death. However, another aspect to consider is that in the early twentieth century, a doctor could confine a patient to a lunatic asylum for a variety of reasons, including homosexuality. If Baines was seen to be colluding with Albert to deny Eric his freedom, this could have contributed to suicidal thoughts, placing them both in a dangerous situation. In which case, he may well have wanted to play down the whole thing.

MARY JOINER RECALLED

When Mary Joiner retook the stand, she was asked if she remembered the conversation with Nurse Rice. She answered that it had taken place three days before Christmas in Western Road and the nurse had asked Mary if she knew a will was going to be disputed. Mary said that she told Nurse Rice that she had heard nothing, which is difficult to believe. Investigations into Eric's life had been ongoing since his exhumation in October and many people had been questioned, It is unlikely Mrs Joiner would not have known the will was in dispute.

Nurse Rice then asked if Mary Joiner thought Eric was insane, 'No,' she replied, 'he is as sane as I or you.' However, there was obviously animosity between the women. According to Joiner, Rice then claimed that 'her references as nurse would go before ours and I replied, "Yes, £50 would go a long way to buy a woman like you!"'.

Benson was surprised, 'You did?' he asked.

'Yes,' said Joiner with emphasis, 'Yes, I did …. She asked me if I was aware that a certain sum of money had been offered by Mr Eric to Dr Baines to look after him, and I said no, I was not aware of any such thing. She also said she had had it on very good authority that we were to be turned out at a minute's notice. Well, we sold up a good home and my husband gave up a good position to come to Hove, and they could not very well do that, because justice would be done to us.'[193]

Despite Joiner thinking it was Eric who had offered Baines money to look after him, it was Albert. Baines confirmed that in his testimony and, given Eric's feelings for Albert, it does not ring true that Eric would simply replace the man he loved for a doctor.

Hanson rose and asked, 'Do you remember a gentleman calling on you on the 20th of September?' This was before Eric had been exhumed and was probably part of the police investigation instigated by Mrs Trevanion's complaints.

'I remember someone coming up the back staircase twice, and also putting a type-written agreement before me which he asked me to put my name to.'

'Your husband signed it?'

'Yes, my husband signed it but I declined.'

'Did you have an interview with that gentleman?'

'No.'

According to Joiner, she never had any conversation with the man who wanted her to sign. He husband told her that: 'he had come to take a statement of what we knew was transpiring or going on in the flat,' but she was not present when the man spoke to her husband.

Hanson warned her, 'Try and be careful, Mrs Joiner.'

'I am being careful,' she told him, and Hanson seemed surprised by her claim that nobody had spoken to her for any testimony.

'Did you say this,' he asked, "I am not surprised that this gentleman is making inquiries, I expected that inquiries would be made and that another inquest would have to take place?"'

'No such words ever passed my lips. I was too indignant with him for coming up the back staircase to have a conversation with him.' The court laughed.[194]

When asked why she thought the man was there, she replied that, in her opinion, he was there to try and gain as much information as possible about life in the flat. When Hanson said it was surely about the death, Mrs Joiner disagreed, saying that it was as much about his life as it was about his death. She said she didn't know what her husband had put in his statement and denied that she had tried to stop him signing but she did eventually sign it herself outside the back door.

Palmer struggled to understand why she had signed a statement that she had never seen. 'And you,' he said to her 'not being a fool, refused to put your name to it?'

'Yes. The man said, "Here missus, I want you to put your name to this," and I said, "I never made that statement and I am not going to put my name to it."'

Why then had Mrs Joiner agreed to sign it after all? Despite the arguments in court about the admissibility of hearsay evidence, the statement the couple signed was never brought into evidence. Of all the people who would have known intimate details of Eric and Albert's life together it would have been the Joiners; but as the wife had pointed out to both Nurse Rice and the court, she insisted 'justice would be done to us' - she wanted a pay-out.

Palmer asked if Eric had liked Nurse Rice and she said no, that he had said something about disliking her smoking in the flat. She denied that Eric had ever wanted the nurse to come back to take care of him telling her, 'If ever that woman comes again, Mrs Joiner, don't let her in the house.' It is possible that Eric was annoyed with Rice when she had taken care of him during one of the August overdoses, as she had wrestled with him to take pills away from his mouth.

Joiner did agree that Eric used to sit and chat and drink champagne with the nurse, which indicates there may not have been that much animosity. She said Rice never said anything against Albert but then changed her mind and said there was an incident she recalled. After the August overdose, Rice was waiting for Albert to come back before she left and Eric suggested she have her hair done by the hairdresser in his bedroom. According to Joiner as the nurse came out, she said, 'I consider Mr Roe is a pig,' because he had gone into the bedroom and had not recognised her.

'Oh, I see, he did not pay her enough attention?' asked Palmer.

'Yes, that's it, sir,' and added, 'I said we had always found Mr Roe a gentleman, and as such I should always speak of him.' She had never heard Albert use disgusting language or say a wrong word about the nurse or anyone else and it had been her who made the £50 comment, not Albert.

Muir wanted to clear up some timing discrepancies on the night of the Eric being taken ill. She had said that coffee was served about 9pm, but couldn't remember if dinner had been served at quarter past or half past eight, although her husband had said it was served at 8pm or a quarter past. She said he wasn't sure about the time.

She remembered that coffee had been served in the den and that she had seen Albert sitting in the dining room about half past nine. When the coffee was served, he left the dining room and went to the den and then she saw him back in the dining room. Albert never mentions returning to the dining room so early; according to him he remained in the den until he went to bed at 11pm and left because Joiner was pouring the wine. Given the trauma that was to follow, it is not surprising that exact timings could not be remembered accurately.

Joiner had not seen Eric again until after dinner when they were called to help with the emetic. She had retired about a quarter to eleven and whilst she did not know the exact time her husband had come to bed, she believed his estimate of 11.05-11.10 to be about right as he always had a smoke after she had left. When they were called, she got dressed and fetched the mustard for the emetic.

'I looked at the clock,' she said, 'because I was waiting to open the door for Dr Baines and when I heard the lift, I opened the door to save him ringing because I did not want my baby to wake up.' That, she said, was ten to twelve and, yes, her clock was right.

After Mary Joiner's evidence had been reported in the newspapers, letters were sent to the Coroner defending Nurse Rice. One from an unsigned source stated that 'all the things said against Nurse Rice are not true' and that they 'ought to be contradicted or steps may go against her in her profession which is her living.' She was, the writer claimed 'quite to be trusted.' Rachel da Costa Andrada Benatar also wrote saying that Nurse Rice had nursed both her mother, her aunt, and herself and wrote, 'I think that you ought not to have allowed that servant woman to swear such lies about one of the kindest and sweetest of nurses whom I have ever met in my life time.'

THE BUTLER AGAIN

Muir recalled Mr Joiner merely to clarify the time he opened the bottle of hock. Joiner said he was not certain but it was about five past ten - not as late as 10.55 as Albert had testified.[195] However, as Albert and the picture framer, Ham, said the discussion about the outstanding bill took place around 10.15pm in the den, it is probable that Joiner was wrong in his timing.

11

DAY 7 – FRIDAY 14 FEBRUARY: THE MISSING WITNESSES

Once again, just as it looked as though the inquest was about to be wound up, the *Cambrian Daily Leader* announced that their representative at Brighton had sent a telegram saying that there were missing witnesses. These were Tom Wilks, an electrical engineer of the Dunvant area of Swansea and a Mr J Campbell, a jeweller of the Swansea Arcade.[196]

Both men had refused to attend and Muir had requested some time to enforce their attendance by formal process. He had been reluctant to delay proceedings yet again but referred back to the Coroner's comments about avoiding any possible criticism over excluding evidence. He added that if it were impossible for Benson to grant the extra week then he would drop the witnesses, adding that he had tried as hard as he could, but the Coroner agreed with Muir. He had read what the men were going to say and felt their testimony should be included even though they might not say in the inquest what they had said in their statements.

In the meantime, Albert's Swansea family had received a number of extraordinary anonymous letters. Although the *Leader* said that, whilst it was aware of the content, it was not in a position to make them public.[197] The letters were forwarded to Palmer and the *Leader* speculated whether he would include them at the inquest as, even though it had been decided it would close on Friday, Palmer could ask they be added as an amendment.

However, the letters were not presented at the inquest and they are not held at the ESRO, so the content is unknown. Perhaps they followed the same lines as the rumours that were swirling throughout Swansea: that a well-known milliner had been interviewed by a stranger about her customers (although why was not made clear); that there had been a motor journey from Swansea to Brecon that was something to do with Albert's marriage but then it turned out Albert was not in the car; that

Albert was already married; that Claude had been to Swansea making his own investigations; and that Detective Inspector Ward from Scotland Yard had also been in town for a few days and subpoenaed several people.[198]

As well as printing such rumours, the *Cambrian Daily Leader* also discussed Eric's will. According to them, 'it has been stated' that the 'principal allegation' in one of the caveats to prevent it being enacted was 'undue influence.'

To clarify, they referred to the case of Wingrove v Wingrove, in which Lord Hannen gave the definitive definition, always quoted in these types of cases:

> To give you some illustration of what I mean, a young man may be caught in the toils of a harlot, who makes use of her influence to induce him to make a will in her favour to the exclusion of his relatives; yet the law does not attempt to guard against these contingencies. Or a man may be the companion of another, and may encourage him in evil courses, and so obtain what is called an undue influence over him, and the consequence is a will in his favour. But that again, shocking as it is – perhaps even worse that the other – will not amount to undue influence. To make undue influence in the eye of the law there must be – to sum it up in a word – coercion. The coercion may be of different kinds; it may be the grossest form, such as actual confinement or violence, or a person in the last days or hours of life may have become so weak and feel that a very little pressure will be sufficient to bring about the desired result, and it may even be that the mere talking to him at that stage of illness and pressing something upon him may so fatigue the brain that the sick person may be induced for quietness' sake to do anything. This would equally be coercion, though not actual violence.[199]

This is a bold statement by the *Leader*. By including a definition that speaks of 'a man may be the companion of another' and 'the mere talking' at a time of illness and fatigue, were they implying Albert exerted 'undue influence'?

They certainly drew attention to their piece by adding a heading in capital letters and quotation marks yet, following Lord Hannen's definition, they made no further comment, leaving readers to make up their own mind as to why they had included it. The *Leader* never identified who had 'stated' that the will would be disputed on these grounds and no other newspaper included this reference. When journalists had discussed the caveats a month earlier, including the *Cambrian Daily Leader,* nobody had mentioned 'undue influence'. It may be that the press chose not to include the reference to avoid influencing the jury and now that the inquest was coming to an end, the *Leader* felt more confident to include the reference; however, they were the only ones who did so.

On the last day of the inquest, the Coroner finally opened proceedings at noon explaining that one of the jurors had been taken ill but as far as he was concerned, they still had two more than was absolutely necessary for a verdict.

Albert arrived with a number of friends from Swansea; accountant, Brinley Bowen; his brother-in-law, Hanlon; Andrew Paton; Edwin Ford from a private inquiry agency; and J. Campbell.

A ROPE AROUND HIS NECK

Jack Cranston (not Fenton as some newspapers reported) Campbell, was a jeweller at the Alexandra Arcade in Swansea and his refusal to attend the inquest had caused a great sensation.

Campbell had made a statement on 5 February to Chief Inspector Ward and was asked to go to Hove on the 7th to appear as a witness but he claimed the statement he had made to Ward was not true and made when he was drunk. He also claimed that Ward had not identified himself as a police officer so he didn't really know who he was talking to.

Unable to get Campbell to give evidence, it was left to Ward to explain to the solicitors and Coroner Benson that the reason the jeweller had refused to sign his statement was that he was unwilling to 'go against a man he had known all his life, and get a rope round his neck.' That, said Campbell, was too far. In the official inquest transcripts, Campbell states that he would 'not get him hanged'[200] but the original statement made to Ward has not been kept.

What could Campbell have possibly said that would put a rope around Albert's neck? The death penalty for homosexuality had been removed in 1861, so it is unlikely that Campbell was referring to that unless it was simply a turn of phrase. It could also, of course, mean that Campbell thought Albert was either guilty of murder or pushing Eric to suicide. Whatever it was, it seemed to be something that Campbell believed was too dangerous to be made public.

In the end, Campbell was subpoenaed to give evidence.

Muir asked if he had made a statement to Ward on the 5 February but Campbell replied that he did not know the date, just that it was a Wednesday. When asked why he would not give evidence, Campbell told Muir that what he had said was not true and that as soon as he was sober, he had told Ward.

Muir asked, 'Was there a man named Ford present when you were asked to sign it?'

'No.'

'Did he tell you not to sign anything?'

'He said something to that effect.'

'Don't sign anything and don't go to London?'

The source Muir was quoting from was not covered but he evidently had access to some sort of information showing that Ford, the private agent working for Albert, had persuaded him not to go.

'No, he did not say that,' insisted Campbell.

'Don't go to London they cannot make you?' Muir continued to quote.

'I cannot say that.'

'Is Mr Ford a private detective?'

'He is a private inquiry agent.'

'Has Mr Ford come up from Swansea with his solicitor today?'

'He came up with me.'

'And his solicitor?'

'The solicitor followed us up.'

'Have you any idea at whose expense the solicitor has come up?'

'I have not, sir.'

Muir decided he did not want to ask Campbell any more questions but would ask Detective Inspector Ward to take the stand. Before that however, Hanson questioned Campbell and asked him if he had taken the statement on the Wednesday or Thursday but all he could remember was that some people fetched him from one public-house and took him to the *Adam and Eve* pub in Swansea at about 5pm. After he had refused to appear at the inquest, Hanson had travelled down to Swansea to meet with him and at the bar had offered him a drink, so he said he would have a whisky.

'Do you remember I said, "Campbell, are you coming up by this next train to London?"'

'Yes, I heard you say that … I refused to go.'

'I know that,' continued Hanson, 'and did I not tell you that I thought you were very silly; that you had already made a statement to Detective Inspector Ward, and that if you did not go, you would probably have to be fetched up?'

'No, I don't remember that but I may have said that.'

'Do you remember my saying, "I take it that the statement you made to Detective Inspector Ward is true."'

'No.'

'Where was Ford then?'

'I don't know where he was then but I believe he had been there previously.'

'He had just that minute left, had he not?'

'He had been gone about an hour before as far as I can remember.'

Hanson continued in his attempt to get Campbell to admit to his Swansea evidence and that he had been influenced by Ford to recant, but the man refused to be drawn simply claiming he did not remember anything and that he was drunk.

Hanson took one last stab, 'Do you remember saying you were not going to give evidence against a man you had known all your life and get him hanged, unless you were fetched?'

'No, I did not say that.'

Unable to get any more out of Campbell, Chief Inspector Ward was brought to the stand.

JACK, DON'T YOU SIGN ANYTHING

Chief Inspector Alfred Ward of the Criminal Investigation

Department, Scotland Yard was one of the most experienced and respected detectives in Britain. Although he had joined Scotland Yard just two years earlier, he had been involved in many high-profile cases. He specialised in poisoning, demonstrating how seriously the police were taking Eric's death.

Ward said that he had met Campbell on the afternoon of Wednesday 5 February in the back room of the *Black Swan* pub and that he had taken his statement down in his pocket book which Campbell then signed. Campbell was quite sober when he signed it.

'Did he mention the name of anybody else who could corroborate him?'

'Yes … Edward Ford.'

The following day Ward spoke to Ford who refused to make a statement, so he went back to Campbell and

found him in the *Adam and Eve* about 10.30am. Ward had taken a room there and Campbell was probably looking for him. Ward had with him a typed version of the statement and asked Campbell to read it and confirm it was correct. When Campbell said it was accurate, Ward asked him to walk around to the Central Police Station to sign but when they got there about 11am, Campbell suddenly refused.

A FAMOUS DETECTIVE.

A photograph of Detective-Inspector Ward, the famous Scotland Yard official, who visited Swansea yesterday.

'Did he then, or at any time, tell you that statement was false?' asked Muir.

'Never.'

'Now, was anyone else in the police office building at the same time?'

'Yes … the man Ford stood in the passage, talking to Mr Hanson, as they walked through. Ford said to Campbell, "Jack, don't you sign anything," after which Campbell refused to sign.'

'What did he say when he refused to sign the statement?'

'He said if it was only a

matter of getting the money back he would not care, but to give evidence against a man he had known all his life, and to get a rope round his neck was going a bit too far.'

Muir had obviously done some research into the private agent's background and was curious who was paying the fees of Ford's solicitor as he was not a wealthy man.

Ward didn't know so Muir asked if he knew the whereabouts of Ford's solicitor the night before. Again, the Detective didn't know for sure and all he could say was that he'd heard that the man had been at Paddington Station with Albert. When asked if he had seen the solicitor that morning, the Detective said yes, with Albert. Muir was obviously trying to stress a link between the solicitor, Ford and Albert.

Palmer got up to defuse Muir's implication and asked Ward to confirm that it was only a rumour that the solicitor had met Albert. In truth, he went on to say, the solicitor had met a friend who had come from Swansea. Ward could not comment but said he had seen the solicitor at Victoria Station talking to Albert but Palmer played that down, saying that almost everybody in the inquiry that day had come down on the same train.

Palmer asked if the Detective had made inquiries in Swansea about Campbell's character. Ward replied he had been working closely with the Swansea police and, as far as he knew, Campbell had never been in trouble. He asked if Ford had said that Campbell had told a pack of lies and the Detective said no.

'That he was one of the biggest liars in Swansea?'

'No. Ford always led me to believe that what he said was true until Tuesday last.'

'How many public houses did you take Campbell into?'

'I never took him into any. He was brought into a public house where I arranged to have a room.' Apart from this meeting in the *Adam and Eve,* he went to no other pub and the only other time Ward saw Campbell was in passing when he was in his shop in the arcade.

As he finished his questioning, Palmer added, 'I don't quite know what Mr Muir insinuates about solicitors coming up with Ford but so far as Mr Roe is concerned, all I have to say is we have got nothing to do with any solicitors coming up with Ford.'

The Coroner then debated whether he should sum up before

lunch but as that would mean separating the jury, he asked if they would be prepared to carry on. The foreman enquired how long the Coroner would take to sum up but Benson would not commit: 'I don't like to mention any precise time … you see, we may have questions to ask you, and you may want a good deal of evidence read over, but I am inclined to think you would be able to get away to your lunch before you were utterly exhausted before the afternoon was very late.'

Before the Coroner could start, Palmer interrupted and said, 'I have been asked to state, on behalf of Mr Ford, that he had never met Mr Roe until last night. He had never seen him before. I am asked to state that in order a false impression may not be created.'

Hanson also wanted to add something, 'Some question was raised,' he said, 'as to the terms the deceased and his mother were on. I put in letters written in 1911 and 1912, which I should like the jury to see. There are other letters in 1906, 1907, 1908 and 1909, couched in the same affectionate terms, and written by the deceased to his mother.'

The Coroner asked, 'You wish the jury to see them?'

'Yes. It was stated that, in 1906, the deceased told Roe that he was on very bad terms with his mother. Their letters deny that.'

Agreeing, the Coroner handed the letters to the jury and told them they had to judge for themselves what inferences if any they wanted to make.[201]

12

SUMMING UP

Coroner Benson started his summary at 12.35. It lasted an hour and forty-five minutes. He began:

> I think I can congratulate you, gentlemen of the jury, on having reached the last stage of this inquiry. I can say with justification that the inquiry has not been insufficient. You have had a great mass of evidence put before you during the seven days of this inquiry. The evidence fills altogether some one hundred and twenty pages of closely typed depositions which require a good deal of digesting. No doubt, you gentlemen have already digested a good deal of what you have heard … it is my duty to put before you the salient points of the evidence so far as they are material, and to make such comment on them as may be likely to be helpful to you…
>
> All counsel can do is to put facts before you without commenting upon them. It is only the Coroner who can properly make any comments upon the evidence, and you are the only judges of the conclusion to be drawn from the evidence. In a Coroner's Court there are no definite issues, nor is there any formal charges against anyone, we are simply holding an inquiry, and the only question that is likely to present any difficulty to you is the question how the deceased came by his death, and with regard to that the material agent of his death is proved, I think, beyond question to your satisfaction. I assume that you are satisfied that it was the drug Veronal, taken in a very large dose on the night of the 9th September…

Now, how did the deceased come to take this fatal dose? Was it taken by the deceased, and, if so, with what object and intention, or was it given him by someone else, and, if so, by whom, and with what object and intention. If you can answer either of these questions fully you have gone a long way, if not the whole way towards answering the other one.[202]

The Coroner then spent some time trying to account for how Eric could have taken 150 grains. He seemed to think, based on the example of Eric buying the drugs at Douthwaite's when he retained just the one, that he usually only took single doses. He did not take into account that Albert had said he usually took two. Benson continued that the dose could not be accidental, or a mishap and reminded the jury that Eric had the idea he could take enormous doses. He said there was a good deal to support the idea of suicide.

He then summarised the timeline of the night Eric died, before asking if Albert had any motive to want Eric dead. Albert had a great deal to gain by the death and any suspicious foul play would undoubtedly fall up him:

Let us examine in some detail the grounds on which suspicion may be entertained with regard to Roe. There is suspicion which precedes proof, and which may exist in the absence of proof. By Trevanion's death Roe gained a fortune and freedom, and a very considerable fortune without restriction of any kind as to its use. Apart from the fortune, he would be gaining absolute release from the duties, whatever they were, of acting as companion and bedfellow to a delicate and eccentric young man. He would at once become free and enjoy £10,000; perhaps marry, and make a career for himself. Roe was a young man still in the prime of life, about 35 years of age. Imagine the life he was actually leading as companion to this effeminate and ridiculous young man, with his incurable addiction to drugs and drink, so that death would be a heavenly relief. Roe would have been more than human in the contingency of Trevanion's death had not occurred to him, and presented itself as a consummation devoutly to be wished for.

I want to examine a more important question, and that is – did anyone else give that to him, or was there foul play of any sort? No, on this point: Who could have given it to him, or who had the opportunity of giving it to him?

Benson said that only Albert and Joiner were present on the evening of the overdose and while there was a possible motive, he added that it would 'be a gross libel on human nature to conclude that every person who was to benefit by another person's death desired that event to occur'.

Benson brought the jury's attention to the conflicting evidence given by Albert and Mrs Trevanion about when Albert became aware of being the main beneficiary of Eric's will. They would, he said, have to make up their own minds, but added:

Is it likely that Roe knew nothing about the will? He lived on extremely intimate terms with the deceased, who spoke freely of his money affairs and his family quarrels, and certainly told Dr Sandifer and Dr Baines what he had done. It is likely, do you think, that Roe knew nothing about the will, or about Trevanion's testamentary depositions, of which he had made many altered and them. Consider carefully how it came about that Roe had so much to gain by Trevanion's death; consider the history of this case and the ever-increasing financial benefits, out of all proportion apparently to the services of a companion to a delicate gentleman. What is the meaning of this extravagant generosity on part of the deceased? ... We may believe the witnesses Sandifer and others who tell us that Trevanion himself said that Roe kept him off the drugs and drink, and other witnesses who say that Roe did his best to check the fancies of this youth for that ridiculous get up, with his painted face,

powdered hair, jewellery and high heeled white satin
shoes and all the rest of it; and that Roe was kind to
the boy. There is a great deal of testimony to that,
and there is no single instance mention of unkindness
… the fact remains that in some way, good or bad, by
fair means or foul, Roe had established a dominant
influence over the boy, and could, by being firm or
severe, get Trevanion to do most things that he
wanted him to do … We know that Trevanion was
devoted to Roe, but an affection not unconnected,
perhaps, with those effeminate characteristics which
were so noticeable in the boy. We know that under
the influence of those mingled feelings of fear and
love, or whatever it was, the boy did in fact heap
ever-increasing financial benefits upon Roe.'

Albert, sitting listening to this, may well have been concerned
about this portrayal and the outcome it might have, particularly
as Benson reminded the jury that it had only taken six months for
him to go from a salary of £50 a quarter to having £10,000 and
then being left an entire estate. He continued:

considering the almost insane infatuation of the boy
for his companion, but it has an ugly look, and can
Roe complain if he is regarded by the friends of
Trevanion and others as an unscrupulous adventurer,
capable of doing anything to secure the fortune of
the boy.

Benson also pointed out that Eric was living far beyond his
means and had he continued to do so, his fortune would have been
lost, making it necessary to ask Albert for the £10,000 back. The
implication was that even if Albert had not known about the will,
it still left a motive for Eric's death. However, Benson had
overlooked one other important fact. If it had been true that Albert
and Baines were planning to have the doctor take care of Eric,
they could easily, given his history of overdoses, commit him to an
asylum. Albert was to be his legal guardian and the doctor's
testimony could have seen Eric locked up and Albert free to enjoy
the rest of the money.

The Coroner then instructed the jury to consider how the Veronal was taken, possibly in either the coffee or the hock. It would have required three quarters of a pint to dissolve the 150 grains; a cup of coffee would only be a quarter of a pint so it was not enough. Eric, said Benson, had only drunk a little coffee and, besides so much Veronal would have to be put into it that Eric could not have failed to notice the extremely bitter taste, unless he was so muddled with drink that he had not noticed. However, Benson does not take into account that there is only Albert's word for how much Eric drank. Joiner was never asked how much coffee was removed and as an average coffee pot would hold about a pint, theoretically there would have been enough to hold the drug.

Anyway, Benson added, the coffee was brought in too early to account for unconsciousness within an hour. This is supported by Ham's evidence; he had no reason to lie and he left at quarter past ten when Eric was still conscious - almost an hour after the coffee had been drunk. There would have been some symptoms of drowsiness so the coffee had to be ruled out.

It was also not possible, said Benson, to dissolve the large amount of grains in half a bottle of hock, as it would have needed five whole bottles to dissolve them all. Taking these facts together, it was simply not feasible 'for a person to administer Veronal in the form of cachets without the knowledge of the person to whom it was administered'. However, he added, no matter what he thought of the facts it was for the jury:

> to say what you think of them – they appear to me to
> make it almost inconceivable that any large quantity
> of Veronal could have been put into the coffee or the
> hock by Roe, or anybody else that night, without the
> deceased's knowledge, but you may not be satisfied
> that these considerations exhaust the possibilities of
> foul play. It is still, perhaps, open to ask whether Roe
> might have not persuaded or encouraged the
> deceased to take an extra-large dose, not letting him
> know, of course, how large a dose it was, by way of
> calming him and securing a good night's sleep after
> the agitating events of the evening.

The motive, Benson suggests, of deliberately but innocently giving Eric a huge dose to help him sleep is not really viable. If, as Albert contended elsewhere, he was always warning Eric about the drug and only letting him have one cachet at a time (as he did on the Cornwall trip), he would have been fully aware of the dangers. He knew about the two previous overdoses and if he was intending to give a large dose to aid sleep, surely it would have been no more than two or three cachets. It also seems unlikely that Albert would have forced the wine down Eric's throat as both Spilsbury and Willcox reported that there were no signs of external violence on the body.

Benson does, however, fail to take into account that Eric may have taken one large dose himself, taunted Albert with it and then Albert goaded him into taking another.

Benson's argument that Albert gave Eric a huge dose to help him sleep after the 'agitating events of the evening' is based only on Albert's evidence. The only people who saw Eric that evening were Mr and Mrs Joiner, Ham the picture framer and Albert. Both Mrs Joiner and Ham said Eric was cheerful; Mr Joiner prevaricated and would not commit to how he thought Eric was; only Albert said he was morose and depressed. It is possible Eric moderated his behaviour in front of the staff but he had cried and been depressed in front of them before, so why pretend otherwise now?

Benson surmised that Eric going off in a huff twice was, according to Albert, because he was trying to moderate Eric's drinking:

> It is conceivable that a second half bottle of hock, and possibly other drinks – there were whisky and sherry, I think, drinks not spoken of by Roe – may have made Trevanion in such a muddled condition not to notice what Roe was doing. It may have done. It is also possible that Trevanion might have requested Roe to make him a good strong sleeping draught, but these are conjectures unsupported by any positive evidence at all, and it is very difficult indeed to admit, when you remember that he always took the powder in the form of cachets, which would require no preparation

> – nothing whatever but just to moisten them in a little
> water – an event that is not absolutely necessary, but
> to make the slip down easily, you moisten them and
> swallow them as you would a spoonful of bread and
> milk, as Dr Sandifer put it.

It is conceivable that Eric used other liquors to take the cachets but no evidence suggested any liquor in the bedroom and nobody saw him in any other room retrieving alcohol or drinking during the day.

As Benson points out, Eric normally took cachets whole, so why would he suddenly switch habits, cut them open and take them in liquid form? Did Eric take one dose by swallowing the cachets followed by a second dose in the wine or coffee? No shells were found on the scene and there was confusion about whether Albert did or did not throw something in the fire. The only empty shell that was found was under a man's handkerchief, not the kind Eric used, so was it Albert's? There are also the questions of why Albert wanted to look around the room the morning after Eric died and why he asked Mrs Trevanion what she had done with the cachets she had found? Had Albert taunted Eric to drink the powder in the hock, it would have been bitter and very grainy but still possible to drink. One of the reasons why there was so much interest in the bottle was to try and ascertain if any wine was left.

The Coroner turned to the issue of Albert throwing something into the fire and the confusion which ensued. Mrs Trevanion, he said, had stated that Joiner told her and Joiner had signed a statement to that effect.

Palmer leapt to his feet.

> I have no recollection, Mr Coroner, of Joiner having
> made a written statement that he had seen Roe
> thrown anything into the fire. Mrs Trevanion gave
> evidence that Joiner had told her that, and Joiner was
> called and said that nothing of the kind took place.

Hanson agreed that this was not included in the statement which leaves the question of what Muir and Hanson were reading from? The statement must have been made to the police and along with all the other police statements, they are not included in the coroner's documents at the ESRO and cannot be found elsewhere. There had been confusion over the signing of statements by Mary Joiner. Perhaps there had been a police statement which Joiner never signed so could not officially be included as evidence.

Even the Coroner seemed confused about the number of statements that had been made and said, 'In cross-examination by Mr Hanson, he (Joiner) was shown a statement, and he admitted that he had made an alteration in that statement, and therefore he said he must have read it.'

Palmer disagreed, 'Not on this point. Mr Hanson agrees with him, Mr Coroner, on this point.'

Hanson did indeed agree and said, 'The statement that Joiner signed did not contain any reference to Roe having thrown anything into the fire.'

Benson asked if other statements had been made and Hanson agreed that Joiner had made other statements which were not submitted, so the Coroner turned to the jury and said, 'Then you must take it, gentlemen, that Joiner did not say this in his statement. I thought he had. He made more than one statement, and it is not in the statement which he signed.'[203]

Even though the reference to Albert throwing something into the fire was not in the signed statement, obviously Joiner had made the comment because both Muir and Hanson read it out. It would have been useful at this point for them to have confirmed what they were reading from but they did not, probably because it was not an officially recognised document. The most likely explanation is that Joiner made the statement to the police but at some point recanted. Despite Mrs Trevanion's dislike for Albert, there was no real reason for her to invent the story but if Joiner was, as his wife claimed, expecting a pay-out from Albert after the inquest, then he did have a reason to lie.

What could have possibly been thrown in the fire that required such subterfuge? A suicide note? A note which detailed their relationship that Albert would have had to get rid of or face jail? Or was it the empty cachets? If Albert played down the number of cachets taken, it would increase the likelihood of the death being written off as just another overdose which is exactly what happened at the first inquest.

Benson ended his summary by saying, 'I fail to see any evidence of actual foul play', arguing that Eric must have known he was taking such a large dose, even if he did not understand what he was taking. If the jury felt it had been administered by someone, even if they had no proof, then they could return an open verdict.

Benson was sceptical about the previous 'accidental' overdoses and asked if that could be seriously considered. If someone had tried to attempt suicide and failed, of course he would say it was accidental, otherwise he would be arrested. Benson believed suicide was indicated because, during the previous overdose, Eric had not only locked the bedroom door but had refused the emetic. 'What', said the Coroner 'would his reason be to do that unless he was determined on suicide?' However, we only have Joiner's testimony that Dr Eccles had threatened to force an emetic if Eric did not take it willingly. Dr Eccles himself was never called to give evidence but he did not challenge the testimony either in the press or by letter to the court. Benson also queried the overdose in the car as it was unlikely to have been taken to induce sleep. As it was during the day, why was it taken? Benson felt it was the same as Eric bolting himself in the room, an effort to prevent interference. Having made several attempts at what Benson considered failed suicides, the excessive dose would then make sense in trying to end things once and for all. He did, however, consider why Eric told Albert to call the doctor. Surely if he was hell bent on suicide, he would have said nothing at all. When Albert had come to bed, he could have simply pretended to be asleep and never wake up and Albert would have been none the wiser. Benson's answer to this was that Eric suffered a sudden change of heart: 'consistent, it seems to me, with that strange hysterical condition he sometimes got into, and it is also consistent with … shrinking from the consequences of his rash and petulant action.'

He added that a motive for suicide was not always present among those who took their own lives but Benson links all suicide attempts from mid-August to when Albert had decided to get married. 'This romantic youth, more like a female than a man (as Joiner had said) was faced with the prospect of losing the companionship of the one human being on whom he could depend for protection from his family, and from some at least of his own weaknesses.'

After mildly criticising Dr Baines for his timidity in not using the stomach pump, Benson wound up his summary.

The foreman of the jury asked if there was any insanity in the family, to which Benson replied no and anyway it was not relevant. Could they read Nurse Rice's note. No, said Benson 'I do not think it would be right' and to do so would mean cross-examining the nurse again which was not possible now the evidence was closed.

THE CORONER'S BIAS

One thing comes through very clearly in Benson's summing up is his bias against Eric. His language is damning, describing Eric as an 'eccentric young man'; 'effeminate and ridiculous'; his 'insane infatuation' over Albert; the 'hysterical condition he sometimes got into'; his 'rash and petulant action' and 'that ridiculous direction to his Executors' over the will.

His language about Albert is much more balanced, describing him as having done 'his best'; that he 'kept him off the drugs and drink'; 'was kind to the boy'; and 'there is no single instance mention of unkindness'. Even when considering the possibility that Albert may have coerced Eric into drinking wine laced with Veronal, Benson suggests he may have 'persuaded or encouraged the deceased to take an extra-large dose' with no mention of the possibility of threatened or bullied.

Benson clearly thought little of Eric but his opinion would have been in keeping with the public's reaction to 'effeminate' men at the time. However, Albert's climb from a humble background to 4th officer on a ship was impressive and he was without doubt a hard-working man which would have created a positive impression. Today, this kind of bias in a summing up to a jury would not be permitted.

THE VERDICT

As the jury mulled over their verdict, Albert stood outside in the corridor chatting to friends; while outside the building a large crowd waited for the verdict.[204]

After just half an hour, the jury filed back in and took their seats. The foreman rose to announce their verdict, which thirteen out of the fourteen agreed upon.

He told the packed court that they believed the deceased came by his death from an overdose of Veronal but 'how or by whom there was no evidence'.

The verdict was greeted with applause throughout the room and 'the public refused to be silenced.'[205] Once the noise finally died down, the foreman added that the jury believed Veronal and its derivatives should be placed on the poison schedule.

Coroner Benson seemed surprised that the jury had ignored him.

'You must have gathered from my remarks,' he said, 'that my own verdict would not have taken this form.' He obviously believed Eric's death to be suicide.

Nonetheless, he told the jury that he understood their difficulty and thanked them for their part in the 'very unusual' inquest.

Albert left the court immediately, accompanied by his solicitor. Outside the large crowd cheered him loudly and several ladies rushed forward to shake his hand. He paused briefly to tell the *Cambrian Daily Leader* that he did not want to say anything for the present, other than to thank the many friends who had supported him. A bank of cameras tried to get photos but he quickly jumped in a car and drove off, accompanied by cheers from the crowd. From London, he and his companions caught the 3.15 for Swansea, arriving shortly before midnight. He was greeted by his fiancée, Mrs Derrick who, despite rumours in some London papers, had never gone to the inquest, Mrs Paton and others. Albert then made his way to his sister's house in Beechwood Road where he had been staying.

The case, wrote the *Leader,* had caused more excitement in Swansea than anything for the past thirty years, bragging that they had provided the most comprehensive coverage of any British paper. It had, they admitted, been considerable in costs for telegram fees but was justified and compensated by the sales of their paper. So enormous had been the demand that they had installed a special wire at the Brighton Post Office just to deal with their requirements during the month-long hearing. They had managed to get the verdict through quickly with the assistance of the *Sussex Daily News*.

In all twenty witnesses had been called and it had been estimated that the cost of the inquiry was around £5,000[206] (about half a million today).

WHO GETS THE MONEY?

Before the echoes of the inquiry had begun to fade, the will was being disputed. Applications were made to set aside the caveats that had been placed on Eric's will that were dependent on the verdict and it was estimated that in about eight weeks an answer would be due.

On 19 February, a Brighton art dealer was in the flat making a valuation of the pictures, which included works by Romney, Reynolds and other famous artists. Albert had arrived in Brighton on the 18th to oversee the valuations, returning to Swansea on the 19th.

In May, the value of Eric's estate was published. The estimated worth was £56,528 1s 4d[207] (about six and a half million today). The executors were Eric's friend, Dr Rees, William Rees, (using the address of 47 Marine Parade, Aberystwyth, not the Swansea one used previously) and solicitor, Leonard James Maton.

Before the details of the will were published, rumours had begun that Albert was negotiating with the family for a settlement and that he would receive a 'substantial sum'[208] on the condition 'that certain allegations on the pleadings made against Mr Roe should be unconditionally withdrawn.'[209] The nature of those allegations was not made clear but it is interesting that Albert should settle when legally the bulk of the estate was his. The allegations must have been very compelling.

As part of this settlement agreement with the Trevanion family, Albert also returned all the family heirlooms to Cecil and Claude.[210]

13

THE AFTERMATH

Four months after the end of the inquest, the Brighton chemist Gibson sued for libel against the *Daily Express,* who had written:

> For a long time Mr Trevanion had been subject to sleeplessness, and had used drugs, notably Veronal, before going to bed. He obtained it in cachets from London, and also from Mr W. A. Gibson, of King's-road, Brighton.

> He used sometimes to buy it in large quantities, Mr Gibson said, but there was nothing in that, for it was put up in cachet form, which makes it easy to determine the correct dose. Veronal is regarded as an eminently safe drug for those who suffer from insomnia, and it would require an enormous dose to have harmful effect.

> That statement was the exact opposite of Gibson's views. No reporter had spoken to him and for years, he regarded Veronal as a dangerous drug so had refused to prescribe it unless by a doctor's order. He had also acted, as a member of the Pharmaceutical Society, in the attempt to get Veronal controlled under the Poisons Act. The paper agreed they had made a mistake, paid him a substantial sum, apologised in court and paid the costs.[211]

> The British Medical Journal referred to the case as one 'of considerable value, since it called attention to many of the important toxicological features relating to Veronal poisoning.' They pointed out that 'Veronal cannot be easily administered with homicidal intent without the person taking the drug being aware of

> the fact that a nauseous substance is being given him,
> which in a normal person would give rise to suspicion.
> No doubt a large dose of Veronal might be purposely
> given to a Veronal taker instead of a moderate dose
> without his being aware of the fact at the time.'[212]

Veronal was put on the dangerous drugs list but it was not banned from being freely available until 1935 after several other high-profile deaths.

Writer, Virginia Woolf, suffered mental health issues, possibly due to sexual abuse and her sexuality; she had several affairs with women, the most famous being with Vita Sackville-West. In September 1913, just seven months after Eric's inquest, she attempted suicide by taking 100 grains of Veronal and nearly died but was saved by having her stomach pumped. She tried again with Veronal a couple of years later but finally drowned herself in 1941.

In 1914, a twenty-year old woman in Bath took a bottle of twenty-five tablets, amounting to 125 grains. Fortunately, the doctor put a cork between her teeth; pumped her stomach with no difficulty; gave her strychnine injections; and other interventions. After three and a half days she recovered. She had suffered from depression and had been inspired by the reading of Eric's case.[213] Numerous other instances were reported, the most famous being whether Thelma Mareo of New Zealand had been murdered by her husband. In the book, *The Trials of Eric Mareo,* the prominent Auckland prosecutor Vincent Meredith was quoted as saying:

> it was extremely difficult to prove that someone had
> been murdered with veronal because 'veronal could
> be bought freely [at least before 1 April 1936] and it
> was impossible to establish that the deceased had
> not himself had veronal and self-administered it.

Indeed, in 1933, there had been another famous criminal trial in Auckland where a nurse, Elspeth Kerr (who would today be a clear candidate for a diagnosis of Munchausen's Syndrome by Proxy), was accused of attempting to murder her adopted daughter with veronal. Although there was clear evidence that the only way in which the child could have taken veronal was through the auspices of her mother, the juries in Kerr's first two trials could not agree. It was only after she had endured a third trial that she was convicted of attempted murder.[214]

Willcox had been wrong about the amount of Veronal Eric had ingested, the real figure probably being around 75 to 129 grains. Others had recovered from a dose of this size after having their stomachs pumped, something Dr Baines refused to do.

WHAT HAPPENED TO…?

Florence Trevanion died four years after her son in March 1916[215] aged sixty and was buried in the family vault alongside Eric in West Norwood cemetery.

Eric's father, Hugh married Caroline Margaret, the mother of his daughter, May Lloyd, in January 1916. However, only six months later, Caroline died. Hugh himself died on 25 February 1918 in Bexhill-on-Sea in Sussex aged fifty-nine.

Cecil joined the Royal Naval Volunteer Reserve during WWI as a lieutenant. He remarried in 1920, had a daughter, Joanna, and died in 1950 aged sixty-four. Claude also served in the war, as a lieutenant in the Royal Army Service Corps and won a medal. He never married and died in 1922 aged just thirty-four.

A year after the inquest ended, on 18 June 1914, Albert married Margaret, the widow of sweet manufacturer, W. H. Derrick, at St Mary's Church, Swansea. They lived at 8 Morgan Street, a modest residence, and hardly somewhere a wealthy person would choose. He had lost the inheritance but what had happened to the £10,000 (a million in today's money) which was supposed to be his if Eric died? His lifestyle did not indicate great wealth and the probability is that he was forced to give most of that back as well.

He died in July 1926 in Swansea aged forty-eight. He had no children.

THE DAMNING LETTERS

The story as outlined above was compiled from two main sources the newspapers and the archive at the East Sussex Records Office. This archive consists of four extensive volumes containing the summaries of the first inquest; letters and documents concerning a new investigation; summaries of the second inquest; and miscellaneous letters. The latter contains some of the correspondence sent to Corner Benson from members of the public, particularly concerning Albert. Some make very interesting reading.

'Alias Tom Fisher' of London had already set sail when Benson received his letter, for 'Fisher' had asked a friend to post it as he was afraid of Albert. He wrote:

> I wish to say my once old friend Albert Roe told me he had great influence over Eric Trevanion and was obliged to keep him in a muddled state or else he would go back to his relations, and if so would then make a will against him, he told me Trevanion was very fond of his family, Roe always kept him well supplied with drugs, he could (do) anything with him. Dr Baines & Roe were often together and if I came near them they talked about something else, all I can say (is) search for the Hock Bottle. I could tell you more if (I) was present but have shipped off for do not want to get in the clutches of Roe.

Some interesting points are raised in this letter: It had been suggested in the inquest that Albert had deliberately kept Eric away from his family and what gives weight to this argument is that Eric never told Albert he had reconnected with his mother. Why would Eric have kept that secret if there was no reason to hide it?

It is well attested that Albert had 'great influence' over Eric but did he keep him 'muddled'? The hairdresser said, 'He was in a drowsy state continually.' Joiner said he was far from strong and both he and Ham said Eric would usually lie down on the couch in the afternoon. However, it is difficult to see how Albert could have kept him drugged, unless in cahoots with the Joiners, as he was rarely there. Taking a barbiturate with alcohol does slow down the heart and lungs which would explain Eric's constant tiredness and wanting to lie down in the afternoons. It is more likely that his drugged-like state was from the drugs combined with alcohol and depression over his worsening personal life.

Another letter from 'a frequenter of the Westend' from Piccadilly Circus wrote:

> You will have the respect of every Englishman if you will do your duty fearlessly & put that Sodomite Rowe (sic) & the rest of them where they should be, but as per usual influence will be brought on you to cover up the filthy business & another shocking & disgusting scandal will be buried because of the position of the parties concerned and the unnatural crime of Sodomy will continue & acceptant in the Westend and in Brighton, far worse now than in the Oscar Wild (sic) days.

The anonymous writer does not elaborate on what other cases were 'buried' and provides no personal knowledge of Albert, unlike a letter from someone who simply signed himself '4th officer', the same rank as Albert in his maritime days:

> Take care how you let Mr Row go off. I have known him intimately for many years he is an Oscar Wilde and money grubber combined a perfect scoundrel having an awful life of Sodomy with this youth and then murdering him for the money. Mr Row has tried this little game all before on board. I've been with him but this is the first time he has succeeded so be careful he is a clever criminal scoundrel.'

The author seems to struggle with writing and this may explain why he misspells Roe's name but he is very explicit in implicating Albert.

The letters incriminating Albert provide no specific details and cannot be accepted as proof as both men may simply have had personal grudges against their old colleague. Both also use pseudonyms which may be because, as 'Fisher' wrote, he was afraid of Albert but it may also be they were afraid of being investigated themselves. Nevertheless, it would be wrong not to include the letters as they are both from men who appear to be sailors, like Albert.

An anonymous slip of paper in an envelope marked Union Castle Line (a British fleet of passenger and cargo ships) contained another accusation against Albert:

> Try and ascertain the gang of card sharpers Roe associated with and inveigled Mr Eric Trevanion into playing cards & losing over 300 one evening coming from Port Said to Naples on July 3rd 1912.

The envelope is postmarked Brighton on 28 January 1913, the same day the foreman of the jury asked Joiner if he had seen any gambling in the flat. There is no indication as to why the foreman asked the question but it seems likely it triggered by the anonymous writer, as the letter is postmarked the same day as this exchange.

The Union Castle Line was based at Southampton, sixty-five miles west, and as the envelope bears a Brighton postmark, it would seem that the anonymous writer was at the inquest.

The difficulty with the letter is that it does not conform to any known dates relating to the travels of the two men. It was certainly not in July 1912 as at that time Eric was in hospital for the hammer toe operation. The trip which did include Naples, but not Port Said, was from December 1910 to April 1911 and it is unlikely, having just spent five months abroad they would go away again so quickly. Besides, on 9 or 10 July Eric had the morphine overdose and nobody mentioned they had just got back from a trip. Perhaps the writer simply got the date wrong or it was malicious.

The final letter of interest in the bundle at the ESRO is from yet another anonymous writer:

> Mr Corner, why not kill two birds with one stone and inquire into the death of the filthy twister who died at prestons whoreshop and Oscar Wild (sic) establishment the Royal York and Albion. Who left pensions to their young (Buffers) and a large sum of money to W. B. Gentle as Exec. and protector from the law. Brighton is one gigantic Twisters Paradise, and Gentle is the ringleader.

Curiously, given the derogatory comments about the Royal York and the Royal Albion, the address on the letter was the

Albion and the writer was probably staying there and attending the inquest.

W. B. Gentle was the Chief Constable of Brighton and Hove but no link can be found between him and cases concerning homosexuality and no name was provided for the 'twister.'

NURSE RICE'S MISSING NOTE

When researching this book, I very much wanted to find the note that Nurse Rice had given to Coroner Benson and I was hoping it was in the records at the East Sussex Records Office. While I was wading through them, I was delighted to find a small piece of white paper with just one sentence, written in pencil. It reads: 'He said that Mr Roe had been his wife for the last seven months.'

As well as the note there is her original statement, which the Public Prosecutor Charles Mathews did not want Benson to show to anyone. It covers her conversation with Eric who told her:

> I don't think you will like Roe much, as he drops his h's so.' She replied, 'Why do you have him with you then?' Eric said, 'Well I never knew what it was to have such good sleep until I slept with him.' As he said it he was kneeling by the side of his bed, and looking at a crucifix which was hanging on the wall. He said to her, 'I swear by the crucifix that Roe has been my wife for the past 7 months'. 'Don't talk such nonsense' she said and he replied, 'I swear that it is true.

At first this may appear curious given the character descriptions throughout the inquest. If anyone was going to be called a 'wife', it was more likely to be Eric. However, sexual orientation cannot so easily be equated with feminism.

Irrespective of sexual orientation, one partner is often more sexually dominant and the other more submissive; and some are comfortable in both roles. Someone who initiates and is more proactive during sex does not necessarily mean they are equally dominant in domestic life. The same applies to those who are more comfortable in a submissive role, it does not mean they are submissive in life.

In 1908, Edward Carpenter wrote that the typical homosexual man did not appear feminine but still possessed the 'tenderer and more emotional soul-nature of a woman.'[216] He believed there are masculine men who do not have so-called 'feminine traits' but who are still emotionally 'feminine'.

Working-class men were less free to express their homosexuality and had to consider their position in the social order. Most could not put themselves at risk. A masculine homosexual man was more of a threat to society because it meant any man could potentially be one, while a 'feminised' man did not pose a real threat as they were seen to be outside society.

Another letter in the ESRO files sheds more light on Eric's sexual activity. It was written on Union Jack Club[19] headed notepaper and was from L. M. Harries who wanted to offer some facts which he thought may, or may not, help Benson.

> Perhaps,' he wrote, 'what I tell you may help you a little in the mystery surrounding the case. Some time ago unfortunately I met Mr Trevanion in Bath and went to his rooms with him and I can honestly say I never met such a disgusting man in my life. His whole mind is centred on immoral actions and as I was out of work I fell to the temptations of the money he offered me. I tell you this because I firmly believe that the same thing has happened with Mr Roe – who probably threatened him with exposure to gain the money he had. To prove to you the state of Mr Trevanion's mind (at the time he was in Bath) he put his arms round my neck in bed and said he would marry me if he could. I do not feel sorry for him at all, he was too filthy for words – but I do think if this Mr Roe forced him to leave his money to him on pain of exposure, he ought to be exposed as no doubt he enjoyed himself on the money he received for the same thing that happened to me.

Harries ends by saying he was now doing well in the army but

---

[19]A club for service personal still in existence today

that he would never forget his evening with the late Mr Trevanion.

The letter, which probably reflects the writer's guilt more than anything else, portrays Eric as an individual who initiated sex but who seems lonely and rather pathetic. The comment about Eric wishing to marry Harries gives the impression he is looking for a long-term companion and while no date is given for the meeting, it was probably either before he met Albert or while Albert was spending a lot of time at sea.

Joiner and others testified that Eric, like Albert, wore a gold wedding-like ring but the subject was not pursued at the inquest, probably because they did not want to delve too deeply into the reasons why. Most of the newspaper coverage skittered past any overt description of their relationship, with just a few hints as to something outside the norm such as the *Daily Mail* referring to 'a romantic friendship' and the time 'they spent almost solely in each other's society. The two men seemed inseparable and few people were admitted to their acquaintance.'.[217] The Australian *Wairarapa Daily Times* used the phrase 'closest companionship'[218] and another Australian paper, the *Glen Innes Examiner*, a 'peculiar friendship.'[219]

It raises the question that if Eric considered Albert to be his wife, how would he have felt knowing Albert was now going to marry someone else?

A SIMILAR TRIAL

Twenty-three years after the final inquest into Eric's death, the Mareo murder trial in New Zealand was, as noted previously, to have eerily similar features.

Eric Mareo was accused of killing his wife, Thelma, with Veronal. He was put on trial twice and on both occasions, found guilty despite the flimsiest of evidence. The official motive given was that he wanted to leave Thelma to be with a mistress despite proof that no such affair existed but underlying this, was the fact that his wife was having a lesbian affair with the exotic dancer, Freda Stark, who later gained fame in WWII by entertaining troops clad only in a feathered head-dress, G-string and gold paint.

Mareo, it was claimed, gave Thelma the Veronal in milk while she was already in a drowsy state and unable to understand what she was taking. It was on the evidence of Stark who was also there, that Mareo was convicted.

A number of matters brought up at both trials impacts on how Eric's death should be considered.

It was attested by a number of people that Thelma and Freda shared a bed together but this was often played down as it was not unusual, even in the 1930s, for people to share beds. Indeed, the whole question of homosexuality in the Mareo trial was, as in Eric's inquest, not considered in depth. Questions, particularly about the women's relationship, were never asked; questions which probably would have been asked if the participants had been heterosexual.

Dr Willcox played a prominent role in the Mareo trials and from his writings, appears to have experience in cases related to homosexuality. In his report Willcox wrote that:

> Thelma was suffering from abnormal sexuality (homosexuality or lesbianism). This condition is commonly associated with addiction to drugs like Barbiton [or Veronal] and to alcoholic excess.[220]

This association between substance abuse and LGBT+ people continues today. It is well documented that discrimination and phobias result in a higher use of drugs and alcohol among lesbian, gay, bisexual and trans people than in the mainstream population.

Prior to the Mareo trials, Willcox's bias against homosexuality had played a part in the banning of Radclyffe Hall's *The Well of Loneliness* in 1928. It was the first English language novel by a woman about two female lovers. Sir Archibald Bodkin, the Director of Public Prosecutions, feared that the book would inspire women to practice lesbianism. In his attempt to ban the work, he wrote to a number of doctors asking for clinical analysis of 'homosexualists' and it was Willcox who gave Bodkin the evidence he needed. Lesbianism was, according to Willcox, 'well known to have a debasing effect on those practising it, which is mental, moral and physical in character.' Adding, 'It leads to gross mental illness, nervous instability, and in some cases to suicide in addicts to this vice. It is a vice which, if widespread, becomes a danger to the well-being of a nation...'[221]

Publication of the book, Willcox said, would risk its being read 'by a large number of innocent persons, who might out of pure curiosity be led to discuss openly and possibly practise the form of

232

vice described'. The book was finally released in Britain in 1949, after Hall's death.

Given that Willcox's attitude was not unusual at the time, it is not surprising that details about homosexuality were suppressed both at Eric's inquest and Mareo's trials. However, in the campaign to have Mareo released, 'the most important opinion' was from Willcox who believed Thelma's dose was self-administered. Like Eric, she was a heavy drinker and constantly took pain medications, often appearing dazed and depressed.

Unfortunately, it was primarily his evidence which had got Mareo locked up in the first place. At the trial, it was presented as fact, driven by the evidence of Willcox, that once the effects of the fatal dose had taken hold and a coma had begun, the patient remained in that coma and subsequently died without ever recovering consciousness.

This was one of the main points in Mareo's trial, that Thelma had become lucid enough for her husband to give her a glass of milk containing the supposed killer dose and that sealed his conviction for murder.

In 1944, Willcox was succeeded in his role as Senior Scientific Analyst to the Home Office by Dr Roche Lynch, who as part of the appeal to quash Mareo's conviction wrote a report in which he stated that whilst he believed the New Zealand medical experts acted honestly, they were inexperienced in dealing with Veronal cases and were mistaken:

> A person who has taken a possible fatal dose of veronal can become completely comatose and subsequently regain more or less complete consciousness, and then relapse into a coma without taking any further doses of the drug.

Thelma was calculated to have taken 100 grains by Willcox's flawed method of doubling-up but the number of grains found by analysis was not given. Lynch, contrary to Willcox, believed that Thelma had taken a dose on the Friday night and another in 'an automatic state' on the Saturday morning.

This is questionable, as from Saturday morning Thelma was in an extremely drowsy state and unable to walk or hold a tea cup, so it is doubtful she could have made her way to the kitchen and prepared the Veronal and something to take it in. However,

Mareo's son had seen her moving about that morning so the possibility is there.

Furthermore, the amount of milk Mareo gave Thelma on Saturday night was so small that if it had contained any Veronal, it would have been a minor amount and not a fatal dose.

It seems more likely that the fatal dose was Friday night and she was conscious, albeit in a very drowsy state for most of Saturday until about 11pm when she went into her fatal coma.

Ham, the picture framer, said that Eric went to bed in the afternoon, something which was unusual as he usually lay on the couch and others had testified that Eric was in a drowsy state during the day. Eric normally took two cachets with no effect and four had put him in a coma during the previous overdose so if he had taken three the night before, it may still have been affecting him. He would have needed to take a minimum of seven cachets as the fatal dose to account for the seventy-five grains could have consisted of one dose or split into two or more.

Mareo's conviction was not overturned and he served twelve years in prison. When Freda Stark died in 1999, she was buried at the foot of Thelma's grave.

That there are parallels with the case of Eric Trevanion is clear and perhaps now it is time to look at whether, unlike the jury in 1912, any conclusions can be drawn.

14

CONCLUSION

Is it possible to determine whether Albert had a hand in Eric's death? Any assessment is made more difficult as the inquest seemed so loaded in Albert's favour.

Of the twenty-two witnesses (excluding Albert), eleven were neutral: Spilsbury the pathologist, the undertaker, the two chemists, the bank, the picture framer, the hairdresser, the two solicitors, Nurse Hawkins and Inspector Ward. Willcox has been shown to have a bias against homosexuality. All were either not involved in Eric's life at all or knew him only slightly.

Mary Geneste, although she gave details of Eric's earlier life, seemed to know little of his relationship with Albert, or was hiding any knowledge. Cecil Trevanion said very little, not even to counter some of Albert's errors. Of the remaining nine witnesses, eight had a close connection to Albert ; the Joiners were still employed by him and receiving their wages (it is not known if they ever received a pay-out) and the chauffeur was still employed; Dr Baines had apparently conspired with Albert to look after Eric, probably against Eric's will if he had known anything about it; and Jack Campbell was Albert's friend who had refused 'to put a rope around his neck'.

Dr Sandifer's business partner was a 'friend' of Eric's according to Albert. If so, how much can we rely on Sandifer's testimony if he knew or suspected a relationship between the two men which could end with Albert in jail and them as witnesses?

This left only Eric's mother and Nurse Rice to speak out for Eric and both were portrayed as somewhat hysterical women, particularly Rice who was described as being offended that Albert had not spoken to her after she had her hair done. Although Rice did say she thought Eric was insane, perhaps she had little knowledge of homosexuality and could not comprehend the idea of Albert being Eric's 'wife'.

We are left with an image of Eric as an isolated, drug addicted and eccentric man with not even enough friends to invite to his funeral. Numerous testimonies speak of his being depressed but was this because of the effect of the drugs or because of his unhappiness that Albert was spending more and more time away from him or a combination of both? In addition, the mental stress of being a homosexual man in a period when it was against the law must surely have played a part.

Was all this enough to make him suicidal? Everyone who knew him said no, despite the depression and the deliberate attempt to lock himself in a room to take an overdose. On the other hand, suicide was a criminal offence and they may have wanted to spare the family public shame.

Were both the August and the September overdoses scare tactics to gain Albert's attention? Possibly.

Or was he forced or goaded by Albert to take more of the drug? Again, that is possible. With his forthcoming marriage, Albert stood to lose a great deal if Eric began to make trouble by talking of their relationship. Eric had discussed this with Nurse Rice, and the hairdresser hinted at a similar conversation, so Albert may have been concerned he would continue to do so. No matter how much money Albert inherited, a scandal about homosexuality would have ruined his social standing, his marriage prospects and possibly put him on trial.

And just what was the deal he made with the family when he returned the inheritance in return for the suppression of 'certain allegations'?

The problem that faced the jury is that, even if they had given a verdict of malicious intent, failing to discount the possibility that Eric had taken the drugs himself left the door open for an appeal. As was stated in the trial of Eric Mareo, it was almost impossible to prove murder using Veronal because it was so difficult to persuade someone to ingest such a large amount. This went in Albert's favour.

Even so, the open verdict brought in by the jury meant they were not swayed by the suicide arguments.

So, did Albert have a hand in Eric's death? Here's my hypothesis:

Albert testified that he told Eric in mid-August he was getting married and Eric overdosed on 31 August. I do believe this was a genuine suicide attempt and the fact that sways me is that he locked the door. Joiner says he also refused to take an emetic but there is no corroborative evidence for that, whereas there is for the door being locked.

On the day of the fatal coma, everyone says Eric was cheerful, but why? He knew the man he loved was leaving him so what did he have to be cheerful about? Albert was due back that evening and I think the reason Eric was cheerful was because he had worked out a plan to get Albert to stay. He could ask Albert to remain with him, or return the £10,000 and if Albert refused, he could blackmail him by threatening to tell everyone of their relationship. He had already told Nurse Rice and probably others who did not want to admit it in a public hearing. Albert probably refused and may have countered that Eric had as much to lose in a public declaration of their relationship as he did. Eric became angry, took an overdose and taunted Albert with it. Albert taunted him back urging him to take another dose, tearing open the cachets putting them in the wine, daring and bullying Eric to drink it. Then he threw the shells into the fire but missed one and when the room was full of people, he spotted it, carefully put his handkerchief over it and intended to retrieve it later but was inadvertently stymied by Mrs Trevanion.

As I said, it is only my theory.

My wife, who edited the draft of this book, has a different one. For her, this is a clear case of murder, believing that a row over Albert's marriage during that last dinner led the older man to believe it was simply too dangerous to risk Eric 'outing' them both or changing his will once more. After Eric took his normal dose of Veronal, Albert dissolved ten or more cachets into the wine and made the drowsy Eric drink it.

You may think differently.

INDEX

'4th officer': letter about Albert, 227

'A frequenter of the Westend': letter about Albert, 227

Alan Turing, 86

Albert Edward Roe: in witness box, 152

Albert Roe: £10,000 from Eric, 68, 170, 181; 10 July overdose, 159; 10 July overdose by Eric, 94; 9 September overdose, 163; appearance, 152; apperance, 19; argument with Florence Trevanion, 169; Asturias, 22; career as sailor, 15; colliery clerk, 27, 80; controversy over funeral, 168; cut telephone wire, 159; cutting of the phone line, 70; early life, 14; employed by Eric, 154; family, 36; illness, 23, 179; inheritance of Eric's money, 222; keeping Eric's jewellery, 171; La Plata, 21; marriage, 174, 193, 225; on the Orotava, 15; row with Florence Trevanion, 130; searching Eric's room, 166; second day in witness box, 159; sharing a bed, 111, 155, 157, 172; single cachet found, 141; taking money from Eric, 173; the single cachet, 182; throwing something in fire, 165; transference of money from Eric, 73; visting Eric in hospital, 128; wanting access to Eric's room, 131; wedding ring, 171, 231; working for Eric, 113

Alias Tom Fisher: letter about Albert, 226

Andrew Paton, 35, 104, 139, 187, 205

anonymous letter about Albert, 228

Anonymous letter about Albert, 228

Auguste Malfaison: in witness box, 105

Baines: controversial conversation with Nurse Rice, 194; recalled to witness box, 194; stomach pump controversy, 97; use of stomach pump, 51

Baines, Dr Harold Athelstan: in witness box, 50

Boulton and Park, 45

Cammell, Laird and Co, 80, 81

Cecil Trevanion: birth, 8; later career and death, 225; letter to Eric, 76; offer of settlement to Albert, 183

Charles Cecil Trevanion: in witness box, 184

Charles Ham, 107

Charles Mathews, 5, 38, 87, 133, 168, 184, 229

Charles Matthews: orders new inquest, 6

Charles Matthews, Public Prosecutor: orders new inquest, 34

Chief Inspector Alfred Ward: in witness box, 207

Chief Inspector Ward, 62, 168, 205, 207

Claude Trevanion: analysis of cachets, 56; birth, 9; case against the cook, 11; later career and death, 225

Conrad Willmore (chauffeur): in witness box, 143

Coroner Benson: bias against Eric, 220; summing up, 211
Denzil Harries, 168, 169
Detective Inspector Ward, 186, 187, 204, 206, 207
Douthwaite, Henry Londesborough: supply of Veronal, 57
Dr Eccles, 115, 146, 219
Dr G. Vere Benson, coroner: first inquest, 4; second inquiry, 37
Dr Henry Stephen Sandifer, 92
Dr Hugh Phillips, 161, 162
Dr Rees, 64
Dr Roche Lynch: contradition of Dr Willcox's methods, 233
Dr Sandifer, 23, 50, 69, 70, 81, 92, 93, 94, 95, 97, 98, 101, 102, 128, 134, 136, 140, 141, 142, 159, 161, 162, 166, 167, 170, 213, 217, 235; 10 July overdose by Eric, 94
Dr Willcox: exhumation report, 5; Mareo trial, 232; return to witness box, 136; Well of Loneliness, 232
Edward Carpenter, 151, 230
Edward Ford, 208
Eric Mareo, 99, 133, 146, 224, 231, 236
Eric Trevaion: appearance, 123
Eric Trevanion: 10 July overdose, 93; 24 August overdose, 50, 68, 114; 9 September coma, 116; 9 September overdose, 33, 50; adjusted figure of Veronal in body, 136; appearance, 19, 24, 32, 85, 105, 116, 122, 149, 170; attitude towards Veronal, 95; attitudes towards Veronal, 67; attraction to Albert, 151; bed sharing, 65, 121; birth, 8; case against the cook, 11; cremation controversy, 81; cutting of the phone line, 70; decorating flat, 30; described as sexual pervert, 44; description of flat, 111; early life, 12; effeminacy, 102, 109; effeminacy, 124;

exhumation, 5, 34, 42; hammer toe, 93, 144; hammer toe operation, 69; ill health, 22; ill health, 13; ill health, 50; in Swansea, 24; inheritance, 13; insomnia, 18; letter from Cecil, 76; meets Albert, 14; morphine use, 95, 135, 145; move to Brighton, 29; on Oratava, 64; on the Oratava, 15; purchases of Veronal, 60; relationship with Albert, 33; relationship with family, 69, 79, 178, 210; sharing a bed, 111; sharing beds, 68; transfer of estate to Albert, 70; Tunbridge Wells overdose, 51, 146; Veronal in the body, 47; wedding ring, 120, 231
Eric Trevanion cremation, 41
Florence Trevanion: Albert throwing something in fire, 118; death, 225; divorce, 10; early life, 7; in witness box, 127; inheritance, 13; notified of Eric's death, 129; row with Albert, 129; searches Eric's room, 131; second marriage to Hugh, 12; single cachet found, 142; visiting Eric in hospital, 128
Freda Stark, 146, 231, 234
Geneste, Mary: in witness box, 63
George Baker, undertaker, 41
Gibson: sues for libel, 223; supply of Veronal, 55
Gibson, William Humphrey: in witness box, 55
Hugh Trevanion: Caroline Margaret, 12; charged with assault, 9; Charlotte Amy Key, 11; death, 225; domestic violence, 8, 12; Evelyn Savage, 9; marriage, 8; second marriage to Florence, 12
Hugo Montgomery, 154, 173
J Campbell, 203
Jack Cranston, 205

Joiner, William Thomas, 109;
   Albert throwing something in
   fire, 118; recalled to witness
   box, 202
Joseph William Bridges: in witness
   box, 139
L. M. Harries: letter about Eric, 230
Lord Alfred Douglas, 27
Lumb, James Dillon: Eric's wills, 73
Magnus Hirschfeld, 26
Marquis of Anglesey, 25
Marshall, John David: analysis of
   cachets, 56
Mary Geneste, 18
Mary Joiner: recalled to witness
   box, 198; row with Nurse Rice,
   198
Mary Joiner (housekeeper): in
   witness box, 125
Mrs Derrick, 186, 187, 193, 221
Nurse Hawkins, 91, 140, 166, 184,
   189, 195, 235
Nurse Rice, Anne, 235; 24 August
   overdose, 116; controversial
   comments about Baines, 189;
   note, 229; return to witness
   box, 189; row with Mary Joiner,
   191

Oscar Wilde, 13, 27, 66, 87, 88,
   123, 124, 125, 151, 227, 228
Rees, 65, 81, 168, 175, 176, 222
Rice, Nurse Anne: believed Eric
   insane, 85; in witness box, 84;
   note, 85
Richard David Muir, 3; barrister for
   Florence Trevanion, 3; requests
   new inquest, 3
Rudolph August Witthaus, 99
Second inquiry, 37
Spilsbury, Dr Bernard Henry:
   pathology report, 43; sexual
   pervert comment, 44
Tardieu, Auguste Ambroise, 44
Tom Davies, 186
Tom Wilks, 203
Trevanion family, 7
Veronal, 45, 47; cachets, 39; cases,
   48; effects of, 101, 137; history
   of, 48; in Eric's body, 47
Virginia Woolf, 224
Willcox: use of stomach pump, 52
Willcox, Dr: exhumation report, 44
Willcox, Dr William H., 45
William Conrad: still in Albert's
   employ, 149
Wingrove v Wingrove, 204

REFERENCES

1. East Sussex Records Office ESRO ref: COR 1/3/25 Trevanion hereafter referred to as ESRO
2. The Times *High Court of Justice* (15 Jan. 1913)
3. Coroner's Society of England and Wales *History* (no date) Accessed online: https://www.coronersociety.org.uk/the-coroners-society/history/
4. Office of National Statistics *A Century of Home Ownership and Renting in England and Wales* (2013) Accessed online: https://webarchive.nationalarchives.gov.uk/20160107120359/http://www.ons.gov.uk/ons/rel/census/2011-census-analysis/a-century-of-home-ownership-and-renting-in-england-and-wales/short-story-on-housing.html
5. Sydney Morning Herald *Mysterious death* (16 Jan. 1913)
6. Cambrian Daily Leader *Mr Trevanion's fortune* (16 Jan. 1913)
7. The Times *Hove poisoning case* (25 Jan. 1913)
8. *ibid*
9. ESRO
10. Davidson, J. W. 'Cooper, Daniel (1785-1835)' *Australian Dictionary of Biography Vol. 1* (Melbourne: Melbourne University Press) 1966
11. Mail News *Maryborough Chronicle* (15 Aug. 1882)
12. Cardiff Times *Sequel to a runaway marriage* (29 Oct. 1887)
13. The Times *The Bankruptcy Act 1883* (18 May 1886)
14. South Wales Echo *A Combination of cruelty and vice* (14 Dec. 1887)
15. Daily News *The police courts* (23 Sep. 1896)
16. Wagga Wagga Advertiser *Twice married to the same man* (18 Apr. 1908)
17. The Telegraph (Brisbane) *Twice wed same man* (19 Aug. 1908)
18. Weekly Mail *Twice married to the same man* (7 Mar. 1908)
19. Daily Express *Exhumation mystery* (15 Jan. 1913)
20. ESRO
21. Weekly Mail *A Single-licence publican's offence at Swansea* 25 Oct. 1884) & Cardiff Times *Breach of the Licensing Act* (25 Oct. 1884)
22. The Cambrian *Births, Marriages and Deaths* (11 Dec. 1896)
23. There seems to be some confusion around who this was as some reports have him as Charles Montgomery whilst others as Hugo Montgomerie
24. Cambrian Daily Leader *The Veronal case* (30 Jan. 1913)
25. Daily Express *Sensational Sequel to wealthy Hove man's death* (15 Jan. 1913)
26. Cambrian Daily Leader *The Veronal case* (30 Jan. 1913)
27. Ancestry.com. *UK, Outward Passenger Lists, 1890-1960* [database on-line]. Provo, UT, USA: Ancestry.com Operations, Inc., 2012
28. Cambrian Daily Leader *Date fixed* (17 Jan. 1913)
29. *ibid*
30. Cambrian Daily Leader *The Brighton flat* (18 Jan. 1913)
31. *ibid*
32. Cambrian Daily Leader *Date fixed* (17 Jan. 1913)
33. North Wales Express *Notes of the week* (20 Sep. 1901)

[34] *Yearbook of Intermediate Sexual Types* - the first journal in the world to deal with sexual variants and was published from 1899 to 1923

[35] Iawn Bloch *Sexual Extremities of the World* (New York: Book Awards) 1964

[36] ESRO

[37] Daily Express *Sensational sequel to wealthy Hove man's death* (15 Jan. 1913)

[38] Walter Adophus von Bissing was born in Silesia and was half-brother to the German Governor-General in Belgium during the war. He had lived in Britain since 1876 but was removed from Brighton and interned in London before he and his English wife and children were interned on the Isle of Man. In 1919 he was found to have done nothing wrong and released.

[39] Wairarapa Daily Times *Trevanion mystery* (7 Mar. 1913)

[40] Cambrian Daily Leader *The verdict* (5 Feb. 1913)

[41] Cambrian Daily Leader *Date fixed* (17 Jan. 1913)

[42] Daily Express *The Veronal mystery* (17 Jan. 1913)

[43] Daily Express *Sensational sequel to wealthy Hove man's death* (15 Jan. 1913)

[44] Daily Express *Exhumation mystery* (15 Jan. 1913)

[45] Daily Express *The Veronal mystery* (17 Jan. 1913)

[46] New Zealand Herald *Hugh Trevanion's death* (1 Mar. 1913)

[47] Wairarapa Daily Times *Trevanion mystery* (7 Mar. 1913)

[48] The Times *High Court of Justice* (15 Jan. 1913)

[49] Daily Express *Sensational sequel to wealthy Hove man's death* (15 Jan. 1913)

[50] The Times *High Court of Justice* (15 Jan. 1913)

[51] Cambrian Daily Leader *Amazing story of a will* (15 Jan. 1913)

[52] Daily Express *Sensational Sequel to wealthy Hove man's death* (15 Jan. 1913)

[53] Cambrian Daily Leader *Amazing story of a will* (15 Jan. 1913)

[54] Cambrian Daily Leader *The Brighton flat* (18 Jan. 1913)

[55] ibid

[56] Cambrian Daily Leader *Mr A E Roe* (20 Jan. 1913)

[57] ibid

[58] Cambrian Daily Leader *The verdict* (14 Feb. 1913)

[59] New York Times *Poison killed earls relative* (2 Feb. 1913)

[60] Cambrian Daily Leader *The Brighton flat mystery* (31 Jan. 1913)

[61] Cambrian Daily Leader *The death of Trevanion* (25 Jan. 1913)

[62] Daily Express *The Veronal mystery* (25 Jan. 1913)

[63] Cambrian Daily Leader *Second inquest opened* (24 Jan. 1913)

[64] The Times *Hove poisoning case* (25 Jan. 1913)

[65] ESRO

[66] Daily Express *Exhumation mystery* (15 Jan. 1913)

[67] The Times *Hove poisoning case* (25 Jan. 1913)

[68] Daily Express *The Veronal mystery* (25 Jan. 1913)

[69] Wellcome Library 'Notes on Autopsies' PP/SPI/A.1, 1/263 Hugh Eric Trevanion

[70] Daily Sketch *The Veronal case* (28 Jan. 1913)

[71] A. A. Tardieu (translated by Scott Long) *Etude Medico-Legale sur les Attentats aux Moeurs* (Paris: J. B. Bailliere, 1859, 3rd ed.)

[72] Burke, Jason 'Tanzania: men arrested for 'gay marriage' face anal examinations' *The Guardian* (8 Nov. 2018)

[73] Daily Express *The Veronal mystery* (25 Jan. 1913)

[74] The Times *Hove poisoning case* (25 Jan. 1913)

[75] *ibid*

[76] Cambrian Daily Leader *The death of Trevanion* (25 Jan. 1913)

[77] Denbighshire Free Press *Insomnia cure said to be found* (24 Oct. 1903)

[78] Rhyl Journal *Drug causes a week's sleep* (25 Jul. 1908)

[79] Cardiff Times *Author's death* (10 Jul. 1909)

[80] Abergavenny Chronicle *Fatal new drug* (20 Aug. 1909)

[81] Willcox, Sir William H, Pickworth, F A; Young, Helen M A *The clinical and pathological effects of hypnotic drugs of the barbituric acid and sulphonal groups* Proceedings of the Royal Society of MedicineVol. 20 (9) (July 1927)

[82] Cambrian Daily Leader *The death of Trevanion* (25 Jan. 1913)

[83] The Times *Hove poisoning case* (25 Jan. 1913)

[84] Cambrian Daily Leader *The death of Trevanion* (25 Jan. 1913)

[85] *ibid*

[86] Daily Mirror *Story of midnight telephone call* (25 Jan. 1913)

[87] ESRO

[88] Cambrian Daily Leader *The death of Trevanion* (25 Jan. 1913)

[89] Daily Mirror *Story of midnight telephone call* (25 Jan. 1913)

[90] ESRO

[91] Daily Express *Sensational sequel to wealthy Hove man's death* (15 Jan. 1913)

[92] Marshall was Manager Director of Bell and Croydon, Chemists and Analysts of Wigmore Street, Cavendish Square, London, still in existence today

[93] Chemist & Druggist *The Veronal mystery* (1 Feb. 1913)

[94] ESRO

[95] ESRO

[96] ESRO

[97] Cambrian Daily Leader *Hove inquest* (27 Jan. 1913)

[98] *ibid*

[99] The Sun (Sydney) *Trevanion inquest* (28 Jan. 1913)

[100] ESRO

[101] Blackstone, William *Commentaries on the Laws of England* Vol. 4 [London] 1795

[102] ESRO

[103] Cambrian Daily Leader *The verdict* (5 Feb. 1913)

[104] The Times *Hove poisoning case* (28 Jan. 1913)

[105] Cambrian Daily Leader *Trevanion's fortune* (17 Dec. 1913)

[106] At 21 Cannon Street London

[107] The Times *Hove poisoning case* (28 Jan. 1913)

[108] Daily Express *The Veronal mystery* (28 Jan. 1913)

[109] *ibid*

[110] ESRO

[111] The Times *Hove poisoning case* (28 Jan. 1913)

[112] Cambrian Daily Leader *Hove inquest* (27 Jan. 1913)

[113] ESRO

[114] ESRO

[115] ESRO

[116] ESRO

[117] ESRO

[118] ESRO

[119] Reid, Dr R. D. 'Letters to the editor: Vice prosecutions' *The Spectator* (3 Jan. 1958)

[120] ESRO Letters

[121] ESRO letters

[122] The Times *Hove poisoning case* (28 Jan. 1913)

[123] National Office of Statistics *Suicides in the UK: 2017 registrations* (4 Sep. 2018)

[124] BBC News *Man jailed for man-slaughter over ex-girlfriend's suicide* (28 Jul. 2017)

[125] The Times *Hove poisoning case* (28 Jan. 1913)

[126] ESRO

[127] ESRO

[128] Willcox W. H., Pickworth FA, Young HM. The Clinical and Pathological Effects of Hypnotic Drugs of the Barbituric Acid and Sulphonal Groups. *Proceedings of the Royal Society of Medicine.* July 1927; 20 (9).

[129] *ibid*

[130] Daily Express *The Veronal mystery* (28 Jan. 1913)

[131] ESRO

[132] Witthaus, R.A. *Manual of Toxicology* reprinted from Witthaus' and Becker's *Medical Jurisprudence Forensic Medicine and Toxicology* Second edition (New York: William Wood and Company) 1911

[133] *ibid*

[134] Ferrall, Charles & Ellis Rebecca *The trial of Eric Mareo* (Wellington: Victoria University Press) 2002

[135135] Grose, Francis *A Classical Dictionary of the Vulgar Tongue* (London: Printed for S. Hooper) 1785

[136] Kersey, John *The New World of Words: Or Universal English Dictionary* (London: Printed for J. Phillips) 1706

[137] Cambrian Daily Leader *Very Weak Minded!* (28 Jan. 1913)

[138] Cambrian Daily Leader *Mr A. E. Roe* (20 Jan. 1913)

[139] He had a salon at 78 King's Road, Brighton

[140] ESRO

[141] ESRO

[142] At 45 Pembridge Road, Notting Hill, London

[143] ESRO

[144] ESRO

[145] Daily Express *Sensational sequel to wealthy Hove man's death* (15 Jan. 1913)

[146] Unfortunately, the plan was not included in the Coroner's Reports held at ESRO

[147] Wairarapa Daily Times *Trevanion mystery* (7 Mar. 1913)

[148] *ibid*

[149] ESRO

[150] Evening Standard *Mr Humphries, a gay icon who was hated by Gay Liberation* (8 Mar. 2007) Accessed online: https://www.standard.co.uk/showbiz/mr-humphries-a-gay-icon-who-was-hated-by-gay-liberation-7266315.html

[151] Cole, Shaun *Don we now our gay apparel* (Oxford: Berg) 2000

[152] Craik, Jennifer *The Face of Fashion: Cultural Studies in Fashion* (London: Routledge) 1993

[153] ESRO

[154] Cambrian Daily Leader *Very weak minded* (28 Jan. 1913)

[155] At 1 Westbourne Square, London

[156] Daily Express *The Veronal mystery* (29 Jan. 1913)

[157] *ibid*

[158] *ibid*

[159] *ibid*

[160] *ibid*

[161] Cambrian Daily Leader *The empty cachet* (29 Jan. 1913)

[162] Willcox et al 1927

[163] Carpenter, Edward *The Intermediate Sex: A Study of Some Transitional Types of Men and Women* (London: George Allen & Unwin Ltd) 1908

[164] *ibid*

[165] Cole, Shaun *Don we now our gay apparel* (Oxford: Berg) 2000

[166] Daily Express *The Veronal Mystery* (31 Jan. 1913)

[167] Daily Mail *Trevanion mystery* (31 Jan. 1913)

[168] Daily Express *The Veronal Mystery* (31 Jan. 1913)

[169] *ibid*

[170] Cambrian Daily Leader *The Hove poisoning case* (31 Jan. 1913)

[171] Cambrian News *Death of Dr Rees*(12 Oct. 1917)

[172] Daily Express *The Veronal mystery* (31 Jan. 1913)

[173] The Times *Hove poisoning case* (31 Jan. 1913)

[174] Cambrian Daily Leader *Trevanion's estate* (3 Feb. 1913)

[175] Cambrian Daily Leader *Mr Trevanion's fortune* (16 Jan. 1913)

[176] *ibid*

[177] Cambrian Daily Leader *Date fixed* (17 Jan. 1913)

[178] Daily Express *The Veronal Mystery* (31 Jan. 1913)

[179] ESRO

[180] Cambrian Daily Leader *The Brighton flat mystery* (31 Jan. 1913)

[181] Cambrian Daily Leader *The Hove inquiry* (4 Feb. 1913)

[182] Daily Mirror *Further delay in Hove inquest* (8 Feb. 1913)

[183] Cambrian Daily Leader *Hove inquest* (6 Feb. 1913)

[184] Cambrian Daily Leader *Sensational rumours* (6 Feb. 1913)

[185] Daily Mirror *Nurse's story at Hove inquest* (5 Feb. 1913)

[186] ESRO

[187] Cambrian Daily Leader *The Hove inquiry* (4 Feb. 1913)

[188] Cambrian Daily Leader *Nurse's story* (5 Feb. 1913)

[189] Daily Mirror *Nurse's story at Hove inquest* (5 Feb. 1913)

[190] *ibid*

[191] Cambrian Daily Leader *Nurse's story* (5 Feb. 1913)

[192] Daily Mirror *Further delay in Hove inquest* (8 Feb. 1913)

[193] The Times *Hove poisoning case* (8 Feb. 1913)

[194] *ibid*

[195] Daily Mirror *Further delay in Hove inquest* (8 Feb. 1913)

[196] Cambrian Daily Leader *The Brighton flat mystery* (7 Feb. 1913)

[197] Cambrian Daily Leader *Anonymous letters* (8 Feb. 1913)

[198] Cambrian Daily Leader *Returned to London* (11 Feb. 1913)

[199] Cambrian Daily Leader *Corrections* (10 Feb. 1913)

[200] ESRO

[201] Cambrian Daily Leader *The verdict* (14 Feb. 1913)

[202] ESRO

[203] Cambrian Daily Leader *The verdict* (14 Feb. 1913)

[204] Cambrian Daily Leader *Cost of the inquiry* (15 Feb. 1913)

[205] Daily Mail *Open verdict* (15 Feb. 1913)

[206] Cambrian Daily Leader *Cost of the inquiry* (15 Feb. 1913)

[207] The Times *Wills and bequests* (21 Aug. 1914)

[208] Cambrian Daily Leader *Trevanion's fortune* (17 Dec. 1913)

[209] The Times *The Hove poisoning case* (21 Jul. 1914)

[210] Cambrian Daily Leader *The Trevanions* (26 Jan. 1917)

[211] Cambrian Daily Leader *The Hove tragedy* (28 Jun. 1913)

[212] British Medical Journal *Veronal poisoning* (15 Mar. 1913) vol 1, issue 2724

[213] Munro, J. M. H. *Veronal Poisoning: Case of Recovery From 125 Grains* The British Medical Journal
Vol. 1, No. 2781 (18 Apr. 1914)

[214] Ferrall, Charles & Ellis, Rebecca *The Trials of Eric Mareo* (Victoria: Victoria University Press) 2002

[215] South Wales Weekly Post *Death of Mrs Trevanion* (25 Mar. 1916)

[216] Carpenter 1908

[217] Daily Mail *The Veronal mystery* (16 Jan. 1913)

[218] Wairarapa Daily Times *Trevanion mystery* (7 Mar.1913)

[219] Glen Innes Examiner *Hugh Trevanion's death* (31 Mar.1913)

[220] Ferrall, Charles & Ellis, Rebecca 2002

[221] Smith, David 'Lesbian novel was 'danger to the nation'' *The Observer* (2 Jan. 2005)

Lightning Source UK Ltd.
Milton Keynes UK
UKHW022209140720
366537UK00005B/424